THE COMMON LOON

THE COMMON LOON

Spirit of Northern Lakes

Judith W. McIntyre

Drawings by Anne Olson

University of Minnesota Press
Minneapolis

Second printing, 1989

Published by the University of Minnesota Press,
2037 University Avenue Southeast, Minneapolis, MN 55414.
Printed in the United States of America.
Page ii photograph by Peter Roberts.
Book and jacket design by Gwen M. Willems.

Library of Congress Cataloging-in-Publication Data

McIntyre, Judith W.
    The common loon: spirit of northern lakes / Judith W. McIntyre.
        p. cm.
    Bibliography: p.
    Includes index.
    ISBN 0-8166-1651-5 ISBN 0-8166-1652-3 (pbk.)
    1. Common loon. I. Title.
    QL696.G33M35 1988   88-4206
    598.4'42 – dc 19   CIP

The University of Minnesota is
an equal-opportunity educator and employer.

Contents

Foreword

This book will be welcomed by every person who is interested in the Common Loon. Those who are entranced by this spectacular bird and who wish to support its continued presence in the face of human population changes will be charmed. The serious student in ornithology will be stimulated by the breadth of original data presented and the extensive bibliography. The author has studied loons for some twenty years in Minnesota, New York, Virginia, and Saskatchewan.

The book begins with an exploration of loon myths, legends, and beliefs from ancient and modern cultures, and deals with breeding biology, ecology, behavior, classification, and distribution. In the last two chapters the author discusses the relationship between humans and loons, and the efforts being made to ensure that the earth is a place where both can co-exist harmoniously.

A great deal of the information was recorded by the author in the field. She also thoroughly extracted information from 240 literature citations. Many points are illustrated by excellent maps, figures, and pen-and-ink drawings. All of these are presented with clarity, conciseness, and at times dry humor.

I was fortunate to work with Sigurd T. Olson on his graduate program, which resulted in *The Common Loon in Minnesota* of 1952. Our work is now thoroughly enhanced some thirty-five years later by this book. I am proud to have had a place in its inception. Judy came to the Lake Itasca Biology Sessions in northwestern Minnesota and said, "I am interested in loons—can I start studying them here?" We went to Mary Lake, where a pair of loons had nested for years. After locating the birds from the shore, we launched a canoe and paddled out to the sedge mat to see their nest.

That was the starting point for the many hours Judy spent observing loons, and this book is the result of her dedication to fundamental research, love of a fascinating bird, and a desire to further the welfare of the Common Loon.

William H. Marshall

Preface

*"Once upon a time there was a bird called a
loon . . ."*

New species arise and others sink into oblivion as evolutionary forces
change: an optimal environment for one species may sound the doom of
another. Climate, habitat, competiton for resources, and predation pressures are always at work, on humans and on every other living creature.
Birth, maturity, decline, and extinction are the natural progression of the
evolution of organisms.

Within historic times, man has witnessed the demise of nearly 130
avian species. Recently the pace of extinctions seems to have quickened,
as massive new environmental hazards are introduced into the environment. Toxic chemicals, air and water pollutants, habitat destruction, and
hunting are only the most obvious of factors at work against many bird
species in the modern world.

The situation of the loon is a conspicuous cause for concern. The loon's
future has seemed clouded to many students . . . and lovers . . . of
this fascinating denizen of our northern wilderness. Studies chronicle
population declines in some areas, but other populations seem stable, and
still others actually seem to be thriving! What is the truth behind this apparent anomaly? Are the prophets of doom correct in their warnings, or
are they unjustifiably alarmist? If some populations survive and thrive
while others sink, what are the causes, and what, if anything, can we do
to assure the stability of all loon populations? Are loons inexorably and
inflexibly bound to their inherited life styles and their historic environ-

ment, or can they adapt in ways that will spare them? This book addresses these questions.

Obviously, all the facts aren't in. They never will be. But today we do have a wealth of information to help us, and so it is time, high time, to examine, compare, and analyze the many recent studies, to look for trends and implications, and for clues that might guide us to help the loon — and the northern wilderness that it adorns — survive.

This book is about the Common Loon, the species that science calls *Gavia immer*. But all loons face many of the same problems, and much in this book is applicable to the other loon species. I hope to separate real problems from illusory ones, and thus point the way toward fruitful avenues of research.

I have lived with loons, summer and winter, day and night, for 20 years. It is my fervent hope that a time will never come when storytellers will say, "Once upon a time there was a bird called a loon . . ." but that grandparents will always be able to take their grandchildren to northern lakes and listen together to that most haunting of boreal wilderness sounds, the call of the loon.

Judith McIntyre

Acknowledgments

Funding for this work has come from a number of sources. I would like to thank the American Museum of Natural History for two Frank M. Chapman Grants, the National Geographic Society for a Research Grant, Utica College of Syracuse University, and both the Dayton Natural History Fund and the Alexander P. Anderson and Lydia Anderson Fellowship, awarded by the University of Minnesota. Contracts were given by the New York State Department of Conservation, the Minnesota Department of Natural Resources and Mercer Industries Inc. The North American Loon Fund, and the Oikos Research Foundation provided monies on many occasions. Much of the research was conducted while I held National Science Foundation grants #GB-12904, GB-19413, and BNS-8106567.

Individuals helped in many ways, too. Volunteers devoted countless hours of time to provide Project Loon Watch reports. Others helped during field work in Minnesota, New York, Virginia, and Saskatchewan: Laurence Alexander, John Brazner, Melody Christoff, Michael Hamas, John Mathisen, Terry Perkins, Captain Walter Reed, Karen Sexton, Ben Thoma, Jim Underhill, Charles Vaughn, Kim Young, and my sons Perry, Richard, and Tony, especially Tony, who gave up five of his own summers and one winter to carry equipment through bogs and along trails, and to maneuver power boats from small Minnesota lakes to the Atlantic Ocean. Special thanks to William Marshall, who, as Director of the University of Minnesota Biology Field Station at Itasca State Park, was the instigator for my work by introducing nesting loons to me one day 20 years ago.

I would like to thank James Gulledge and Andrea Priori and the Library of Natural Sounds at the Laboratory of Ornithology, Cornell University, for assistance with tapes and loon recordings. A special thanks to Bill Parker for help with everything from photographs to sound recordings, and especially for preparing the acoustic glossary at the back of the book. Lee Herrington and the SUNY College of Environmental Science and Forestry at Syracuse lent me most of the sound equipment used in playback experiments.

Others were good sports to read parts or all of the manuscript and offered valuable advice. Some were biologists and some were not, for I want the book to be enjoyed both by ornithologists and by the general public. To Laurence Alexander, Jack Barr, Dotty Deimel, Marcia Gallo, Theodora Jankowski, Terry McMaster, Helen Mather, Robert Nero, Robb Reavill, Charles Sibley, Robert Storer, Paul Strong, and Harrison Tordoff, thank you for reading and commenting.

Patty Burchard and Emmett McSweeny were invaluable in researching library material. Virginia Marsicane and Elizabeth Welch helped with typing, and Bruce Brodsky patiently helped in answering my computer questions. William Barklow, Jack Barr, Scott Sutcliffe, and Keith Yonge shared their loon study sites with me, and Al Smith hosted me at a summering site for immature loons in New Brunswick. Dwain Warner not only served as my adviser in graduate school, but has continued to be my mentor throughout my career, and I am grateful for his support. I have a special thank you for my husband, Pat, who has continued for 20 years to help with field work, keep equipment in working order, and support my single-mindedness as the Loon Lady.

The staff of the University of Minnesota Press have been helpful during all stages of the preparation of this book, and I thank them for their patience with me for several years.

I thank Craig Borck, Robert Furness, Tom Martinson, and Peter Roberts for use of their photographs. Anne Olson's wonderful loon drawings greatly enhance this book, and I thank her for them.

Finally, thank you loons, for sharing your lives with me. It has been a thrill and a privilege to watch your courtship, nesting, and territorial defense; to see your young hatch as black chicks and grow into gray and white juveniles; to feel your soft feathers in my hands as I banded you; and to hear you calling to each other across northern lakes.

Myths, Legends, Beliefs

Loons have occupied a place in the daily lives of peoples for thousands of years. Loon bones and fragments have been found in middens of early peoples in many parts of the world. Loon remains have shown up in diggings from ninth-century settlements on islands off Great Britain (Ticehurst 1908). Far away, on the other side of the world, native Americans included loons in their list of "good food" (Seton 1911). Loons were considered delicious by Inuits, and their skins were used for ornamentation on pouches, bags, and articles of clothing by Barbinzians and Inuits (Wilson and Bonaparte 1831). Loons are still eaten by native Americans. Recently the James Bay and Northern Quebec Native Harvesting Research Committee verified a large harvest of loons by the Cree from communities in the region (Desgranges and LaPorte 1979).

Loons have also occupied a central place in the cultures of many peoples. In fact, some stories are told with only slightly different versions around campfires on both sides of the world. This could be because the same characteristics have caught the imagination of people in general, but anthropologists believe it indicates cross-cultural transmission. Stories about loons, the kinds of stories that become the legends, the mythology, the believable magic of societies, focus primarily on loons' diving ability, their calls, or their distinctive black-and-white feather patterns. These characteristics of call, dive, and pattern are uniquely *loon*. There is something mysterious about each. Loons disappear when they dive. Where do they go? What are they doing? Their *calls* echo across moonlit lakes with the eerie magic of a supernatural being. What are they saying? To whom are they saying it? Their black-and-white feather *pattern*, especially the spots on their backs and stripes around their necks are so precise they could have been painted on. Why? Who put them there? What do they mean?

The story of a miracle performed by a loon is one fireside legend repeated in several ways. The Copper tribes, far to the north in Canada, tell of a blind boy who was made to see again by a loon. In other tribes, a slightly different version tells of a shaman or medicine man who was cured by a loon. But whoever it is, man or boy, the story is much the same. Someone who is blind has his vision restored by a loon, who carries him on his back to the bottom of a lake, again and again, until his eyes are clear. In gratitude, the boy or man gives a necklace to the loon. In the story from the Salish people of British Columbia (Leechman 1968), Kelora the Medicine Man throws his magic shaman's necklace of dentalium shells over the loon's head. As it falls over the neck of the bird, it becomes the white pattern of feathers which we know as the Loon's Necklace.

Folktales say that loons were once land birds. One of those stories, passed down by generations of Micmac Indians, tells about the time when loons lived on land (Robertson 1969). One loon was so tame, yet clumsy, that it annoyed all the villagers as it ran in and out of the wigwams, knocking over belongings and spilling food and drink. The Micmacs could finally stand it no longer, caught Loon, and threatened to throw him into the water. Thinking quickly, Loon begged them not to throw him into the water, but to throw him in the fire instead. The Indians, thinking they could finally get even, were sure to throw him into the water. When he was safely away from the village he called back to them with his wonderful laugh, saying, "Just what I wanted, just what I wanted." And that is how the Loon Became a Water Bird.

The birds we call loons in North America are known by many different names in other parts of the world. Our word *loon* comes from the early Scandinavian word *lom* or *lumme*, meaning clumsy. Loons cannot walk very well on land, but must shuffle on and off their nests. They look awkward, and come to land only for mating and nesting.

One of the original five clans of the Ojibway Nation was the loon, or *Mang* clan. A unique quality was ascribed to each clan, such as being very clever or extremely swift. One interpretation for the loon clan's special characteristic is that Mang was proud (Robert Gawboy, pers. comm.). Other translations indicate Mang was considered the most handsome of birds. Cooke (1884) mentioned that the word *loon-hearted* was given to an individual who was thought to be extremely brave, used much as our expression *lion-hearted*.

Sometimes *huart*, French for *cry*, is used to refer to loons in French-speaking Canada, and the Russian word for loon, *gagara*, sounds exactly like the cry of the Arctic Loon. There are also many stories about the loon's cry, such as a legend from North American Indians, The Crow and The Loon. Once upon a time both crows and loons were men. They were friends, and did everything together. But one day, as they were fishing, Loon caught all the fish, while Crow caught nothing. In a jealous rage, Crow hit Loon, then cut out his tongue and threw him overboard. All he could say was the cry we now call a wail, but the Great Spirit took pity on him and turned him into a loon, while his friend was turned into a crow.

In the languages of Indians from the northeastern United States and Canada, loons are called by versions of the word *Kwe-moo*, for example, *Kwimuuk* and *Hukweem*. These names sound like the long, drawn-out wail, especially if said slowly as in Kwe-moo-oo-oo. The Passamaquodie, Micmac and Algonkin tribes share a legend about how the loon got its call. Each is a slightly different version of the same story told about *Kwe-moo* and *Glooscap*, *Kulocap*, or *Clote-scarpe*, the Indian hero sometimes referred to as the Hiawatha of the northeastern tribes.

In the story told by the Milicete Indians (Long 1900), Hukweem was Clote-Scarpe's hunting companion long before there were dogs. All the animals fought with each other, and after Hukweem returned from hunting, he tried to keep peace. Finally he became frustrated as he found he was unable to make the fisher and the wolf and the panther get along with the other animals. In desperation, he called for Clote-Scarpe to come back and live with them. But Clote-Scarpe never came, and today the loon is still calling, asking him to return.

The Micmac version is quite different. Glooscap came to visit the Micmacs one day in their lonely wilderness home in Newfoundland. The people didn't want him to leave, but after three days and three nights he had to move on. To help the loneliness of the Micmacs, he appointed Kwee-moo as his special messenger. He said he would return whenever Kwee-moo called, because his call could be heard anywhere. Then he gave him the special call that we call the wail. He still calls today, and the call you may think is just an echo is Glooscap's answer to Kwee-moo.

Another tale from Canada tells about the loon's echo. Sinikielt was a brave warrior who set off to rescue beautiful Lalita. He traveled far, up and down hills, until it grew dark. He kept walking, unable to stop until he found her. But his foot found the edge of a cliff first, and over he fell, to the water below, calling all the way to the bottom. When the loons call today, the echo you hear is Sinikielt, still calling for Lalita.

Many tales surrounding loon calls involve superstitious beliefs, several from the Faeroe Islands. It is said that if a loon gives its flight call during a burial, the soul is being accompanied to heaven. When the Red-throated Loon mews like a cat, wet weather is coming to the Faeroes, but if the weather is going to be fair, the loon has a different call. Loons are considered weather prophets in the Shetland Islands, too, where they are known as "rain-geese." Indians of British Columbia believe loon calls foretell rain, and they imitate them during their rain ceremonies. In Norway, both Arctic and Red-throated Loons predict stormy weather, and another Norwegian belief says that a loon call means someone will drown (Armstrong 1970a,b,c). An English nickname, *spotted loo*, brings to mind eerie calls announcing a coming storm (McAtee 1957).

The ability to forecast the weather has been attributed to loons because they have traditionally been considered special, even being thought to have supernatural powers. They were used as shaman ornaments in Siberia, and were believed to accompany the shamen on their journeys to the spirit world. Corpses with artificial eyes placed in the sockets were buried in early Alaskan graves. A loon buried near human remains was found to have been prepared in the same way. This suggests that loons were believed to accompany the dead to the Beyond. The Faeroe Island belief concerning the accompaniment of the dead to heaven may share the same legendary background.

The most northern of the Mongol peoples, the Buryats, thought spirits appeared as loons. Loons have also been sacred to other northern cultures, among them the Tungus peoples of northern Siberia, the Norwegians and the Japanese. As recently as 1931, Arctic and Red-throated Loons were made national monuments in Japan because of their importance to Japanese fishermen of the Inland Sea. Fishermen use loons to guide them to lance, a small bait fish, which they net in great numbers (Austin and Kuroda 1953). If a loon is killed by becoming entangled in fishing nets, it is put in the bottom of the boat so as not to disturb other loons, and later is taken to shore where it is gently placed at a shrine. Perhaps the most recent example of an honorary award for loons was the 1961 designation of the Common Loon as Minnesota's State Bird. It was lauded as exemplifying the special wilderness quality typical of northern Minnesota, its call said to denote the spirit of wilderness.

Loons have been implicated in a series of stories telling how the world was made. The story of creation describing how earth was made from mud originated in India. In the earliest version known, a boar leapt into the water and brought up mud on its back, which then floated and became the earth (Armstrong 1970c). As the legend spread north, west, and east, the boar was replaced by a diving bird or mammal. In all northern legends, including those brought across the Bering Strait into North America, the creator of the world is thought to have been a diver. This series of stories is interesting to trace because of the gradual shifting from bird to man. The Voguls live along the Ob River basin in western Siberia, occupying a central position in the north-to-south expansion of this tale. Their legend tells of cooperation among the raven and Red-throated and Yellow-billed Loons. The loons dove and brought mud to the surface, while the raven flew overhead to check on their progress.

A story from southern Siberia describes God and man as two geese. As the man-goose dives for mud, the God-goose flies overhead and supervises the building of the world. Farther to the west, the Latvian interpretation says that it is the Devil who lives in the water, and he brings mud to the surface in his mouth and spits it out to make mountains (Armstrong 1970c).

Native people along the Nensei River, eastward from Khanty-Mansino, attributed mud-fetching to Red-throated Loons. Still farther, from the Lena River and beyond to the lake region of eastern Siberia, the Yakuts tell of the Yellow-billed Loon and the Mother Goddess. The loon was directed to dive deep and bring up mud to make the world. But when it returned to the surface, it claimed it was impossible to do so. Mother Goddess saw mud on its bill and knew it was lying. To punish the loon, she condemned it to live in the water forever.

There are such stories of creation among native Americans. The Chippewa Indians of the central North American lake region tell their version. Long ago, when the world was all water, the Great Spirit told the animals it would be good to have land so animals could walk, and there would be grass and forests and flowers. He asked the animals, one at a time, if they would dive far down to the bottom and bring up a little mud so he could make land. Muskrat, Otter, and Beaver all tried and failed. Finally he asked Loon to go down as far as he could. After a long while he surfaced, but was sad because he thought he had failed. He waved his foot to say good-bye to the Great Spirit, but as he did so, a little mud glistened in the sun. That was enough to make land, and Loon became a hero. Loons still bring their feet out of the water and wave them in the air to remember their hero, the Loon Who Made the World.

Stories and legends about loons are very old. Many have passed into books of myths, no longer told and passed down from father to son, from mother to daughter. Apollo took the form of a diver when he guided emigrants to their new homes (Gray 1964), a story that is now almost forgotten. Other stories are remembered as superstitions, and some are still believed. Many people still believe that loons call just before a storm. When they hear a long lonely wail they believe the loons are announcing a coming thunderstorm. Others think loons do something mysterious while underwater. When loons are pursuing a long series of dives and underwater swimming, it may be difficult to see them come up for a gasp of air. They sneak their heads above water like periscopes and submerge immediately, a behavior that has led to the belief that loons can stay underwater for long periods of time, engaged in some "underwater magic."

Legends from northern people go back to the earliest civilizations of the taiga and tundra. The earliest evidence of all is a drawing done during the Stone Age in Norway. It shows a loon underneath an elk. What does it signify? Is it evidence that some stories about loons, now forgotten, surrounded their importance as food? Or is the loon under the elk because it provided good luck during the elk hunt? Was a loon charm worn to ensure a successful hunt? Perhaps we will never know.

We do know that today loons continue to provide much of the magic of the northern wilderness. Their haunting calls become the raw material for our own dreams and imaginations, just as they did for our ancestors when they created the myths and legends about Kelora, Glooscap, and Hukweem.

This book attempts to bring together much of what we now know about loons: what and where they are, what they do, what their problems are, and how we can help. But the mystery will remain. For the more we learn, the more questions we ask.

CHAPTER 1
Arrival and Territorial Behavior

On boreal lakes, spring's announcement and summer's promise are heralded by loon music. As newly thawed lakes sparkle under an April sun, the loons fly in, drop down, and land abruptly on their summer homes. They look quickly beneath the water's surface, then raise their heads and tell the world that the spirit of northern lakes is in residence.

The timing of arrival is correlated with latitude. In north-central Minnesota, from about 46° to 47°N, most pairs are on territory during April. Some early arrivals are present by the end of March (McIntyre 1975). Farther north, in the Boundary Waters Canoe Area of Minnesota (47° to 48° N), loons are present by mid-May (Olson and Marshall 1952, Titus and Van Druff 1981). Sutcliffe (1980) found that 50 percent or more of the summer's population was always present by April in New Hampshire. Loons are on territory in northern Alberta and northern Saskatchewan (54° to 55°N) somewhat later, usually by mid-May (Vermeer 1973a, Yonge 1981). In Iceland, even farther north at 65°N latitude, Sjølander and Ågren (1972) reported the arrival date for one pair as 30 May, but that was the only pair for which they could be certain of arrival time.

Loons do not return on the same date every year. Their return follows ice-out, as might be suspected, since they need open water to land. Arrival time depends on how early or late the lakes open. When lakes opened exceptionally early in Minnesota, I found that loons came back an average of eight days after lakes were ice-free. When the ice went out very late, the average interval between open water and loon arrival was shortened to three days. In a more typical year, loons were on territory an average of five days after there was open water. Yonge (1981) said that loons returned to his study site in northern Saskatchewan as soon as they could. As each section of his study lake opened, more and more territorial claimants arrived. Loons were on territory as soon as there was open water, and Yonge reported that seven of 10 territories that he could view were occupied on the evening of the day when the first open water was seen. Three days later, all 10 territories had residents.

Loon territories provide all the needs of the birds during the summer: a place to nest, to raise young, and to find food. It is important that loons return as early as possible in order to claim a good territory, protect and defend it, but the timing is restricted by weather and feathers. Frozen lakes cannot be used by loons, and in that way, weather restricts the time of arrival. Because loons undergo a complete remigial molt, or loss of all flight feathers at one time, on the wintering grounds, they are without flight feathers for a period of time. They are forced to remain on the ocean until molting has been completed and they can fly again.

With such limits placed on the earliest arrival time, it is probably advantageous to arrive no later than conspecifics to assure the best choice of territory. I had suspected they might arrive together, and finally, in 1976, I was lucky enough to see the arrival of male loons to Itasca State Park, Minnesota. At 1040 on April 13, I was sitting at Elk Lake, having just checked all the lakes in my study area. Lakes were starting to open and the smaller ones had become ice-free during the night. I heard flight calls, looked up, and there, in a tight flock, eight loons were circling Elk Lake. One peeled off and landed, while the others flew on. I quickly rechecked my lakes, and found that male loons occupied many of them. By evening, nine lakes had territorial loons patrolling and giving occasional yodel calls. Were the males I saw arrive a group of territorial neighbors? It certainly seemed that way.

Although males seem to arrive at about the same time to any one region, the pattern of female arrivals is different. Loons have been reported to return in pairs to lakes in the northern parts of their range (Yeates 1950, Sjölander and Ågren 1972, Yonge 1981). But along the southern edge, for example in New York, New Hampshire, and Minnesota, males arrive first, and are followed shortly by their mates (McIntyre 1975, Sutcliffe 1980).

I checked arrival times of pair members and compared them with yearly weather patterns. In years when spring came earlier than usual and lakes were open and ready for loons by early April, males arrived before females. Males were also alone on territory longer than in years when lakes stayed frozen until late April. In years with late springs, loons waited around, forming larger and larger groups on open water, particularly on rivers and the inlets and outlets of large lakes. When they were finally able to take up residence on their territorial lakes, loons could be seen arriving already paired. This suggests that females did not fly back with males, but returned separately a bit later. When males were forced by weather conditions to wait for lakes to open, the females caught up with them, so both pair members arrived together, or close to the same time, on territories. This also explains why loons arrive paired at more northern lakes, for, as males are held back periodically en route, females are more likely to catch up with them.

Some loons arrive later, after territories have been established and nesting has begun. I suspect these may be younger birds, perhaps wearing their black and white feathers for the first time. Many are nonbreeders and remain unpaired throughout the summer. Second-year immatures molt their flight feathers later than adults do, and are flightless early in the summer. Is it possible that the remigial molt moves up a little earlier each year until loons reach adulthood, so that three-year-olds molt in April or May, and have just finished molting when they arrive?

In places where all suitable habitat is occupied, it is expected that nonnesting birds would linger at the borders of good territories, waiting for a chance to secure one for themselves. In healthy populations of other species of birds, nonbreeding individuals wait to take over a territory. However, there are also single and nonnesting pairs of loons occupying locations that seem to be potential territories. Is it possible that young birds spend at least one summer getting acquainted with a prospective site before attempting to breed?

Common Loon territories are used for all activities during the breeding season, such as nesting, care of the young, and feeding. For that reason, there are several factors that make habitat optimal or just marginal for a loon territory. The first is size. Loon territories are often referred to as "large," "far apart," or "one to a lake." Actually, territories come in many sizes. The smallest are five- to six-hectare lakes. Adults defending these

Table 1–1. Sizes of Common Loon Territories

| Study Area | Lakes | | Size(ha) | | Source |
	Type*	N	x̄(SE)	Range	
Minnesota	S	38	20.3(3.8)	4 -124	McIntyre 1975, 1978
New York	S	23	53.5(8.5)	10.5-178.9	Parker 1985
New York	M	20	74.3(7.6)	27 -168	Young 1983, McIntyre (unpubl.)
Ontario	M	16	77.8(9.4)	49 -140	Rummel and Goetzinger 1975
Saskatchewan	M	28	26.2(1.52)	9 - 36	McIntyre 1983

*S refers to small lakes, sufficient for only one territorial pair.
 M refers to lakes with many loon pairs.

tiny ponds use adjacent bodies of water for their own feeding, but food for their young comes only from the territorial lake. Lakes smaller than 80 hectares generally support only one pair of loons, but the shape of the lake also influences the number of pairs it can support. Lakes of only 60 to 70 hectares may support two pairs if physiographic features such as bays and islands form visual barriers.

Larger lakes, especially those of several hundred hectares or more, may have many pairs. The size of each territory is often determined by natural features, and deep bays may permit large, but easily defended, territories. For example, Young (1983) studied one pair with a very deep bay as its territory. Its enormous holdings amounted to 168 hectares—the size of 377 football fields! We called this a territory, but it is a moot point whether or not all of it was truly a defended area.

Territory sizes using data from several studies are shown in Table 1–1. Olson and Marshall (1952) said they thought defended territories could be quite small when there were adjacent neutral sites where loons could do much of their feeding. On the other hand, I found that territories on the larger lakes were larger than those on small lakes. Territories on a large lake in northern Saskatchewan with nearly 100 pairs were larger than those on small Minnesota lakes. Both Saskatchewan and Minnesota have large and stable populations. Larger territories are found in New York, where the population has declined and is less dense than in Minnesota or Saskatchewan. There is also a difference in territorial size between large and small New York lakes, larger territories on large lakes, and smaller holdings on small lakes.

Territory size changes during the breeding season. Some workers found that it increased for pairs raising chicks and shrank for pairs that were unsuccessful at hatching young (Rummel and Goetzinger 1975, Christoff 1979). Other indications are that territory size is established in the spring and is the same when juveniles are being raised, but appears to shrink during the time adults are nesting or raising small chicks. Activity is then limited to smaller sectors of the territory, subsets of the total defended area (Young 1983). Territories may expand when chicks hatch, but this depends on whether or not expansion is possible. If the potential expansion area is unoccupied or weakly defended, a pair with young often moves in; if such an area is not available, activities are restricted to holdings already established. Territory size on small lakes is nonexpandable. Adults with small territories on small lakes feed themselves elsewhere with increasing frequency as young grow older, and they leave the food resource at the natal lake to the juveniles. The young also move as soon as they can fly, and they go to larger lakes where they establish their own feeding stations.

It has been suggested that birds may initially defend a larger area than they really need at the time they first establish territories in the spring in order to prevent other loons from nesting, and thus gain a reproductive advantage (Verner 1978). Loons do not fit this model; in fact, they do just the opposite. They may enlarge territories, but those I have noted as shrinking have been those held by unsuccessful nesters.

Water depth and clarity may be marginally important to loons. I found loons nesting and raising young on both deep and shallow lakes. Some use ponds no deeper than 1.5 meters, ponds almost choked with emergent vegetation. Alvo (1981) tells of loons in Ontario nesting in marshes no deeper than 0.5 meters. He speculates that loons were using portions of the lakes which were undisturbed by human recreational use, and I suspect that loons using shallow lakes in my study areas did so for the same reason. Those lakes provided no sport fishing or swimming and were rarely visited by people seeking recreation.

Loons are frequently encountered during the course of duck-banding operations on many of the big waterfowl lakes in northwestern Minnesota. Biologists from Minnesota's Department of Natural Resources have banded more than 100 adults and juveniles in the past five years. Most were caught on shallow lakes, which suggests that shallow water does not prevent loons from nesting and raising young.

Most lakes across the Canadian Shield of North America are not shallow, marshy ponds, but are lakes of varying depths, including rocky shoals, deep holes, shallow bays, and marshy inlets. This is the heart of the Common Loon's breeding range, and is considered optimal loon habitat. Loons use the varying depths of these lakes for different purposes. When possible, they nest adjacent to steep slopes so they can slide off the nest into the water, feed over rocky shoals where there is an abundance of food, and raise their young in shallow, marshy, safe areas (McIntyre 1975, 1983). For large Maine lakes, Strong (1985) found consistent use of specific depths for feeding by adults to be more shallow than depths either Barr (pers. comm.) or I have recorded (one to two meters). Chick-rearing activities took place in even more shallow areas and social interactions in deeper waters of the Maine lakes. It would seem that lake depth does not make or break a potential territory, but the best lakes I have encountered have both deep and shallow portions.

Loons are visual predators. They locate fish by sight, then dive and chase them underwater, twisting and turning with their prey. Hence water clarity is important. There are a few records of loons caught in nets as deep as 70 to 75 meters, but in general they hunt in water between two and four meters deep. Visibility should be good at least to a depth of three or four meters and preferably should be clear to a much deeper level. Secchi disks are black and white, round metal plates that are lowered into the water to check visibility. Secchi disk readings taken in the Chippewa National Forest study lakes averaged 2.18 meters on lakes with territorial pairs and only 0.91 meters on lakes without loons, suggesting that visibility was important, since it was more than twice as great on lakes with loons than on lakes without them.

During a study in northwestern Ontario, Jack Barr found that turbidity was an important factor. Potential territories were assessed on the basis of many characteristics, primarily physiographic features and food resources. In some locations, less than five percent of the predicted sites were occupied. The single factor shared by all lakes without loons was turbidity caused by hydroelectric plants, fluctuating water levels, and industrial effluents. Some of the useless portions of these lakes had Secchi disk readings as low as 0.3 meters.

Loons can compensate for conditions of low visibility by using only the shallow parts of a lake, parts so shallow that birds can see to the bottom even if waters are not clear. However, the usual hunting depth is between two and a half and five meters. A loon's mobility is somewhat restricted in water that is more shallow than that. However, I studied loons that nested and raised young on black-water bog lakes, and they fed only in the shallow parts. I have also seen loons choose the marshy parts of larger lakes when open water was turbid. In spite of good food and appropriate nesting islands, as long as water is murky, loons choose other locations in which to spend their time. Clear water is critical for loons.

One would expect the food base to be important in selecting a territory. Loons eat fish. They also take other prey, including some crustaceans, especially crayfish. All lakes where I have studied loons have had fish. Some contained only suckers or bullheads, and some of the bog lakes with pH readings as low as 4.0 had sticklebacks and mudminnows, both acid-tolerant species. Mudminnows are exactly the right size to feed young, growing loons, and they provide suitable food for adults, too.

Most others who study loons also report fish in lakes occupied by loons. For example, Vermeer (1973a) found that loons in central Alberta used only lakes with fish. On the other hand, Munro (1945) reported that 11 of his 35 study lakes in British Columbia had no fish. Both he and more recently Parker (1985a), who worked in the Adirondacks of New York, found that adults fed insects and aquatic insect larvae to their chicks in lieu of fish, and Parker (1985b) also saw adult loons carry fish from one lake to another.

Good places to nest and raise young are certainly considerations in the choice of a territory. Nest sites should be built where both the eggs being incubated and the birds incubating them are safe from scavengers, predators and weather vagaries. Islands are preferred nest sites in most studies that have checked for nest-site selection (Olson and Marshall 1952, Vermeer 1973b, McIntyre 1975, Yonge 1981). However, Strong (1985) found that at least some loons are more successful when they place their nests in backwater sites.

Do islands "make or break" potential territories? I was curious to find out, and knew that John Mathisen, biologist in the Chippewa National Forest in Minnesota, had built some floating islands for Ring-necked Ducks as loafing sites, and that loons nested on them (Mathisen 1969). In 1970, John, his staff, and I built artificial nesting platforms on the Chippewa National Forest study lakes, which had no natural islands. I was hoping to answer two questions: (1) would loons prefer them to traditional shore sites? (2) would they attract loons to lakes where territorial loons had not nested in recent years?

Pairs quickly took to the small islands, increasing their nesting success significantly, by 58.9 percent (McIntyre and Mathisen 1978). However, islands alone were insufficient to lure new territorial pairs to unoccupied lakes. Platforms were checked and repaired during four subsequent years, but still no loons took up residence. Apparently, by themselves, islands do not change the character of lakes sufficiently to attract loons, suggesting other factors are more important.

Nest sites are best if they include some overhead cover to hide eggs from the eyes of avian predators, good visibility of the territory by the sitting bird, a steep incline just off the nest so loons can easily approach and leave underwater, and some shelter or protection from wind and waves. No single characteristic is an absolute requirement, and does not determine whether a lake or part of a lake is selected as a territory, but such factors do help to ensure nest success.

Loons generally select an alternate site for a new nest following a loss. A territory that provides two or more good locations is better than one with only a single appropriate site (McIntyre 1975). A location found by a predator will probably be visited again, and if a replacement nest is placed in the same location as the original one, it is more likely to be depredated than a nest built elsewhere.

A place to raise young is often overlooked as an important habitat consideration. When I began to watch loons 20 years ago, I noticed that adults moved chicks away from the nest as soon as they were dry. Christoff (1978) documented use of an area for the early chick-rearing period and called it the nursery. Later, in 1981 in Saskatchewan, I mapped the locations and measured the physical features of nurseries. Quiet bays, sheltered from wind and waves, were consistently used. The availability of such places adds to the value of the territory and are reused from year to year for the same purpose (Strong 1987).

Territories are used by pairs throughout the summer, nearly until fall migration. However, adults of both sexes leave periodically throughout the breeding season. In 1968 I monitored time off and on territory for one pair that did not renest following a loss. They had been visiting other lakes to eat, because their territory was only a small pond. The female was in residence only 10.5 percent of the time from 22 June, when the nest was lost, until 27 August, when my observation periods ceased; the male spent 87.9 percent of the time during the same period on territory.

Adults, including those with young, leave their territories with increasing frequency and duration late in the summer. Young can supply much of their own food by the time they are eight weeks old (Barr 1973), so adults are able to leave for prolonged periods by this time. If their territories are on small lakes, adults go to other lakes; if territories are on large lakes where there are many pairs, adults swim to neutral places on the same lake. Either way, adults leave their territories in early morning and toward evening for social gatherings. This is described in more detail in Chapter 6.

Most territories have loons in residence for a minimum of four months, and if young are raised, the time increases to between five and six months. Nest failure often results in earlier abandonment, in some cases by late July. I suspect that birds which are among the early arrivals in spring may have the best territories with the most abundant food resource, and are therefore the same ones that leave late. It has been suggested that birds holding optimal territories are physically superior to residents on marginal territories because they have a better food resource and, therefore, are capable of migrating early (see Gauthreaux 1978). Loons do not fall into this category; the earliest to arrive are the last to leave.

Use of the same nest site, approximate similarity of boundaries from year to year, and immediate occupancy in the spring all argue strongly for site fidelity. In the early 1970s, an adult loon with a chick in tow was banded, and was recaptured the following year on the same territory (McIntyre 1974). More recently, several banded adults have been recaptured on the same territory in subsequent years during banding by Minnesota's Department of Natural Resources (Eberhardt 1984). In 1975 Keith Yonge banded and color marked 10 adult loons in Saskatchewan. In 1976 he returned to see if any marked loons had also returned and found several tagged loons, all on the same territories where they had been captured the previous year.

Most recently, sonograms of the yodel call have been used to check whether or not the same individuals occupy the same territories from year to year. Yodels are distinctive, and throughout the summer they sound the same for each loon. Sonograms are printouts of vocalizations. They allow for a quantitative analysis of calls and provide a more reliable way of looking at similarities and differences among calls than just listening to them. Sonogram analysis confirms that during the summer, each individual male loon gives the same yodel, distinctive from those of other male loons in the population.

William Barklow recorded yodels from the same territories in Maine for more than 10 years and found that the yodel from each territory was the same each year. He assumed that meant the same individual had returned to the same territory year after year. Ed Miller had the same results from his vocalization studies in Michigan, and so do I from my recordings in New York (all, pers. comm.) So far, none of us has been recording the calls of marked individuals, but the evidence seems overwhelming that each male loon has a distinctive yodel, which remains constant from year to year, and which can be used to vocally tag individuals. Yodels from several males are provided on the record at the back of the book, and sonograms are shown in Chapter 7. Altogether, the evidence indicates that each male defends the same territory for many years. There is not yet a way to mark females through their vocalizations, and banded loons have not been sexed. Other evidence indicates that loons may form the same pair bonds from year to year, as discussed in Chapter 2. If so, that means that both males and females retain the same territories in subsequent years.

Loons return to breeding territories each spring as soon as there is sufficient open water for them to land. They defend just what they need at any one time during the breeding season, and enlarge their territories, when they can, only after chicks hatch. Males arrive slightly ahead of their mates in the southern portions of the breeding range, but pairs often arrive at the same time in lakes farther north. Optimal territories have clear water, a good supply of fish, a variety of bottom types and depths, nesting islands with a steep drop-off and a good view of the territory, and quiet, protected places in which to raise chicks.

People often say, "My loons are back again this summer!" They are probably right. Loons may live for 25 or 30 years, and there is a growing body of evidence that they return to the same territories every year. Loons divide their time between freshwater lakes of the north and coastal marine waters. Many species of birds hurry north to breed each summer, and then, within a matter of weeks, hurry southward again. Loons are different. They spend about five to six months of each year on their northern lakes, and five to six months on the wintering grounds. The remainder of the time they are en route from one place to the other.

CHAPTER 2

The Pair Alone: Courtship, Mating, and Nesting

Courtship and Copulation

For all the spectacular behavior that loons exhibit, such as aggressive combats over territorial rights, night choruses, late-summer calling flights including a dozen or more birds, and ritualized late-summer gatherings, one might expect an equally exciting pattern of courtship behavior. That does not happen. Loon courtship is quiet. Published descriptions of spring behavior include chasing, running, and calling, and sometimes they have been termed courtship. But they aren't. Because only two birds are involved in many of these sequences, some observers have been wrong in concluding that they were engaged in mating displays.

It is suspected that pair members remate from year to year, and if they do, courtship should be primarily a renewal and recognition ceremony. It is possible that courtship preceding the initial pairing is different, and may be a more lively display. If this does happpen, it has yet to be witnessed and described. Courtship begins as soon as the pair is on territory and continues throughout June, providing nesting has not begun. Loons

Figure 2-1. Copulation by Common Loons. Notice that the male's feet are resting on the female's shoulders and his head extends over and beyond hers.

are physiologically ready to initiate and respond to courtship for about two months, a prolonged period of readiness which permits them to renest if a first nest is lost.

Before nesting, the pair spends most of its time together in back bays and near nesting islands engaged in feeding and caring for feathers and other body parts, which behaviorists call maintenance activities. Periodically throughout the day, but especially in the morning and evening, they move close to the shoreline, where they swim close together, either side by side or in tandem. Males and females share the same displays, which they usually give at the same time. As pair members swim together, their posturings tend to reduce direct visual confrontation. They avert their heads from each other by turning them to the side, and they engage in short dives. Chapter 7 provides detailed descriptions of visual and vocal signals, and Figure 7–2 shows the sequence of visual displays.

The "mew" or "ma" call is given by both sexes, but most often by the male when he swims to shore and invites the female to come onto land for copulation. As he faces away from her, he turns his head slightly toward her, he calls, and she responds by either moving toward him or swimming away. As long as she remains nearby, he continues to call. Males invite more frequently than females accept. A male may remain sitting quietly, pointing toward the shore, call, invite, and wait over and over again before his mate accepts. It is common for females seemingly to ignore their mates, then initiate copulation themselves by climbing onto land at a site

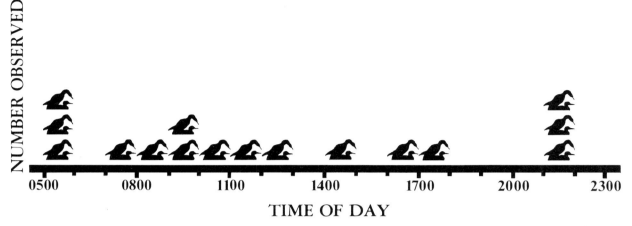

Figure 2-2. Times of day when Common Loons have been observed to copulate (N = 5 pairs).

of their own choosing. Courtship sequences vary in duration from a minute or two to a quarter of an hour, but most last from three to 10 minutes. They end with much preening, whether or not a copulation results.

Copulation is highly stereotyped. If the male is the initiator, he swims to shore, assumes a modified pelican posture by alternately facing land and turning his head away (Figure 7–2e). He sometimes climbs onto land, and if he does, and his mate follows, he returns to the water, swims around so that he can be in a position to climb up and mount her from behind. If the female initiates copulation, she climbs onto shore first, and may or may not lower her head and face away from the male.

The male shuffles over the back of his mate until he stands half upright to establish cloacal contact (Plate 1). She raises her tail and moves it to one side, and copulation follows (Figure 2–1). He does not grasp the female's neck as waterfowl do. After a few seconds, he dismounts by walking over her shoulder and sliding into the water, then he swims a short distance from land and preens. The female continues to hold her tail high and stays on lands for two to three minutes longer before she leaves, swims out a short distance, and preens. The copulation site sometimes becomes the nest site, and when it does, nest-building frequently follows copulation. If this is the case, the female may stay on land longer. Even if she does not move nest material around with her bill, she stays on land at least two minutes longer than the male does.

Copulations are more common in the morning and evening than at other times, but occur throughout the day (see Figure 2–2). I don't know if loons copulate at night, but suspect they do not, because at night they raft away from land over deeper water. The same location may be used repeatedly for copulations. I have seen loons try to climb onto land in some places where they immediately fall back into the water, unable to stay on a hummock or islet that isn't large enough for two birds. I once saw a male walk onto his mate's back, then fall off sideways when the weight of the two loons caused a shift in the floating island under them. I also saw a female accept a male's invitation, climb onto land, then slowly sink deeper and deeper into the water as the fragile sedge mat they were occupying collapsed beneath them. It would seem reasonable that a site once found to be appropriate might be used over and over again. So, quietly and without fanfare, chases, running, aerial displays, or extensive vocalizing, loons court, mate, and begin the business of raising young.

Nests

All loons build their nests on the ground adjacent to the water, and on a variety of anchored or nonfloating substrate. Eggs are sometimes placed directly on rock, covered with duff, needles, or leaves. Some are on sedge mat, and occasionally loons use a cranberry patch or the half-rotted part of a semisubmerged log. Muskrat houses may be slightly rearranged to include a depression, and a small island is perfect. In Saskatchewan, 84 percent of the nests were placed on islands (Yonge 1981). Just to the west, in Alberta, 92.3 percent were on islands (Vermeer 1973a). What is important is that nests be on something surrounded by water. If vegetation is available, loons use it; if not, they make no structure. Table 2–1 summarizes published descriptions of loon nests and demonstrates that variability occurs wherever loons nest. From Alaska to Maine and from the Yukon to New Hampshire, loons use whatever materials are on hand.

When they do construct a nest, loons are opportunistic in their choice of vegetation. Materials have been examined during studies in New Hampshire, Saskatchewan, and Minnesota (Table 2–2). At the southern limit of the loons' range, there is an abundance of vegetation available for nesting material; in the Canadian Shield country, rocky islands provide most nest sites, and vegetative materials are limited. Even so, there is sufficient diversity among nests in each of the three regions to indicate that loons are not fussy in their choice of nest materials.

I collected two nests that loons built on artificial islands, so I was sure they were composed only of materials used to build a single nest. Clumps of vegetation formed more than 80 percent of each nest, both by weight

Table 2–1. Nest Types throughout the Breeding Range of Common Loons

Masses of Vegetation consisting of material at hand, both terrestrial and aquatic, usually partially rotted

    Iceland: Sjølander and Ågren 1972
    Maine: Bent 1919, Sim 1923, Palmer 1949
    Minnesota: Olson and Marshall 1952, McIntyre 1975
    New Brunswick: Raine 1892
    Newfoundland: Peters and Burleigh 1951
    New Hampshire: Sutcliffe 1980
    New York: McIntyre unpubl.
    Nova Scotia: Tufts 1961
    Northwest Territories: Raine 1892
    Saskatchewan: Yonge 1981
    Western Canada: Taverner 1926, Munro 1945

Depressions in old muskrat houses

    Alaska: Gabrielson and Lincoln 1959
    Alberta: Salt and Wilk 1958
    British Columbia: Munro 1945
    Massachusetts: Forbush 1925
    Michigan: Manville 1952
    Minnesota: Roberts 1932, Olson and Marshall 1952, McIntyre 1975
    Ontario: Snyder 1951

Scrapes, bare, or nearly bare, made on sand or rock

    Alaska: Gabrielson and Lincoln 1959
    Alberta: Salt and Wilk 1958
    British Columbia: Munro 1945
    Iceland: Yeates 1950
    Maine: Palmer 1949
    Massachusetts: Forbush 1925
    Michigan: Manville 1952
    Minnesota: Roberts 1932, Olson 1951, McIntyre 1975
    Newfoundland: Bent 1919
    New York: Davie 1898
    Nova Scotia: Tafts 1961
    Ontario: Raine 1898
    Quebec: Dionne 1906
    Saskatchewan: Yonge 1981.

Moss only
    Quebec: Harper 1958
    Saskatchewan: Yonge 1981

and by volume. The clumps had either been plucked from around the nest or brought up from the bottom of the lake. Yonge (1981) also found that clumps accounted for the largest percentage of materials used in any one nest in Saskatchewan. Apparently, loons use chunks of vegetation as the major material when it is available. In fact, a former nest suspected to have been a loon nest can be confirmed as one by finding that it is made of a collection of individual matted clumps. Loons also use other things, for example, old reeds or cattails, which have dried and been washed ashore.

I weighed the two nests I collected: one weighed nine, and the other, 18, kilograms. Loons can and do build substantial nests, and if water levels rise during incubation, they continue to build their nests higher to prevent flooding. Nest diameter is over half a meter. Table 2–3 gives nest sizes from more than one hundred nests in Minnesota and New Hampshire. New Hampshire nests are a little larger than Minnesota ones, and this may be a reflection of the larger body size of New Hampshire loons. Larger loons may need larger nests on which to sit for four weeks.

Nests are rarely built far from water. Loons are awkward on land and are vulnerable unless they are able to enter the water quickly. Nests are almost always placed at the water's edge when they are new, but if water levels fall, nests become farther and farther away as incubation proceeds. Most nests are placed next to a drop-off, an abrupt slope in the lake bottom immediately offshore. This is not mandatory, but is preferable, as deep water assures that a loon can swim underwater and undetected to and from the nest. A swimming loon measures 0.2 meters from belly to back, and it is interesting that water depths off 28 successful Saskatchewan sites were more than 0.3 meters deep at five meters from the nest and had an average slope of 30° (McIntyre 1983).

There are two advantages for placement near deep water: Water levels fluctuate, both naturally, from droughts and heavy rainfall, and from artificial conditions such as dam impoundments. Loons continue to incubate if their nests are stranded by water drawdowns, but there is a limit to how far they will move overland to reach their nests. If a nest is left stranded high above the water, loons will continue to incubate even when they must climb two or three meters up to it. I have seen loons scramble up a steep slope for 45 minutes to reach a nest after it was left perched atop a small island following a drop in water level. Yet, from such a site, a loon can enter the water quickly if disturbed. Vulnerability comes from being stranded inland, unable to leave rapidly, and not from having to make a long return trip back to the nest.

Table 2–2. Vegetation in Common Loon Nests (N = 243 nests)

Study Area and Source	Material	Percentage Occurrence[a]
Saskatchewan Yonge 1981	moss chunks	75
	Carex spp.	73
	twigs	40
	leaf litter	23
	detritus from lake bottom	12
	Phragmites communis	9
	Scirpus spp.	9
	Typha spp.	2
New Hampshire Sutcliffe 1980	detritus	31
	grasses	20
	twigs	20
	rhizomes	5
	Bryophtes	5
	unidentified leaves	5
Minnesota McIntyre 1975	*Carex* spp.	87
	Typha latifolia	47
	Scirpus acutus	40
	moss, other than sphagnum	33
	Dryopteris thelypteris	27
	Eleocharis sp.	20
	Lycopus uniflores	20
	Scuttelaria epilobifloia	20
	unidentified rhizomes	20
	Alnus sp.	13
	Campanula aparanoides	13
	Hypericum virginicum	13
	Utricularia sp.	13
	Calla palustris	7
	Dulichium arundinaceum	7
	Iris versicolor	7
	Salix sp.	7
	sphagnum	7
	Thuja occidentalis	7
	pine needles	7

[a]Figures indicate the percentage of nests examined in which a vegetation type/species occurred.

Table 2–3. Sizes of Common Loon Nests in Minnesota and New Hampshire

Study Area and Source	N	Outside (cm)	Inside (cm)	Depth (cm)
Minnesota				
McIntyre 1975	47	56.9	24.4	3.1
Olson and Marshall 1952	12	55.9	33.0	7.6
New Hampshire				
Sutcliffe 1981	54	66.0	32.4	4.1

Loons leave and return underwater to their nests when they can. During experiments in 1971 and 1972 to identify potential predators on loon nests in north central Minnesota, mainland experimental sites were depredated nightly and island locations were left untouched. I had constructed artificial loon nests, packed a mixture of wet sand and clay around them to permit footprints to remain after the predators left, and placed double-yolked turkey eggs, dyed to look like loon eggs, in each nest. The nests were checked every morning and evening and eggs were replaced as needed (see Plate 2).

During the 1971 trials, 71 percent of all egg losses on the mainland were caused by raccoons and the rest by skunks. In 1972, raccoons were responsible for 89 percent of all losses, most during the night (72 percent). At the same time, there were no losses on island sites (McIntyre 1976). Opportunistic scavengers that wandered along the shoreline quickly learned about the availability of eggs and returned nightly to eat the replacements.

Small islands, on the other hand, do not harbor shore-wandering mammals, and random mammalian depredation consequently is reduced. However, there are also avian predators, primarily gulls, crows, and ravens, which survey prospective sites from the air. I wondered why no birds had found the experimental nests. Then I realized that the major difference between my experiments and a real loon nest was that I had not gone back and forth to the nests (I checked them through a spotting scope)—there had been no activity to attract attention to the nest.

The assumption is that the same thing is happening to loon nests in the wild as is happening during the experiments. When loons are able to return to their nests underwater, they don't have to surface until reaching shore, and when leaving, they slide head first into the water off the nest and make an underwater exit. Deep water and a steep slope permit unobtrusive nest exchanges, reducing the chance that predators will find the nest.

All nests are not sheltered, but most are placed away from the wind, in a small bay, or on a promontory on the lee side of an island. In Minnesota, where the prevailing winds are from the northwest and where the southeast shores are swept clean, the northwest sides often have boggy, marshy shoreline. As expected, nests are placed mostly on the northeast, east, south, and southwest sides. Of those I measured, only 16 percent of the nests were along the southeast.

On the other hand, when loons use islands as nest sites, they choose the side closest to the mainland; or if a small nesting island is near a larger one, they locate on the side toward the larger island (Yonge 1981). The larger land mass offers shelter and nests may be on any side whether north, east, south or west, if the mainland is close by. Other commonly chosen sites are in bays or along slight indentations in the shoreline. In view of the increase in human recreational pressure, it may be that back bays, or the backwaters that Strong (1985) describes, have fewer intrusions from campers and canoeists, and so offer the privacy loons seek; otherwise it seems incompatible with another preference for loon nests, that of visibility of their own territory.

On a pristine Canadian lake where human intrusion was slight, I measured the ability of incubating loons to view their own territories by placing myself on their nests, and, at loon's eye level, taking compass readings over as broad a distance as I could. The average angle of their line of sight was 130° (McIntyre 1983) and it seemed that nests are positioned to compromise maximum shelter with maximum visibility.

Two studies in the Boundary Waters Canoe Area of northern Minnesota reported that 92.6 percent and 77.9 percent of loon nests were on islands (Olson and Marshall 1952, Titus and Van Druff 1981). The more recent study was done after the region had become tremendously popular as a canoe route. The investigators found that pressure from island-camping canoeists had forced many loons to abandon traditional territories, which had been centered on the area around islands along the canoe route. Loons had shifted their nests to bays and shorelines away from people. The higher figure of 92.6 percent from 30 years earlier probably indicates the loons' preference if they could nest anywhere they chose to. The lower, more recent figure shows only what the loons did do, and not what may have been optimal for them.

Sutcliffe (1981) reported that 69 percent of New Hampshire nests were on islands, and in Minnesota, I found that just over 50 percent were. When

I offered artificial platforms, island use increased to 88 percent. Evidence indicates that islands are the preferred nest sites, but in some of the more developed sectors of the breeding range, where islands have been taken over by summer homes and campers, loons are able to nest on alternative sites. Strong (1985), for example, found that Maine loons chose both islands and backwater sites.

If a first clutch is lost, loons frequently renest, usually in a different place. Consecutive nest sites may be in the same location following success (hatch) or in a different place following failure (loss of eggs) (Figure 2–3). The same nest site is often used year after year, but if a nest fails in one year, there is an increased chance the next nest will be built in a different location. If a renest is attempted during the same breeding season, a different site is almost always used, and if a nest is lost but the loons do not renest during that breeding season, a different site will most likely be chosen the following year. If a nest placed on the secondary site is then destroyed, they frequently go back to the previous site for the next nesting, and so rotate nest placement between the two sites.

Nests are built by both members of the pair. They do so by pulling or retrieving nest material and throwing it from side to side on the nest site. Harrison (1967) described the many ways in which birds build their nests, and called sideways-throwing the most primitive form of construction. When a loon "pulls" nest material, it reaches out as it sits on the nest, and either drags nearby material toward itself, or pulls vegetation up by the roots and lays it on the nest site. Moss is gathered in this way, and dead material, such as dried reeds or cattails which have been washed ashore, are sometimes used, too.

"Retrieving" refers to fetching material from the bottom of the lake, bringing it to the surface, and throwing it onto the nest site. Retrieved materials are primarily partially rotted vegetation and roots of aquatic plants, and they provide the characteristic appearance of a mound of clumps typical of loon nests. Throwing is inaccurate early in nest-building, and I have seen loons bring up billsful of vegetation only to throw them back into the lake. In 1971 I watched a loon dive, bring up a large bunch of rootlets, and throw it onto its own back! Fortunately, the bird's aim improved during later building stages.

When loons work as a pair, one member is on the nest and the other is nearby in the water, although sometimes both may climb onto the site and build. Whenever I have watched Common Loons build a nest, both pair members have been working together. On the other hand, Drury (1961) watched Red-throated Loons, and said they worked one at a time.

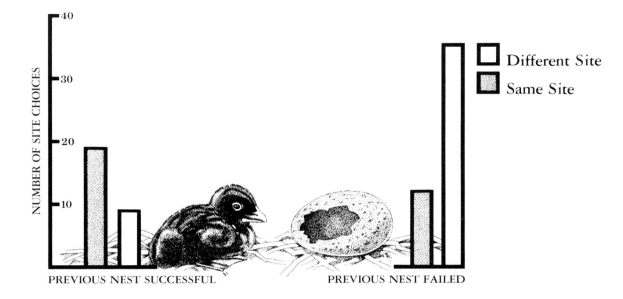

Figure 2-3. Nest-site selection relative to the preceding nesting attempt and its success or failure. At *left* are sites at which there was a successful hatch during the last nesting attempt; at *right* are sites at which eggs were lost before hatching during the preceding attempt. The same site refers to the same location as the preceding nest; a different site is somewhere other than the previous location.

While one bird worked alone, its mate loafed on the opposite side of the territory. Sjølander and Ågren (1972) thought Common Loon females in Iceland did all the nest-building; Lehtonen (1970) stated that male Arctic Loons in Finland built alone. I doubt this is sufficient evidence that building differs among loon species; the sample sizes in each study (one to four pairs) are simply too small to form such a conclusion. It may be that there is simply a great deal of variability from one pair to another.

In 1981 I built an artificial nesting islet directly offshore from my observation post. I wanted to be able to monitor one pair from the onset of nesting through incubation. The loons accepted the structure immediately, but unfortunately lost their first egg to high waves during a storm and renested in another location. However, I was able to monitor them continuously during their first nest-building sequence. The time spent in all aspects of nest-building, both the number of times each bird got on and off the nest and the total amount of time each bird spent actively building, was equally divided between the two (McIntyre 1975). Both parents incubate, and trading places during nest-building by getting-off and getting-on may be important in establishing a pattern of nest exchange, but as far as I know the idea has not been tested.

Some nest-building continues during incubation. Loons act out some nest-building behavior immediately after a nest exchange, and as the new incubator settles on the eggs, it picks at and sometimes picks up plants around the nest. This may result in vegetation being added to the nest, but unless the nest is threatened, little real building will be done. During times of rising water levels, birds actively build, and as water rises, so do nests. Pair members build during storms, during flooding and heavy wave action, and if the nest is in jeopardy, both adults may vigorously dive and add new material from the bottom of the lake.

Nests that haven't been used for many years are still recognizable as loon nests. Much nest material is roots, and old nests sprout new plants. Nests used in subsequent years have material added to them each year, but small eggshell fragments from previous years can usually be found buried beneath them.

Eggs

"Anyone who has seen a loon egg is apt to remember it first for its size. Any female loon who has ever laid one no doubt remembers it for the same reason." I wrote this a long time ago in my doctoral thesis. I have looked at it since and wondered if I really put that flip statement in a dissertation or if some invisible hand wrote it while I wasn't looking. The statement is true. I am looking at a loon egg as I write. It isn't big as loon eggs go, only 52.8 mm x 89.5 mm, and it weighed only 116 grams when collected. Some loon eggs weigh half again as much, and most are between 140 and 160 grams. Nevertheless, it is a big egg. It is thick-shelled, dark, and impressive.

Egg sizes vary among populations. The smallest are in North Dakota and the largest in the northeast and northwest, in Alaska, eastern Canada, and Iceland (Anderson et al. 1970). Measurements were taken from eggs in museums, eggs collected before 1946, the year DDT was first added to the environment. The authors were interested in comparing their size and thickness with that of eggs laid later, to measure the effects of chlorinated hydrocarbons. I measured eggs from Minnesota, New York, and Saskatchewan. These more recent measurements, together with others

Table 2–4. Common Loon Egg Sizes by Geographical Region
(West to East across the Breeding Range)

Study Area[a]	N	Length x Breadth	L/B Ratio	Volume (cm³)	Collection Date	Source
Alaska, British Columbia	32	no data	1.54	143.7	pre-1946	Anderson et al. 1970
Washington, Idaho, Montana	10	no data	1.58	130.9	pre-1946	Anderson et al. 1970
Alberta, Manitoba, Saskatchewan	70	no data	1.60	128.0	pre-1946	Anderson et al. 1970
Saskatchewan	148	87.1x54.7	1.59	129.5	1975	Yonge 1981
Saskatchewan	11	86.4x54.3	1.59	126.1	1981	McIntyre unpubl.
Alberta	40	86.5x53.9	1.60	124.3	1972	Vermeer 1973b
Minnesota, Wisconsin, Michigan, southern Ontario	49	no data	1.58	140.5	pre-1946	Anderson et al. 1970
Minnesota	53	87.6x55.6	1.58	134.1	1970–74	McIntyre 1975
Minnesota	30	87.0x54.0	1.58	129.7	1949	Olson and Marshall 1952
Ontario, Quebec	69	no data	1.62	142.7	pre-1946	Anderson et al. 1970
Maine, New York, New Hampshire, Nova Scotia, Labrador, Newfoundland	38	no data	1.61	146.3	pre-1946	Anderson et al. 1970
New York	45	91.56x57.14	1.60	148.3	1978–83	McIntyre unpubl.
Iceland, eastern Greenland	43	no data	1.56	150.3	pre-1946	Anderson et al. 1970

[a]Geographical area designations from Anderson et al. 1970.

from Alberta and Saskatchewan, are nearly the same as those made earlier (see Table 2–4).

A loon's second egg is smaller than the first. Yonge (1981) said that second eggs averaged about two percent smaller; when I compared the first and second eggs from a sampling of New York lakes, an even greater difference was apparent. It was between 0.3 and 10 percent, with an average of 3.5 percent (N = 21). Eggs in replacement clutches are smaller than those from the original by about four percent according to Yonge (1981). Neither he nor I found that size was related to hatchability, either within a clutch or among clutches.

Loon eggs are subelliptical to ovoid in shape. Their color varies from a deep olive to a light brown, although most eggs are a deep olive brown and have dark brown or black irregular spots (Plate 3). Color varies from

Table 2–5. Number of Eggs in Common Loon Clutches

Study Area	1-Egg	2-Egg	3-Egg	N	Source
Alberta	1	16	2	1	Henderson 1924
	5	18	1	24	Vermeer 1973b
Minnesota	21	26	0	47	Olson and Marshall 1952
	18	32	1	51	McIntyre 1975
	56	73	0	129	Titus and Van Druff 1981
New York	6	32	0	38	McIntyre unpubl.
Saskatchwan	54	197	1	252	Yonge 1981
	15	47	0	62	McIntyre unpubl.
Totals	176	441	5	622	
Proportion of total	.283	.709	.008		

clutch to clutch in the same population, and even eggs from the same nest are sometimes different from each other. Eggs laid by the same female are similar in shape and size.

Most clutches contain two eggs (Table 2–5). A quick glance shows that there are many one-egg clutches, more than one-fourth of the sample, so perhaps it should be said that loons lay *either* one or two eggs in each laying cycle. However, many of the one-egg clutches are "partial clutches," that is, they are left when one of a clutch of two is taken by a predator, lost to flooding or some other cause. During one study I found that only seven of 18 one-egg clutches were the product of a one-egg laying cycle. Other researchers have also reported that most one-egg clutches are laid after the first egg of a two-egg laying cycle had been lost (Titus and Van Druff 1981, Yonge 1981).

Three-egg clutches are rare. Only five have been reported from the seven studies supplying information presented in Table 2–5. Five of 622 is less than one percent! More recently, there have been other reports of three-egg clutches, and even the discovery of two four-egg clutches, one in Minnesota (Zicus et al. 1983) and one in New Hampshire (Nelson 1983). I have seen two broods of three partially grown young that I could verify had come from the same nest. Apparently, a three-egg clutch can be laid, incubated, hatched, and reared, at least for a few weeks. Whether or not young from a brood of this size can be successfully fledged is not known.

Two-egg clutches have a higher hatching rate than do one-egg clutches. By combining the results of several studies and 314 clutches, I calculated that 33.8 percent of the one-egg clutches hatched, but more than twice as many, 70.2 percent of the two-egg clutches did (Olson and Marshall 1952, Vermeer 1973a, McIntyre 1975, Titus and Van Druff 1981). Hatching of each egg in a two-egg clutch is not an independent event. Titus and Van Druff (1981) pointed out that only 12 percent of their two-egg clutches hatched a single egg and lost the other. Either both hatch or neither do.

All eggs for which I have recorded laying times were laid in the afternoon at two-day intervals. However, Yonge (1981) counted nine instances of a three-day interval between eggs. The three for which I have notes were laid at 1408, between 1308 and 1715, and between 1700 and daybreak, respectively. The literature offers little information on laying times for any species of loon, although Drury (1961) reported seeing a Red-throated Loon lay an egg in the afternnoon between 1640 and 1655.

I was lucky to witness egg-laying by one female after watching her throughout the nest-building period. It was the first egg she laid that year, maybe the first ever. The following description is taken verbatim from my field notes, and it gives a step-by-step description of egg-laying.

Time of Day	Observation
1305–1327	Female on nest, building.
1327–1402	Female sitting, no building behavior.
1402	Male approaches nest, goes up to female, then slowly swims back and forth in front of her. He leaves.
1402–1408	Female raises body up and down 19 times. The first 17 times were 5 seconds each, the 18th time took 12 seconds, and the last time was 16 seconds. At this time the egg was laid. Female stays semi-upright, gives a tail-shake, moves tail up and down more than 15 times. I lost track of the number. She grips the side of the nest with her toes and she pants.
1408–1425	Female continues to grip side of nest with toes, she is facing me and I can see her from head-on. She pants and periodically opens and closes her eyes.
1428	Female stops panting. Sits.
1429–1433	Female pecks at vegetation, then slides off nest and leaves. The male meets her as she swims

	away from the nest. They turn their heads away from each other. Female dives, comes up in front of her mate, swims past him using crouch swimming posture.
1433	Male swims to nest, looks at it, returns to female, swims again to nest, climbs on.
1434–1436	As male stands semi-upright on nest he rolls egg with his feet, rolls it forward, then repeats the rolling 4 times. He finally sits on the egg, pulls vegetation around himself and arranges it.
1436	Female swims to nest, dives directly in front.
1439–1442	Male moves to one side of the nest, off the egg, and keeps building. The female climbs on, and both pair members continue to work on building the nest.

Drury (1961) described the egg-laying he saw by a Red-throated Loon and said she laid it in 15 minutes with "no noticeable movement." I know of no other published accounts of egg-laying.

Loons may lay replacement clutches if the first one is lost. I know of four nesting attempts by only one pair, but the last two were parts of a single laying cycle. The first egg was lost almost as soon as it was laid and the bird moved to a new nest site before laying the second. Loons do not always lay replacement clutches. Less than half the pairs that lost nests while I was studying them laid a second clutch. Yonge (1981) kept records on 148 destroyed clutches, and noted that 66, or 45 percent, were replaced, slightly less than half. He found that the date on which a clutch was lost was the best predictor for the possibility it would be replaced. If a nest was lost early during the nesting season, within the first 18 days, there was a greater than 80 percent chance it would be replaced; if later, the chances fell, to less than 19 percent if the nesting season had continued for more than a month.

Replacement clutches are not laid immediately following loss of a nest. Second nestings were initiated between 11 and 13 days following loss by loons in Minnesota. Sutcliffe (1980) reported that New Hampshire loons renested after an interval of eight to 18 days. Yonge (1981) made a thorough analysis of replacement intervals using data from 27 lost nests. He found a positive linear relationship between the time of year when the original nest was lost and the time lapse until a replacement began. For example, if nests were lost early in the summer, the interval until a new nest was started was likely to be eight, nine, or 10 days. Later in the breeding season, longer intervals followed before a new attempt began. There was no relationship between the length of time it took to start a second nest and the length of time the first clutch had been incubated.

Incubation

Both pair members incubate and they do so for nearly a month. Loons I studied spent between 26 and 31 days incubating clutches that hatched. The first egg may hatch one day earlier than the second, and sometimes they hatch simultaneously or within the same day. Even without taking into account hatching differences for the two eggs, there is some variability in the length of incubation. Yonge (1981) found that the average was only 26 days for any one egg, and he thinks the longer incubation time of 28 to 29 days, which is reported so often in the literature, may mean the total time between the laying of the first egg and the hatching of the second.

At times loons may continue to incubate long after the appropriate time. Sutcliffe (1982) kept checking on loons that sat and sat and sat, and he found that each of two pairs sat for 66 and 74 days, by far the longest times on record. I had always attributed extended incubation to infertile eggs, and thought that adults continued to incubate eggs that never had a chance to hatch in the first place. Now some disturbing new evidence shows that many overincubated eggs from my New York study site contained chicks almost ready to hatch. Why did they fail? Tests on these eggs are being conducted by the U.S. Fish and Wildlife Service, but so far there are no answers.

The nest is covered by one adult for more than 99 percent of the time during an incubation period. Only rarely are nests left untended. When people approach too close, the loons slide off into the water. Nests are left at other times when an intruder loon enters the territory, and both adults swim out in defense. Occasionally an adult slips from its nest and goes a short way out in the water to preen or bathe, but it returns quickly, and is never out of view of the nest site. Loons do not cover their nests when they leave them, so eggs are exposed.

Loons do not have a brood patch with loss of all feathers in a specific region of the abdomen. They do, however, have increased vascularization in a part of the belly which rests on the eggs. Plate 4 shows egg placement under the bird. In both males and females there is an increased blood sup-

Figure 2-4. Incubation postures of Common Loons. *a.* Turning the eggs. *b.* Panting. When weather is hot, loons spread their wings away from the body, open their bills, and pant. *c.* Incubation posture seen most frequently, the "normal" position. *d.* Upright posture. This is an alert position and is taken following initial recognition of a disturbance. *e.* Hangover posture. This is incipient to leaving the nest, hence is an intention movement. Loons assume this posture when they are approached or when disturbance is prolonged, and if it continues, they will quietly slip underwater from this position.

ply to the abdomen, confirming that both incubate. Birds that have nested, but have completed the annual cycle, show a modified extent of vascularization; those that have not nested at all have no proliferation of blood vessels (Barr, pers. comm.).

I have never been able to find a general pattern of nest exchange. Taylor (1974) tells of "setting his watch" by nest exchanges, but I cannot find a pair with such a reliable schedule. Some pairs exchange duties approximately every hour and a half for two weeks, then the time interval changes; other pairs have longer bouts, and may sit for several hours at a time before relinquishing nest and eggs to the mate. Many pairs do have a regular day/night pattern. Exchange times during the day may vary, but at dawn the males of these pairs relieve their mates, and late in the evening, when there is barely enough light to record nest exchanges, females climb onto their nests and males move into open water.

Does this mean that females are always on nests at night while males patrol? The pattern of nocturnal calling by males would seem to support this idea. Young (1983) reported that yodels are given most frequently at night during the nesting stage. Yodels are male calls, used as territorial statements, and are the only calls not given by females. Young's results suggest that males are off their nests at night and are out patrolling their territories. Conversely, Yonge (pers. comm.) told of capturing both pair members on the nest on subsequent nights, one on one night, the other the following night. Perhaps pairs set their own, unique schedules, or maybe close to hatching, both members are more attentive and males are more likely to take their turn on the nest during the night. There is much work to be done to determine the pattern of nest exchange.

Loons reach their nests from the water's edge by "walking" one foot at a time with their bodies in a semiupright position. If the distance from water to nest is great, they may periodically stop and flop to their bellies, or they may walk a couple of steps, flop, and slide along like a feathered seal. Late in incubation, pathways from shore to nest resemble beaver runways, especially where the water level has fallen and vegetation has grown between the shoreline and the nest.

Incubation postures are shown in Figure 2–4. Most of the time loons sit as shown in Figure 2–4c, but if there is disturbance, they raise their heads (Figure 2–4d) and look around. If the disturbance continues, or if an intruder remains nearby, they hang over the nest, an intention movement indicating that they are about to leave the nest and slide into the water (Figure 2–4e). When weather is hot, loons remain on the nest, even though they could cool themselves quickly by entering the water, but they do spread their wings and pant as they continue to incubate (Figure 2–4b). Eggs are turned every time there is a nest exchange, and occasionally, in between.

Finally, after nearly a month sitting on a nest, hot sun beating on their backs, blackflies biting their heads, summer storms spilling rain and hail on them, rising water levels sending them scurrying to add nest material, their eggs hatch. The loon family is free to leave.

CHAPTER 3
The Loon Family

Beginning about midsummer, at the time of the longest day of the year, and continuing until mid-July, loon pairs become loon families. The group of male, female, and one or two chicks stays together throughout the summer. Both parents nurture and nourish their young, and the group remains a cohesive unit until close to the time of fall migration.

Hatching

Loon chicks hatch within 24 hours of the time they pip (break through the shell of) their eggs. They begin to peep while still in the shell, as early as four days before hatching, and they continue to peep as they peck open the egg. It is easy to determine whether an egg has been hatched or predated. The membrane of a hatched egg has "bite" marks left by the chick's egg tooth. The chick circles the large end of the egg as it opens the membrane, and a distinctive pattern is left.

Siblings usually do not hatch at the same time, although there are exceptions. I found that all chicks from the same nest hatch within 24 hours of each other. Yonge (1981) did a detailed study on hatching intervals of 39 broods, and he found a greater variability of hatching intervals than I did and offered some explanations for optimal timing. He suggested that a fine line exists between selection for synchronous hatching and longer intervals between the time chicks emerge. If chicks hatch together, they share an equal chance of surviving. Neither has a priority advantage over the other, both are off the nest at the same time, and initially are fed at approximately the same time.

When there is a long interval between hatchings, the first chick leaves the nest for a short time, is fed, and is stronger and heavier than the second to hatch before the family moves away permanently from the nest site. It maintains a weight advantage and outcompetes its smaller brother or sister for all resources. On the other hand, if food is scarce or not readily available, synchronously hatched young would share what food there is and the chance of the parents raising even one young is reduced.

The optimal strategy is to produce chicks that both stand an excellent chance of fledging if there is sufficient food, but where at least one will survive if there is only enough food for one. Yonge (1981) found that chicks hatching less than 12 hours apart had a lower survival rate than those hatching at longer intervals, but among those hatching more than 30 hours apart, survival of both was still more unlikely. He concluded that broods of chicks that hatch 18 to 24 hours apart have the best chance of fledging.

Chicks are dry within a few hours after hatching and stay on the nest overnight if they hatch in the afternoon or if the weather is severe. One generally hatches first and it may leave the nest for a swim with one parent while the other parent remains on the nest with the still-hatching chick. The older chick eventually returns to the nest where both offspring are brooded under the sitting adult until they are dry and able to move away from the nest site. Chicks on the nest spend much time crawling over, under, and around the parent bird, as well as crawling under the wing and onto the back. This instinctive behavior follows the same patterns used when chicks initiate back-riding. It may serve as a practice session for the chicks before their permanent move to the water.

Once a pair of chicks is off the nest they do not return. However, Sjølander and Ågren (1972) reported that loons and their young frequently went ashore in Iceland, although they didn't suggest they came onto land at the nest site. I surprised an adult and chicks resting on the shore in northern Saskatchewan, but have never encountered loons anywhere but on the water in New York or Minnesota. It may be that in places where human disturbance is rare, loons go ashore from time to time to brood their young, but where people pressure is great, loons have given up this habit and stay in the water.

Figure 3-1. Diagrammatic interpretation of loon chick following its parents as it is led off the nest. As it swims toward one, that adult turns away, while the second comes closer. This, in turn, seems to stimulate the chick to turn and swim toward the other adult, which then turns away and the chick returns to the first parent. Thus, the chick is forced to zigzag between the two as they lead it off the nest and to the nursery.

Chicks may come back to the nest site shortly after initial nest-leaving, but this is only temporary, and happens when something is not quite right. I watched this sequence in the Adirondacks of New York:

Two chicks had hatched the previous day and been brooded on the nest overnight. At 0930 the adults called them off the nest and moved a short distance out, into open water, one on either side of their young.

Suddenly they were attacked by a dive-bombing Herring Gull. The male loon defended by treading water and penguin dancing, but did no calling. The chicks remained with the female.

After the gull left, the loons, chicks in tow, returned to the nest site. The female climbed on, and after she moved eggshell fragments around with her bill, the chicks scrambled onto the nest. They moved under her, were brooded, and stayed for two hours.

At 1130 they quietly left the nest, and the family moved silently across the open water to the nursery. Chicks swam all the way and there was no back-riding during the move.

At 0930 the weather had been drizzly following an all-night rain. By 1130 the sun was out and the day was clear. Was it weather or predator that precipitated their return to the nest? Either, neither or both may have been the cause.

Adults coax chicks off the nest from the water, facing them and giving little calls similar to the mew calls used during courtship, but with an added frequency component, so that they sound like soft two-note wails. The young scramble off the nest, tumble into the water, and swim out to their parents. They may swim to the adults and stay in the water, not on the adults' backs, for up to an hour.

Chicks are soon moved to a nursery area, and those I watched swam all the way. During the voyage, chicks try to climb onto an adult's back, and as they do, the nearer adult swims away and the other moves closer. The chicks then move toward the approaching parent, and when they get too close, it swims off and the first one returns. In this way the chicks follow a zigzag path to the nursery (Figure 3–1).

Chicks don't always zigzag, but they follow, either between their parents or lagging behind, during the trip that may take two hours or more. I suspect that following the parents permits imprinting by the chicks. If the distance is great, or if there are other problems such as wind, waves, or potential predators, the adults may stop enroute at a quiet sector and permit the young to climb onto their backs, and may feed them before proceeding. When they continue, the little loonlings are made to swim once again. They stay in nurseries for the first two weeks, or, if the location is suitable and has prey items of various sizes which are suitable for larger chicks as well as for the tiny ones, they may use the same location for several weeks.

Nurseries

Habitat suitable for rearing small loon chicks is different from that which makes good nest sites, and is not the same as places for feeding or social gatherings. While I was studying loon response to vocalization playbacks in northern Saskatchewan, I had the opportunity to examine the requirements nurseries had to meet on a large lake with 86 pairs of loons (McIntyre 1983; Figure 3–2). I assumed that if many pairs of loons partitioned a lake, the nurseries would all have some features in common. Perhaps these could provide clues to what factors are important for a good nursery.

The major similarity was protection from strong winds and waves. Most nurseries were located in back bays, but if that was not possible, there was another form of shelter. Sometimes it was just a strip close to the mainland along the west side, with protection from westerly winds, or in small coves, with protective islands between them and the main body of the lake.

Nurseries are shallow and have both emergent and submergent vegetation. They average 1.75 hectares, or about 15 percent of the territory, and are less than a meter and a half deep. These measurements were taken during the Saskatchewan study, but I have also made random measurements during field work in other places, primarily in New York and Minnesota, and they are similar. Nurseries are uniformly shallow, usually in bays, and have an abundance of small fish. One other feature they all share is their distance from the nest site. My Canadian study revealed that nursery locations were variable, yet averaged half a kilometer from the nest (509 meters) and were nearly 300 meters farther from the nearest neighbor's territorial line than the nest was. On small lakes where so great a distance was not possible, nurseries were at the opposite side of the lake, or around a peninsula from the nest site.

Nearly 15 years ago I received a letter from one of the volunteers in Project Loon Watch in Minnesota. She told of a small lake where loons nested and of a larger nearby lake where the adults took their young to raise them. She found tiny chicks walking/crawling/scooting along a roadway, preparing to cross to the larger lake on the other side, while overhead the parent birds called and circled. I thought it rather strange behavior, but every year she reported the same thing. Sometimes she located the chicks and sometimes her neighbor did, and sometimes they were even able to calculate when to expect hatching and to be ready to carry the chicks by hand to the nursery lake so they wouldn't have to cross the road.

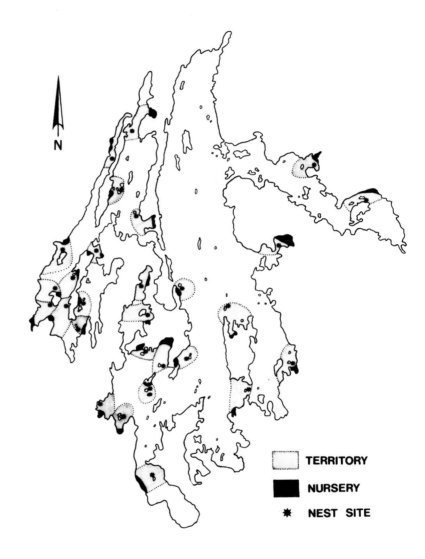

Figure 3-2. Hanson Lake nurseries, shown in relation to the locations of the nest sites and adjacent territories. Each territory is defined by a broken line, each nursery is shown as a black area, and the nest sites are indicated by asterisks.

▢ TERRITORY

■ NURSERY

✳ NEST SITE

A paper from Sweden also documents movement from one lake to another by Red-throated Loon chicks (Von Braun et al. 1968). The young were nearly a month old, when, pressured by increasing disturbance on their natal lake, the adults vocally encouraged the chicks to cross through a woods to a new lake. During the move parents and young called to each other using a call that had previously been interpreted as having a solely territorial function. Then, in 1974, I had reason to believe it could happen in my study area, too.

I had been monitoring pairs in Itasca State Park, Minnesota, some on very small lakes. A shallow, marshy, six-hectare lake had a pair with newly hatched young. A larger lake nearby, which usually also had a pair in residence, had none in 1974. When the young were just a few days old, they disappeared from the tiny lake. I found a pair with two small chicks on the larger lake, riding high in the water. I have no doubt that they were the same birds, but what I would have given to have been there when they moved from one lake to the other. Loons may be more flexible in their behavior than we thought, and they may have more tricks up their checkered sleeves than anyone could have guessed.

Parental Care of Young

Common Loon chicks are dependent on their parents for at least some of their needs until they are three months old. Chicks can swim, dive a little, stand in the water to shake their tiny wings, and skitter about the nest quite handily a few hours after hatching, but they are helpless to defend or feed themselves. Parents must feed, carry and defend their chicks (Figure 3–3) for several weeks.

It has been well documented that the hormonally driven urge of loons to care for their young is particularly strong for the first week or two after hatching. However, there are also reports of loons caring for young other than their own, suggesting that recognition of their own offspring is weak. Periodically, the Loon Preservation Committee of New Hampshire includes a story in its annual report about adoptions by Common Loons. In a paper concerning Red-throated Loons in Scotland, Dymond (1980) described the adoption of a single chick by a pair with two chicks of their own. They fed and cared for all three young, and all survived to fledge.

A more unusual case was reported by Abraham (1978). During the course of his studies on Alaskan waterfowl, he observed a pair of Arctic Loons with a brood of five Spectacled Eider ducklings in tow! He reasoned that adults and chicks were those incubating or being incubated on nests 10 meters apart on an island close to where he initially saw them. Both eider and Arctic Loon young feed on small invertebrates; ducklings feed themselves, but loon chicks must be fed by their parents. The ducklings Abraham watched secured most of their own food, but were also

Figure 3-3. Adult Common Loons caring for their young. *a.* Feeding the chick. *b.* Carrying the young in back-riding position. *c.* Defending the young by running across the water and calling with the tremolo vocalization. Note the calling loon's open bill.

receptive to being fed by the loons. They rode on the backs of the loons, and responded to vocal warning signals. Apparently, neither adult loons nor young eiders have strong mechanisms for identifying their own biological family.

Juveniles can secure quite a bit of their own food by the time they are eight weeks old, but before then, one or both adults are with them most of the time and provide almost all their food. Chicks peck at anything from insects to nest material while they are still being brooded, and they readily accept whatever their parents offer. Small chicks are fed mostly aquatic insects, small fish, and crayfish. Adults dive for suitable prey items, and initially, when chicks are only a few days old, one adult stays on the surface while the other hunts underwater.

Barr (1973) noted that chicks beg by pecking adults next to the bill and side of the head, and those he hand-raised became imprinted on him as the parent figure and begged from him in the same way. Chicks also beg vocally, using a series of single notes which increase in intensity if food is not quickly presented. If begging continues, it ends with a whine and a wail. Adults also make soft calls as they deliver food to their young, and examples of both calls are on the record at the back of this book.

An adult holds a fish crosswise in its bill and the chick takes it, then shifts it 90° so that it will go head first down the throat (Plate 5b). Chicks frequently drop the fish when they are young, and the adults retrieve it and offer it again. During their first week of life, chicks often drop the fish as they shift it in their bills, and later, chicks drop or refuse food if they are not hungry. A retrieved fish is splashed in the water, then offered again. Retrievals may continue for several mintues. Barr (1973) found they could be repeated for as long as 20 minutes before adults gave up and ate the food themselves.

Both parents feed the young. There have been no exhaustive studies to find if there is a pattern to parental feeding, a time schedule, or parental division of responsibilities. During the summer of 1978, Melody Christoff, then a student in the College of Biological Science and Forestry at the State University of New York in Syracuse, worked with me in the Adirondacks. She monitored one loon pair and their two chicks for five weeks by spending all daylight hours for 31 days observing them and recording their behavior (Christoff 1979). It was a pilot study that she planned to follow with her graduate research, a study of the interactions between adults and their young. Tragically, Melody died before her projected work could be completed.

Although her preliminary report represented the behavior of only one pair and its chicks, nine days old when she began her observations, it was the first detailed study of its kind and it included some unique information. Christoff found that when the chicks were small, the male did most of the feeding, but by the time they were four weeks old, the feeding role was divided almost evenly between male and female. Between one-third and one-half the time both pair members fed the chicks simultaneously (Table 3–1).

According to the Christoff data, intensive feeding was not evenly spaced throughout the day as Sjølander and Ågren (1972) reported from

Table 3-1. Parental Feedings to Common Loon Chicks
When Sex of Feeding Parent Was Known (N = 111)[a]

Age of Chick (days)	Male when Only One Feeding[b]	Female when Only One Feeding[b]	Both Male and Female Feeding[b]
9–14	75.0%	25.0%	30.0%
15–20	72.7	27.3	31.0
21–26	61.3	38.7	44.0
27–32	56.0	44.0	47.0
33–40	53.8	46.2	25.0

[a]From Christoff 1979.
[b]Columns two and three give the percentage of time when only one adult was feeding; the last column gives the percentage of total time the chicks were being fed.

their Icelandic study. They noted that chicks were fed at approximately one-hour intervals all day long, but Christoff found that chicks were fed in the early morning, with a peak of feeding at 0900. Adults then fed themselves until afternoon, with only occasional food offerings to the young. Their feeding efforts turned again to the chicks between 1600 and 2000.

Small chicks stay on the surface when adults dive for food. During the first week one parent remains with the chicks when the other one dives, and the returning loon swims toward the chicks to offer the food item. During the second week, one adult is usually, though not always, with the young, but the young stay where they are left and the adult with food moves toward them. When chicks are older than two weeks, they swim alongside the adult as it searches, wait as it dives, and approach as it surfaces with fish. By the time chicks are approaching their fourth week, adults drop food for them to retrieve. Adults grasp fish to paralyze, or at least impair them, and on many occasions, I have seen them run a fish back and forth in their bills, action that results in spinal-cord injury. Young chicks have only to pick up the fish; they do not have to chase it.

Barr (1973) reported that the female extends the area in which she forages with her chicks during the first several weeks. Christoff (1979) mapped and measured the expansion of locations used by adults and young during the weeks she watched them. She found that adults usually fed themselves away from the sites where they fed chicks, often outside the previously mapped defended territory. Later, as feeding locations expanded for the chicks, these "adult-only" feeding places were added to the chick-feeding sites, until by the end of her study, the total territory increased by 222 hectares. A map of this expansion is shown in Figure 3–4.

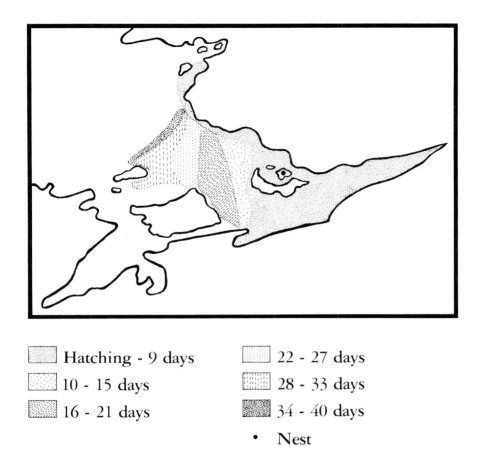

	Hatching - 9 days		22 - 27 days
	10 - 15 days		28 - 33 days
	16 - 21 days		34 - 40 days
		•	Nest

Figure 3-4. Territory use for feeding the young and its expansion with increasing age of the chicks. (From Christoff 1979.)

As chicks grow older, they are left alone more and more frequently, and for longer times. Even when they are small, there are some times when one or both adults go away. Tiny chicks are often with only one parent, usually the female (Christoff 1979). I combined records from Christoff's study into one table that shows that for the first two weeks, whenever one adult was alone with the young, it was always the female (Table 3–2). Although the male occasionally was found alone with the young after that time, the female continued to be the primary attendant.

Young remain in the same place whenever they are left. I mapped these locations on several lakes, and found they were in the same vicinity where adults fed the chicks. I mapped hiding places for four years on one lake in Minnesota. The sites alternated between the same two places every

Table 3–2. Percentage of Time Each Parent Stayed Alone with Chicks When Sex of Attendant Parent Was Known (N = 141 Incidents)[a]

Age of Chick (days)	Male Only[b]	Female Only[b]
9–14	0	100.0
15–20	14.8	85.2
21–26	20.5	79.5
27–32	11.5	88.5
33–40	33.3	66.7

[a]From Christoff 1978.
[b]Situations include times when one adult left to dive for food, to defend the family, to feed itself, or to swim ahead and leave the other adult alone with the young.

year. Hiding sites are about five to 10 meters from the shore in shallow water from two to five meters deep. Small chicks sit quietly during their wait, much like young fawns that lie immobile on the forest floor when left alone. Older chicks crouch low in the water, hunched, with their heads lying along the surface of the water if they are alerted to danger. When adults return, they give soft two-note wail calls. Little chicks stay where they are and do not move out to their parents until the adults are directly in front of them. Older young move toward their parents when they call, slowly swimming out to meet the returning adults.

By the time juveniles are eight weeks old they are able to supply at least half of their own food, and adults may leave them for extended periods throughout the day, returning in the evening to stay with them overnight. This may or may not be representative of Common Loon behavior patterns. In fact, all the behavior patterns given between adults and young are not necessarily the same every time. I imagine there is considerable individual variability for much behavior, but consistent behaviors include quiet hiding near shore by small chicks, two-note wails given by returning adults, and moving out to meet parents by young after they are between two and three weeks old.

Adults actively defend their young, using defensive behavior that includes posturings showing both fear and aggression. Adults rise to an upright posture and tread water while giving tremolo calls. Barklow (1979) stated that the three gradients of the tremolo correspond to increasing intensity, with progressively higher levels of agitation. My observations agree with his.

In the acoustic glossary at the back of this book, there is a sequence of tremolo calling, starting with a low Type 1 tremolo, given as we approached a loon family by boat. Call variation moved next to a Type 2, and finally to a Type 3 as we got closer and closer and posed an increasing threat to the loon family. Finally, both adults can be heard on the record calling together, with the patter of the male's feet in the background as he raced across the water. Plates 5a and c were taken at the same time as the recording was made.

Adults defend their chicks underwater as well as on the surface. Small chicks are vulnerable to predation by turtles and large fish, and adults frequently peer whether they are feeding or not. They even patrol underwater, coming to the surface periodically to give tremolo calls. It is difficult to identify chick predators, especially those that are underwater. Some evidence was secured by Yonge (1981) when he checked records from fish-processing companies in Canada and discovered that loon chicks had been identified from time to time in the guts of large northern pike. I have also seen small chicks killed by other loons that come up underneath the little ones and spear them in the abdomen. Large snapping turtles are also capable of eating loon chicks, as they do ducklings, although I know of no verified records. In view of the many potential underwater predators, it is not surprising that adults check beneath the surface from time to time when they are caring for chicks.

Back-riding may be one mechanism by which predation is reduced (Plate 5d). Chicks are safe while they are on the adult's back, although I have noticed that when danger is imminent, chicks are dropped into the water, and kept close to the adults. Herring Gulls pose a serious threat if chicks stray from their parents. They swoop down and grab them from overhead with their bills. Chicks scamper onto the back of either parent by squeezing under the wing and coming over the side. When older, they sometimes crawl over the rear just to one side of the tail. They can face in either direction, but usually they face toward the head. They may ride high or they may snuggle half under one wing, with their feet touching the most sparsely feathered region of the adult's back. Most back-riding ceases after two weeks. I have not seen a chick ride after it was three weeks old.

Adults also shelter swimming chicks under their wings (Plate 5e). They are almost completely enfolded, with only their heads peeking out, but relatively little time is devoted to wing-brooding compared to back-riding, and it is confined to chicks less than a week old.

I have observed back-riding for many chicks and their parents, but had not been able to make continuous observations for any prolonged periods. In 1976, Tammy Black, then a student in SUNY's College of Biological

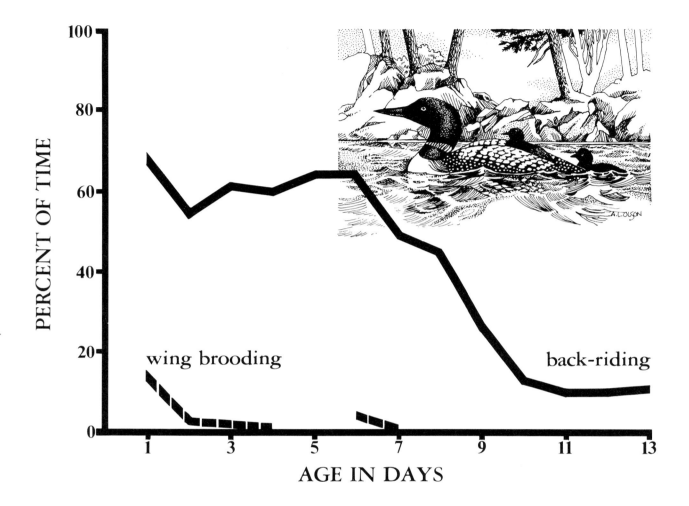

Figure 3-5. Time spent back-riding and being brooded under the wing by a Common Loon chick during its first 13 days. (From Black 1976.)

Science and Forestry in Syracuse, was able to do that while attending the University of Minnesota Field Biology Station at Itasca State Park (Black 1976). For more than 167 hours during 13 days she monitored a pair and their single chick on a lake where there was no human disturbance. For the first week, it spent more than half its time riding, plus more time being brooded under the wing, but after eight days there was a sharp drop in the amount of time the chick back-rode. Figure 3–5 is based on Black's work.

It is possible that back-riding serves to warm the chicks, providing for a kind of mobile brooder. I made some measurements of body temperature on young chicks kept in the water for prolonged periods, away from their parents. When they were in the shade, their body temperatures fell, but in the sun there was no difference. Thermoregulation was operative by day four, but perhaps the metabolic cost is high for a chick kept in cold water compared to one riding on its parent's back, even if it can maintain its temperature. I suspect that chicks lose heat to the water through their enormous feet, and heat is conserved when they are back-riding. The question deserves further testing.

Development of the Young

Loon chicks are covered with soft blackish down, except for their white bellies. The sequence of their molts and plumages is given in Chapter 9. Loon chicks weigh less than a stick of butter at hatching. Their weights differ individually, and there is a difference in weights of chicks from different populations reflecting size differences among adults of the same groups. Those from the central part of the breeding range, from Minnesota through central Canada, weigh less than those from the more eastern parts. I know of no hatching- weight data from the western part of the range for comparison.

Yonge (1981) weighed chicks in northern Saskatchewan and found they ranged from 77 to 99 grams with an average of 85.5 grams. I weighed chicks in northern Minnesota and found they were between 77 and 99.2 grams, averaging 85.4 grams, or almost exactly the same as Yonge's report. Barr's (1973) chicks in Algonquin Park, Ontario, weighed between 71.4 and 108.5 grams at hatching, averaging 93.9 grams, considerably larger than the others. I have been able to weigh only two newly hatched chicks in New York, largely because I am reluctant to disturb chicks with Herring Gulls standing by. The two I weighed were 108 and 112 grams, both larger than the largest of the Midwest chicks.

Yonge (1981) checked 29 newly hatched chicks and found that the weight of the second-hatched chick was greater than that of the first one out of the egg by an average of 3.2 grams. However, by the time the second chick had hatched, the first weighed about six grams more than its younger sibling because it was being fed while the younger was still emerging from the egg. Barr (pers. comm.), on the other hand, found that siblings hatched at shorter intervals and weighed more nearly the same than Yonge reported.

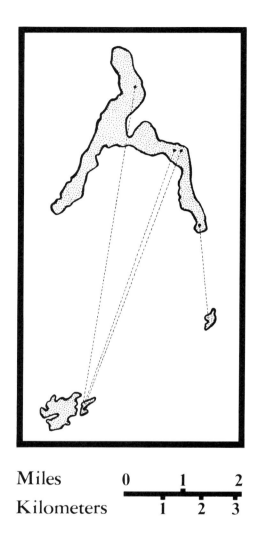

Miles

Kilometers

Figure 3-6. Locations of the small natal lakes for Common Loon young that subsequently moved out to Lake Itasca, shown as the largest lake.

Barr (1973) followed growth and development of the young from hatching to one year of age. He said that most structures have achieved their full growth by two months, except for the bill and primary feathers. These continue to grow for the next several weeks and flight feathers are not fully developed until young are about three months old. Juveniles on my study site could fly by the time they were 11 to 12 weeks and those Barr studied also made their first flights by the same age.

Loon chicks are dependent on their parents for food for many weeks, but after they are able to secure their own food, and have flight feathers permitting them to make short flights, they may leave the parental territory. I banded and marked four juveniles with wing tags in two different years at Itasca State Park, Minnesota. All had been raised on small lakes, and there was some evidence that young from the many small lakes in the park were moving away from parental territories at the end of the summer. The movement pattern for these four is shown in Figure 3–6. Two were siblings from one lake, a pair I was able to follow throughout the fall until they migrated; one was a single chick from the same lake, raised the following year; and the fourth a young from another lake in the park. The siblings I followed staked out individual claims and remained on them until November.

Juveniles generally leave later than do adults, although a few adults remain on northern lakes until just before freezing. The young I followed (their behavior is described in Chapter 6), left in a large group composed only of juveniles. I have seen no evidence on the fall staging grounds, nor on the wintering grounds, that family units remain intact, and all evidence points to a separation of adults and young by fall.

It would be nice to end this chapter by coming full circle, with juveniles grown up and becoming breeding adults. Then all the parts could be filled in, and a conclusion reached whether the family gets together again or whether the unit is permanently dissolved. But, so far, there are no answers to questions about this part of a loon's life.

As far as anyone knows most loon families stay together for about four months. They migrate separately, adults leaving before the young. There is no indication that parents and offspring have any contact later, and it is a mystery whether or not young eventually establish territories near those of their parents. Recently, Eberhardt (1984) was able to recapture immatures he had banded the previous year, and discovered they had returned to their natal lakes. Is this a clue that young loons will also return to the place where they were raised after they mature, or is this news from Minnesota only a report of unusual events?

CHAPTER 4
Parasites, Disease, and Loon Populations

Loons and Blackflies

Blackflies, mosquitoes and Punkies: a cosmopolitan police
detailed by Divine Providence to guard the great hunting park of
the Republic from the incursions of Cockney poachers and mur-
derers of deer in summer. Long may they wave!
                    —toast from North Woods Walton Club, 1858

What a delightful way to look at the insects most of us regard as the
scourge of the north! We view them as a nuisance or worse, and Common
Loons may also consider blackflies their peskiest pest. Loons are plagued
by any number of parasites, both ectoparasites and endoparasites. Those
we can relate to best are blackflies. If loons feel the same way, it may be
because there is one species, *Simulium euryadminiculum*, that attacks only
Common Loons. This simulid's life as a flying, biting, blood-sucking
adult is timed to coincide with loon incubation. I have seen incubating
loons with heads crawling with blackflies, unable to leave their nests to

dive and free themselves from these insects. One afternoon I watched a sitting loon shaking its head while surrounded by blackflies; it shook its head an average of once every 9.6 seconds!

S. *euryadminiculum* was first described by Davies (1949) at Algonquin Park in Ontario, and has now been identified in New York and Minnesota (Jamnback 1969, McIntyre 1975). Lowther and Wood (1964) ran a series of interesting tests using museum skins of a Pied-billed Grebe, a Common Merganser, a Herring Gull, and a Common Loon, plus the skin of a freshly killed Common Loon and the water in which it had been washed. S. *euryadminiculum* came in swarms to the fresh skins, the wash water that had been poured on the beach, and the Common Loon museum skin, but ignored skins of other species.

When loon and duck skins were placed on a beach together with live ducklings, S. *euryadminiculum* was again attracted only to the Common Loon skin, even though a living host was available (Fallis and Smith 1964). The uropygial gland of Common Loons secretes a substance that apparently provides an olfactory cue to this species of blackflies.

It is suspected that S. *euryadminiculum* may also act as a vector and transmit a blood parasite to loons. Other species of simulids are well known to carry leukocytozoa from duck to duck. Recently blood parasites known to be carried by other simulid species and thought to be parasitic only to ducks were found in tissue taken from two loons in Florida (Anderson and Forrester 1974). It was assumed the parasites were acquired on the breeding grounds. However, it is not known if S. *euryadminiculum* was the vector, biting ducks, and then transmitting parasites to loons, or if a different simulid species was the causal agent. The next time you are bothered by blackflies, think of the poor, vulnerable, sitting loon. It must stay put for hours, incubating its eggs, and it has neither screened porch nor insect repellent to combat the blackflies.

Parasites

An extensive list of internal parasites has been described for Common Loons (Appendix 3). Two parasites have received attention because of their economic importance; one affects a popular game fish, and the other has a commercially important crustacean as its intermediate host.

The life cycle of black spot disease of trout (*Apophallus brevis*) and its relationship to loons was first described by Miller (1941, 1942). Common Loons are the final host for this parasite, and there are two intermediate hosts, a snail and a trout (Figure 4–1). Trout carry the encysted metacer-

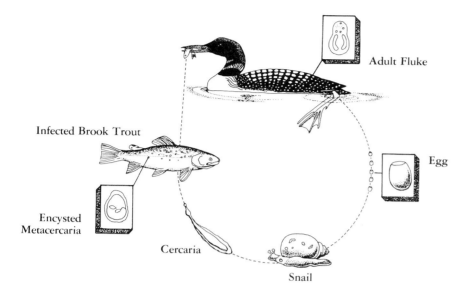

Figure 4-1. Life cycle of *Apophallus brevis*, the trematode causing black spot in trout.

Labels on figure: Adult Fluke, Egg, Snail, Cercaria, Encysted Metacercaria, Infected Brook Trout

caria, or second larval stage, which loons ingest when they eat infected trout, and flukes reach the adult stage in the loon as soon as three to four days after being taken into the intestine.

The blue crab serves as the major intermediate host for a microphallid trematode, another fluke, now thought to be the primary parasite recently found in the gut of Common Loons. Examination of emaciated loons from a massive die-off in 1983 off the gulf coast of Florida showed high concentrations of these flukes in the intestinal tract, an average of 9,300 flukes per loon. Loons were thin and weak and suffered from hemorrhagic enteritis (Stroud and Lange 1983). Until then it wasn't known that loons fed so extensively on invertebrates, particularly on crabs, during the winter. I have a concern that this feeding pattern is not normal, but may result from neurological incapacitation following mercury poisoning. Nerve damage destroys muscle coordination, and makes it difficult for a loon to chase a moving fish. It would be much easier to capture a slow-moving crab as it walks along the ocean floor.

Diseases

Two diseases that seem to have the greatest impact on loons are aspergillosis and botulism (BOT). The *Aspergillus* fungus is airborne as spores in the environment, and probably is found in most wild birds. When loons are under stress, the spores initiate mycelial growth which forms a creeping plaque, forming a "spreading fungal sheet" (Locke and Young 1967). It literally covers cardiac vessels, lungs, and air sacs. The threat to birds is not so much an interference with their lungs as it is the damage it renders to air sacs. *Aspergillus* grows over air sacs until it completely covers them and destroys their ability to function. Growth begins following parasitic infestation, botulism, severe weather conditions, or the anxiety of captivity. Any one of these factors causes sufficient stress to initiate growth of spores already present in the loon's respiratory system.

Kaben and Schwarz (1970) demonstrated that germination of spores in *Aspergillus* is greatly reduced under the influence of saltwater, although to the best of my knowledge, no experiments have yet been conducted demonstrating the mechanism of this retardation. Preliminary findings indicate that loons should be less susceptible to aspergillus on the wintering grounds than on the breeding grounds. I have found aspergillosis to be a problem when trying to maintain loons in captivity. A fungicide, such as mycostatin, seems to lessen the effects of the fungus, and keeping loons in a cool to cold environment also reduces the rate of mycelial growth.

Both *Clostridium perfrigens* and *Clostridium botulinum* have been implicated as causes of mortality to loons on Lake Michigan as well as on their coastal wintering grounds. *C. perfrigens* was found in specimens examined at Patuxent, following the 1972 Florida die-off, and considerable evidence implicates *C. botulinum* as a major contributor to the Great Lakes' epidemics.

C. botulinum, which causes botulism, or food poisoning, does its damage with a toxic by-product rather than by itself. Under anaerobic conditions, vegetative growth begins, and the toxins released can cause illness and death. Muscular paralysis follows because botulism blocks the release of neurotransmitters at the end bulb of nerve axons, thus preventing muscle contraction (Kao et al. 1976). Paralyzed water birds cannot hold their heads out of water and they drown. Fatalities in some years have numbered several thousand.

Fish are susceptible to residual botulinum spores in bottom sediments of Lake Michigan (Huss and Eskildsen 1974). Alewives frequently become contaminated with BOT, and stomach analyses of dead loons reveal that loons feed heavily on alewives, thereby ingesting the deadly toxin. Feeding experiments confirm that loons are truly susceptible to botulism toxins (Monheimer 1968).

Type C BOT has been recognized for nearly 50 years as a major cause of waterfowl mortalities, but it wasn't until 1963 that Type E BOT was

Table 4–1. Mortalities of Common Loons Reported on Lake Michigan
under Conditions of Botulism Type E Poisoning

Year/Month	Number Dead	Study Area	Source
1963/Nov-Dec	more than 3,000	west side	Kaufmann and Fay 1964
1964/late Oct	3,570	north end	Fay 1966
1965	no figure; fewer than previous years	north end	Fay 1966
1967/Nov-Dec	48	south end	Fay 1969
1968/Oct	no figure	north end	Fay 1969
1976/Oct-Nov	759	south end	Brand et al. 1983
1981/Nov	69	south end	Brand et al. 1983

discovered. Its association with Lake Michigan loon mortalities was first reported a year later by Kaufmann and Fay (1964) after they examined carcasses from the 1963 die-off. Since then both Type E and Type C have been found in serum taken from dead birds. Even low levels of each can be dangerous if both are present, because they have a lethal synergistic effect (Jensen and Gritman 1966).

In 1964 there was another major epidemic, and die-offs continued to be reported. Sometimes only a few birds died, but in other years hundreds or even thousands of dead loons washed up on Lake Michigan shores. A summary by Brand et al. (1983) noted a trend that losses were concentrated along the north end of Lake Michigan during October and along the southern shores in November and December. Geographical distribution of the die-offs is probably related to the location of loons during migration rather than to shifts and changes in sources of botulism.

Most die-offs happen in the fall, but in 1980 a Ring-billed Gull colony in Lake Michigan was hit with an outbreak of Type E BOT in June. In 1981, 13 dead loons were found on the shores of Lake Superior in July and Type E Bot was again identified. Apparently, the potential for die-offs is in the lake throughout the summer and fall, but loon mortalities are more apt to occur in autumn because that is when large numbers of loons stage on Lake Michigan during migration. Lake Michigan Common Loon mortalities during the last two decades are summarized in Table 4–1.

Populations and Productivity

If loons are plagued by parasites and disease, and have suffered such extensive losses in some years, at times thousands in a relatively small area, what abilities do they have to counteract the losses? In other words,

Table 4–2. Population Density and Productivity of Common Loon Pairs in Several Populations across Their Breeding Range

Study Area	N	Ha/Pair	Fledged/ Hatched	Fledged/ Pair	Source
New Hampshire	93	481	0.89	0.55	All four studies:
	89	503	0.89	0.45	Loon Preservation
	82	546	0.78	0.44	Committee Report 1979
	94	476	0.82	0.59	
Vermont	127	no data	no data	0.56	VINS Report 1984
New York	56	308	no data	0.84	Trivelpiece et al. 1979
	105[a]	373	no data	0.83	Trivelpiece et al. 1979
	105[a]	207	0.80	0.73	McIntyre unpubl.
	132	384	no data	.97	Parker and Miller 1988
Minnesota	22	48	no data	0.27	McIntyre 1978
	29	39	no data	0.31	McIntyre 1978
	14	296	no data	0.93	McIntyre 1975
	25	11	0.94	0.80	McIntyre 1975
	9	37	no data	0.22	McIntyre 1975
	73	35	0.80	0.54	Titus and Van Druff 1981
	73	35	0.82	0.42	Titus and Van Druff 1981
Ontario	29	no data	0.68	0.66	All three studies:
	38	no data	0.75	0.87	Heimberger et al. 1983
	35	no data	0.86	0.69	
Saskatchewan	96	43	0.69	0.50	Yonge 1981
	102	40	0.67	0.57	Yonge 1981
	96	43	no data	0.64	McIntyre unpubl.
	87	47	0.90	0.78	McIntyre unpubl.
Alaska	33	52	0.70	0.48	Smith 1981
	Average		0.80	0.60	

[a]These are not the same 105 pairs; both studies were done in the Adirondacks, but not with the same loons.

is annual productivity sufficient to maintain stable populations in the face of periodic epidemics? Reproductive success, or the number of fledged juveniles per pair, averages just over half a young per pair per year. The data in Table 4–2 represent information from more than 1,500 pairs, including loons from busy lakes at popular resort areas, remote lakes in northern Canada where people are a rarity and loons are common, little four-hectare ponds, and 4,000-hectare lakes shared by many loon pairs.

If eggs hatch, chick survival has always been considered high. Yonge (1981), who reported more fledging data than any other individual researcher, indicated that 68 percent of hatched chicks fledged. Titus and Van Druff (1981) found that 81 percent of hatched chicks survived among the 146 pairs they monitored. Chick mortality has been viewed as low after the first two weeks, and if a chick reaches two to three weeks of age, its chances of making it have been thought to be very good. Most tiny chicks die because they are gobbled by something; gulls, fish, or turtles are among the possibilities. Young loons are much safer after they acquire some diving skill.

Recently some disturbing new information has been reported. Alvo (1985) compared loons using lakes at three stages of acidification and found that older young were dying on lakes with low pH readings. Apparently, these lakes had a scanty food base for the loons to use, but there were some invertebrates and plant material available. Sufficient to feed small chicks, the food resource was not enough to permit older young to continue growing, and without fish in their diets they starved to death.

Dulin (1988) studied sibling rivalry and dominance hierarchies in Michigan. His work is presented in greater detail in Chapter 6, but with reference to this discussion, he reported that under conditions of food shortages, one of a sibling pair went without and sometimes starved to death after it had reached three to four weeks of age. Both his study and Alvo's indicate that fledging cannot be assumed at such an early age as we once thought. Young should be at least a month old before being counted as survivors. When I was working on north-central Minnesota lakes in the early 1970s, I assumed loons would be fledged if they were three weeks old because few young died after that time in my study area. State surveys have also used three weeks as the critical time to record "fledged." These recent studies by Dulin and Alvo indicate this may not be valid everywhere in the breeding range.

Productivity varies considerably from population to population (Table 4–2). Three New York studies show that resident birds seem to have a higher rate of productivity than loons in most other parts of the range. In general, if the number of fledged young per pair is compared to the hectares of water surface per pair, it seems that in locations of high density, productivity is lower than in places with sparse breeding populations. Even within single sites (see the Saskatchewan figures in Table 4–2), as population changes, so does reproductive rate.

I interpret this as showing that adults in a population with few loon pairs have the chance to secure the best territories, those with excellent nest sites, abundant food resources, and optimal nurseries. Without the conflict and encounters that occur when pairs nest in close proximity, time needed for territorial defense is reduced and more time can be devoted to caring for the chicks.

The single exception in Table 4–2 is New Hampshire, but there is heavy recreational use of most New Hampshire lakes, resulting in high disturbance factors. Even if loons need not engage in territorial conflicts to the same degree as do loons in more densely populated places, "defense" from human intrusion may steal time from parental duties in the same way that intraspecific conflicts do in populations from the heart of the breeding range.

There is little information on replacement within populations. Yodels identify individual males, and are being used to confirm if the same male is on territory from one year to the next. However, there is no marked population anywhere, and still no way to identify females. Habitat suitable for one pair is suitable for another, and even the same nest site may sometimes be used by different pairs in different years.

For the past decade I have kept track of a loon population on the Adirondack lake where I have been conducting most of my summer research. Shifts and changes in population show both gains and losses. During that time, three new territories became established. Although one lasted for only a single breeding season, the other two continue to be active four to five years after they were established. Overall I found that between 75 and 100 percent of males that I could identify by yodels returned in subsequent years. This is not so different from Nilsson's (1977) findings. He constructed a life table for Arctic Loons using the 1929–1941 banding data Schuz gathered during his annual study of migrants on the Baltic Sea. Using meaningful recovery data for 76 loons, he estimated that 89 percent of the adults return each year. Nilsson estimated that to maintain a stable population, an annual reproductive rate must be 0.47 fledged juveniles per pair per year, and he built into this an estimated juvenile mortality rate of 22 percent.

Juvenile mortality may be somewhat higher for Common Loons. Of 82 juveniles banded in Minnesota, 13, or 16 percent, were recovered during their second year, one during its fourth and one at age seven. (A recovered bird is one that has died and its band has been "recovered"; the bird is therefore identified.) Nearly 30 percent of the juveniles I banded were recovered during their first winter.

Banding data for Common Loons are few, but there are 37 usable records, defined as those for which loons were banded at one place and time and recovered at another. There are many records of loons banded after they were caught by hand as injured or oiled birds. Birds taken and

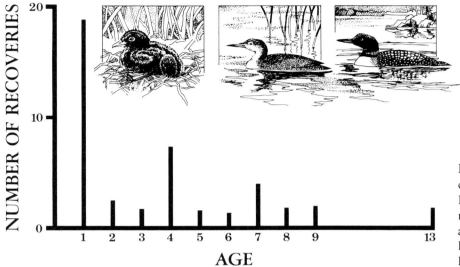

Figure 4-2. Survivorship curve (in years) of Common Loons based on 37 banding records from the U.S. Fish and Wildlife Service Bird Banding Laboratory in Laurel, Maryland.

cleaned up following oil spills are sometimes banded before being released, but they are frequently found dead just a short distance from where they were released, often within a few days. This gives a clue about the high mortality that oiled birds suffer, but does not help in the construction of a life table.

Survivorship information is graphed in Figure 4–2. By far the largest loss occurs during the first year, when young are initiated to the rigors of a diversity of stresses. Fewer and fewer are lost from subsequent age classes. Nilsson (1977) thought loons probably had a life span of 20 to 30 years, and I agree with him. In fact, it may be even longer, provided they can survive the first year. On the basis of identification of individual yodels, several males in my study area are more than 15 years old, assuming their age at first breeding to be at least four years.

It may be that loon life spans are so long that we will have to wait many years to understand mortality rates and be able to make accurate predictions about stable populations. It is important to be able to understand replacement rates needed to maintain healthy populations, to be able to compare them with present replacement rates, and finally to have sufficient information to suggest life expectancy for loons after they achieve adult breeding status. Insurance tables for humans are surely more easily derived than life tables for loons. With our present information, we are able to suggest that loons are capable of living a long time, especially if they survive the first winter. In the movie *On Golden Pond*, Katherine Hepburn called out, "The loons are back, the loons are back." How many summer lake dwellers say the same thing every year when they return to their cottages? And they may well be right, for the very same loons probably do return year after year after year.

CHAPTER 5
Behavioral Ecology

Loons spend most of the daylight hours in feeding and maintenance activities. They swim, they fly, they lay their heads over their backs and doze, but mostly they pursue, capture, and eat fish, and take care of their feathers.

Maintenance

Loons bathe, preen, scratch, and wiggle their feet, all maintenance behaviors. Care of the feathers occupies loons throughout the day. After diving, sitting on a nest, or engaging in social interactions, they preen, bathe, shake, and rearrange their feathers. Preening realigns the individual barbs lining both sides of the feather shaft. These tend to come unhooked during physical activity, and if feathers are to provide a protective covering, all the parts must stay tightly "zipped" together to form a smooth and waterproof surface.

Loons preen either after dipping their bills in the water, or after squeezing oil from the uropygial gland at the base of the tail (Figure 5–1a and b). I have used the term *water dipping* to distinguish it from *bill dipping*, which refers to a social display. Water dipping is done by dipping the bill

Figure 5-1. Common Loon feather-care postures. *a.* Water dipping used during preening. *b.* Oiling from the uropygial gland. *c.* Head rubbing. *d.* Wing flapping.

in the water and immediately preening. Bill dipping is a rapid immersion of the bill tip in the water directly in front of the bird followed by a rapid flick of the bill to one side.

Oil glands are covered with a tuft of feathers and can be seen protruding from between the closed bill of a bird as it squeezes out the oil. Loons oil most feathers directly, but to reach the back of the head and neck, they must first rub their bills across the contour feathers to leave oil on the surface. Then they throw their heads backward, twisting and rubbing against back and shoulder feathers to transfer oil onto head and neck feathers (Figure 5–1c).

Loons preen by grasping individual feathers and pulling the vanes through the bill. Manipulation of individual feathers is called nibbling in some species, in waterfowl, for example (McKinney 1965), and it is also an apt term to use for loons. Loons nibble most body feathers while they are sitting in the water, including those on their sides and under their wings. However, to preen feathers on their abdomens, they roll onto their sides, almost all the way over onto their backs. This is called the rolling or belly preen. Both are appropriate terms for the posture of upside-down loons, and the flash of white as loons roll over in the water is a familiar sight to loon watchers.

Individual wing and tail feathers are pulled through the bill as wings and tail are spread to make access to them easier. More time is spent on body feathers than on wing and tail feathers, and more time is spent on belly feathers than on those of the back. It may be that the feathers that spend most time in the water are the ones that get most care, or it may be that wing and tail feathers can be easily straightened by shaking and that contour feathers need individual attention.

Care of the feathers includes both preening and shaking. Body shakes are usually part of a bathing sequence, and wings and tails are shaken during preening whether or not bathing is included. Wing flaps are usually given at the end of a preening sequence, and may be done several times during an entire preening period. During a wing flap a loon rises high in the water with neck outstretched and bill held above the horizontal as it shakes its wings. Compare Figure 5–1d with Figure 7–1f. In the latter, the bill is held at or below the horizontal and wings are spread but unmoving, signaling aggression. During wing flaps, the bill is held in such a way that no aggressive intent is showing.

Tail wags are also given at or near the end of preening sequences. The tail is raised slightly above the water and shaken from side to side. It does not seem to have any social significance, and I have never seen tail wagging during social interactions. Both wing flaps and tail wags serve only to arrange feathers.

The following sequence, taken directly from my field notes, is typical of a preening bout. There are many variations of preening sequences, but there is a basic theme, moving from oiling to preening to flapping and finally to settling.

1. Loon squeezes oil from the uropygial gland.
2. Loon wipes bill across its back.
3. Loon gives several head rubs across the back where it has just wiped the oil.
4. Loon preens its breast feathers. Head is held straight down from high neck position. Looks much like a loon in its pelican posture, and its bill digs into the breast feathers, occasionally pulling one out.
5. Loon dips bill in water and begins to preen flank feathers.

6. It moves its head up from the flank to the lining of the wing. As it does so, its wing is elevated, and its head lowered to approach the feathers from an upside-down position.
7. Loon now changes sides and works on the other flank and wing.
8. Loon squeezes more oil from its preen gland and wipes its head across its back.
9. More head rubs follow.
10. Another sequence of belly preening begins, this one even more vigorous than the one before.
11. Bird rises in water, lifts its head and gives several wing flaps.
12. Loon settles, wiggles a bit, then carefully folds its wings across its back.
13. Loon tips the other way, elevates its tail and wags it.
14. Loon remains drifting, head low and neck withdrawn, and this signals the end of preening.

Bathing involves a more vigorous approach to feather care. It is not always a part of a body-care routine, but often follows copulation or a period of incubation. Bathing loons flap their wings and raise great splashes of water around themselves. Interspersed between splashings are occasional nibbles, directed primarily to belly feathers. Loons frequently turn onto their sides while bathing, and may make a complete rollover onto their backs, then turn over to the other side before righting themselves. Schreiber (1977) has described similar behavior in pelicans as "thrashing the water with partially-opened wings." Loons do the same thing, so it is appropriate to adopt his terminology and call it wing thrashing.

Loons may intersperse wing thrashing with tipping and lower their bills into the water, but I have never seen loons use water from their bills to splash over themselves. I suspect that rather than using water by moving it around with their bills, they are washing their faces when they immerse them. Bathing usually ends with a wing flap and a body shake.

Most preening sequences are between five and 15 minutes long, but the addition of bathing may extend the period to nearly an hour. The longest sequence of body-care behavior follows an incubation sequence. After a loon leaves its nest, it swims a short distance offshore and begins to preen,

Figure 5-2. Sequence from foot waggle to sleeping posture. *a.* Foot waggle, shaking water off one foot while the other foot remains in the water. *b.* The right foot has just been shaken and can barely be seen tucked under the wing; the proximal part of the tarsus is just above and to the right of the left foot, which remains in the water. *c.* Normal sleeping posture for adult Common Loons. The left foot is in the water, the right is tucked under the wing and cannot be seen in this drawing. The head lies over the back facing the tail, with the bill buried in the scapular feathers.

working especially on belly feathers. Loons scratch indirectly, that is, they hold their feet above, rather than under, the wing when scratching head or neck. This should be expected because their feet are placed close together, far to the rear of their bodies, rather than on the ventral side. Scratching, like bathing, is not part of every maintenance routine.

Another typical loon foot-moving behavior is the foot waggle; it has several functions (Figure 5–2a). It is frequently used near the end of a preening sequence. During a foot waggle, one foot is raised in the air, and held there for a short time, or shaken at once. Afterward, the foot may be dipped in the water again and the foot waggle repeated, or it may be placed under the wing. With one foot tucked and one foot in the water, a loon can remain drifting but is still able to maintain its stability and control the direction of its movement. The foot in the water serves as both keel and rudder.

I suspect that feet are used in the regulation of body temperature. Loon feet have a large surface area and a well-developed vascular system. When they are brought out of the water, shaken and held in the air, evaporative water loss cools them and the cooled blood returns to the body. Conversely, heat loss is reduced when one foot is taken from the water and sheltered under the wing.

Before sleeping, loons do a foot waggle and tuck one foot under a wing. Healthy loons sleep with their heads turned toward their tails, faces buried beneath scapular feathers, with bills obscured by feathers but eyes uncovered. Figure 5–2 shows the sequence from foot waggle to sleeping posture. The foot remaining in the water continues to move gently back and forth and, as it paddles, it stabilizes the bird. Small chicks turn their heads to one side rather than over their backs. Sick adults also position their heads to the side; a sleeping adult in chick sleeping posture should be considered injured, sick, or disabled.

Chicks engage in comfort movements similar to those of adults and they begin them at a young age. The first is the foot waggle, begun the first day after hatching. By the second day chicks can preen, scratch, and tuck their heads to one side or under the wing, but at this time, although they preen, they do not squeeze oil from the uropygial gland. By the third day they wing flap, tail waggle, and engage in head rubs, even though they have no wing feathers to straighten, virtually no tail, and no oil to rub on their backs. By the fourth day they dip their bills in water (water dipping) before preening, and they begin to pick up gravel to take into their gizzards as grit. They peer by the fifth day, make underwater turns during dives, go through complete bathing sequences, and spend a great deal of time belly preening.

By the end of the first week, chicks use oil from the uropygial gland and they continue to spend more and more time caring for their feathers. At this time they use all the comfort movements of adults, even though several of them do not result in actual feather care, and they also begin some underwater maneuvers, which will be useful to them later when they begin to hunt for and capture their own food.

Feeding and Diving

Loons are primarily fish eaters. They eat some invertebrates, and on lakes where there are no fish they take whatever is available. They are opportunistic and will eat anything they can easily see and readily capture. Loons have been said to compete with sport fishermen by taking game fish, and if trout and whitefish are available to them, there is no doubt they will eat them. Presence and availability are not the same thing, and loons must be able to capture their prey before they can eat it. Trout have a very fast burst speed and they move in a straight line, making their capture more difficult than that of some other species.

There is some evidence that loons will eat trout on lakes that are managed for salmonids and where fish of other species have been removed. Trout on several stocked lakes were marked with jaw tags during a New York fish-management study (Flick 1983). Loons were using the same lakes and when three loons were caught and drowned in trap nets, their stomach contents were analyzed. As I write this, I have 18 jaw tags in front of me, tags removed from the stomachs of the three loons.

Weights and measurements of the trout were recorded before the fish were marked and released. The recovered tags suggest the average trout eaten by the loons was 25 centimeters long; the largest was nearly half a meter long and weighed half a kilogram. That is an exceedingly long trout for a loon to eat, but a trout of that weight and length would be shaped more like an eel. Still, Flick's (1983) publication claimed proof that at least some loons are able to consume exceedingly large fish. Another study conducted in the northern part of the lower peninsula of Michigan included examination of stomach contents from several species of fish-eating water birds. Ten of the 12 loon stomachs contained some trout remains (Alexander 1977). However, lakes on which loons were taken were also managed exclusively for trout, and if loons were to eat, they had no other choice.

Examination of stomach contents from loons feeding on lakes with a broad species diversity of prey items showed different results. During the Lake Michigan die-offs of the 1960s it was possible to analyze stomach contents from a large series of specimens because thousands of loons were available (Peterson 1965). The most common prey item in stomachs from 134 Common Loons was alewives. Other species eaten by loons included smelt, sea lamprey, coregonids, mottled sculpin, and yellow perch. Some plant material, insects, and crayfish remains were also found. Alewives are the most common Lake Michigan fish in the size class preferentially taken by loons, so it is not surprising they were feeding heavily on them.

Four populations were sampled by Olson and Marshall (1952) and Barr (1973). Loons breeding on lakes in Ontario, Minnesota, Wisconsin, and Michigan ate mostly yellow perch. This is not surprising, since yellow perch is the most common species in the majority of lakes in the heart of the loons' breeding range.

Thirteen of Munro's (1945) study lakes in British Columbia had no fish, yet he found that loons nested and raised young on them. They substituted mollusks, caddis flies, amphipods, and dragonfly nymphs for fish, both for themselves and to feed their young. In each of the five studies just mentioned, loons were eating whatever was in the greatest abundance or most readily captured.

Young loons feed from an extensive menu. They eat small fish, mostly minnows and perch, aquatic insects, and crayfish. Juveniles continue to eat both crayfish and small fish when they begin to capture their own food. Recently, Parker (1985) reported that young loons were fed a diet of aquatic insects and newts when lake acidification denied them their traditional prey.

I made daily observations of a pair of siblings in the fall of 1974. At night they rafted together over deep water. Early in the morning they swam side by side to a bed of rushes along the shore, where they fed together. Leisurely they poked along in water less than a meter deep, making short dives for crayfish. Twenty minutes to half an hour later they separated and moved to deeper water sites, where they spent the balance of each day feeding and caring for their feathers. They reminded me of a pair of human youngsters, hungry in the morning and heading for the quickest breakfast. But instead of cold cereal from a box, the young loons dipped into the shallow water for cold crayfish, each in its own, individual box.

Although most evidence for what loons eat comes from examination of stomach contents, plus a few observations like the one just described, there are data from one experimental study (Barr 1973). Captive hand-raised loons were offered a variety of food under controlled conditions. Some experimental trials involved size-preference choices, by making available to loons different size classes of one or several fish species. Fish choices in other trials were between smooth versus rough, slender versus broad, and normal versus fish with clipped fins, which made them less efficient swimmers and thus easier to capture. Results from all experiments showed that loons preferred fish with small heads, soft scales, slender bodies, and no spines. Cisco were preferred to perch, suckers, bullheads, lake chub, and pumpkinseed, as long as all species were equally easy to capture.

If these were the results of experimental studies, why did Barr find yellow perch to be the most common fish in stomachs of the wild loons he examined? Wild yellow perch swim erratically when pursued, that is, they zigzag, twist, and turn, and are easy to see and follow. Trout and suckers swim in a direct, straight line and head for the deeper and darker parts of a lake. It is easier for loons to capture perch because loons are also experts at turning, pivoting, and other quick underwater maneuvers. In addition, perch follow the 20-degree isotherm. This is within the upper five meters on lakes, thus in a stratum where light is excellent. Because loons are visual predators, it is important that they be able to see their prey.

There is a big gap in our knowledge about food for wintering loons. Forbush (1929) noticed them eating flounder, and during my study off the coast of Virginia, I did too. However, I attributed that to the fact that flounder were so large that loons had to bring them to the surface for additional handling before they could swallow them, making the flounder easy for me to see. I suspect there are other fish, smaller or slimmer ones, that are eaten underwater, and are never seen by observers. The finding of crab remains in loons killed during the 1983 Florida die-off was discussed in Chapter 4. As mentioned, it is not known if crabs are a common food for wintering loons, or are just marginal, and were taken at that time because loons were ill and unable to capture fish. A study of the winter feeding habits of loons is desperately needed.

I once watched a captive loon consume 124 fathead minnows during a single feeding session, all ingested underwater. The loon literally sucked them in with the speed of a swimming-pool vacuum cleaner. On the other hand, large fish are brought to the surface, where they are billed, run back and forth through the bills, until they are semiparalyzed or even killed, making them easier to shift to a position for ingestion. I have never seen loons swallow fish in any direction other than headfirst, whether the food item was living or dead.

Before they feed, loons lower their heads into the water and look around, in a gesture called peering (Figure 5–3b). When a prey item is sighted, the loon dives underwater, compresses its feathers, and holds its wings tight to its body. The loon jerks its head back and forth between an extended and an S-position, to fix its eyes on the prey. Barr (1973) described loons' underwater swimming as especially skillful when turning. They are capable of a very rapid pivot turn which they do while thrusting with their feet. Wings may be used to stabilize the turn, but power is

Figure 5-3. Feeding postures of Common Loons. *a.* Swimming loon on the surface of the water. *b.* Peering loon; note its head is lowered so the water just covers its eyes. *c.* Diving with feet moving simultaneously and neck retracted in an S-position. *d.* Capturing prey, with fish grasped sideways in bill.

derived from the feet alone. The foot is extended on the side to which the bird is turning, and the toes are spread. That foot serves as a braking pivot about which the loon swings its body, and as it does so, its tail is flexed downward and the body moves with the back forming the outside of a curve. As the body turns, the extended foot pushes to accelerate the move. If the fish is just ahead of the loon's beak, it is caught.

The bill is clasped so the fish is held crosswise between the mandibles and cannot escape. The bill is tightly closed only at the tip. A slight gap occurs along the length of the rest of the bill, and this helps to hold the fish and prevent its slipping out the front. In addition, the tongue is extended forward when a fish is first touched, then it moves backward and upward during capture to press the prey tightly against the roof of the mouth. Together these actions add to the security of holding wiggly, often slippery, food. Barr (1973) described in detail both the action of a loon's bill during food capture and the musculature associated with it.

The tight grasp on the fish has another advantage when feeding the young. Although chicks peck at anything, such as nest material, sticks or anything nearby, as soon as they hatch, their parents must feed them for many weeks. From the first day, adults feed whole fish to young in addition to aquatic insects, crayfish, and leeches.

Fish are presented to the chicks crosswise, and young must manipulate the fish themselves, shifting them so they can be swallowed headfirst. Pressure exerted just behind the operculum of the fish by the adult's bill partially paralyzes the fish (Barr 1973) and an immobilized fish can then be readily positioned by a small chick. Fish are dropped in front of older chicks, and young must pick them up. An impaired fish can be "captured" by a juvenile, but a normal fish might swim away. In this manner, chicks gain experience in capturing their own prey even while their food is still being provided by their parents.

Chicks begin to peer and follow parental hunting during their first week. When they are two weeks old they often dive immediately after the adults do, following them to probe and search along the bottom (Barr 1973). Young loons do not use the same locations to feed themselves as adults do to capture food for the chicks. Adult feeding areas continue to move out farther and farther toward the territorial periphery as chicks grow older. Locations where chicks go to hunt food for themselves are far back in the recesses of the territory, and in shallower water than that in which adults hunt. At one-meter depths, chicks scout around sunken logs, stumps, debris, all of which are good hiding places for the small fish and crayfish they seek to capture (Christoff 1979).

Even so, with optimal habitat, an abundance of prey items, and shallow water with good visibility, Barr (1973) found that loons at three weeks of age caught very few uninjured fish, and even by six weeks were able to capture only a small part of their daily needs. By eight weeks, when adults leave their young for prolonged periods, juveniles are able to catch about half their own food.

Diving, probing, peering, searching, are all done by young chicks. When they are less than two weeks old, they can remain underwater about 30 seconds at a time. Adult feeding dives average 42 seconds. Many loon biologists have accumulated diving time records, and we have reported approximately the same times, for example, 41.4 seconds (Reimchen and Douglas 1980) and 42.9 seconds (McIntyre 1983).

Parker (1985) monitored adults on large lakes and small ones, acidified lakes and those not affected by acid rain, lakes with excellent fish populations and those with depauperate fish stocks. After analyzing more than 5,000 dive times, he found that the average feeding dive lasted 42.6 seconds. On acidified lakes, dives were longer than on normal ones, and the longest dive times of all were on acidified lakes smaller than 50 hectares. The shortest dive times were recorded for loons feeding on small lakes least affected by acid rain and with good fish populations. Parker attributed longer dive times to greater difficulty in finding or capturing food.

Dives on the wintering grounds are somewhat shorter. Robinson (1923) timed dives of wintering loons off the English coast and reported that they averaged 34 seconds. The loons which I monitored in an inshore bay off the coast of Virginia had feeding dives averaging 39.5 seconds. They were feeding in shallow waters from one to three meters deep. Wintering loons fed most heavily when the tide was ebbing, and I suspect fish may lag behind receding tides and become more readily available to the loons at that time (McIntyre 1978).

Duration of dives has not been monitored for individual loons on the fall staging grounds because most feed in groups and it is impossible to tell which is which when they are all diving together. During studies on Mille Lacs lake in Minnesota, feeding associations were composed of 15 to 25 loons that stayed together and dove together, although not all loons dove at the same instant. Duration of the group dives was 20 to 30 seconds, or considerably less than feeding dives on either the summering or wintering grounds (McIntyre and Barr 1983). We attributed it to the greater efficiency of group foraging, and the abundant population of yellow perch, cisco and emerald shiners in Mille Lacs.

Loons dive at times other than when they are feeding. Courtship dives are short, and pair members dive simultaneously, with dives averaging only six to seven seconds. During intraspecific interactions, especially during late-summer social gatherings, dives are also short, averaging only 15 seconds. Somewhat longer dives are made at the end of aggressive encounters by the territorial loon or loons when they make long underwater swims to check the territory for any loons that may still be on their territory. These are called searching dives.

Diving physiology of the loon has not been studied. Presumably loons, like other diving birds, utilize modifications that permit extended dives if necessary. Their feathers are compressed and air is forced out from between them as well as from the air sacs, to change the specific gravity at the beginning of the dive. Perhaps their heart rate is lowered, perhaps there is an automatic switching of available oxygen to the brain and away from the extremities, and their dark muscles must surely have a high concentration of myoglobin to allow for extended periods of anaerobic metabolic activity. No experimental work has been done to provide evidence that loons share these adaptations with other diving birds.

Loons begin to dive when they are young. Day-old chicks can make short dives of two to three seconds. Chicks are like corks in that they can submerge for only a few inches underwater and then they pop up. Within a few days they can dive to depths of 50 centimeters. When less than a week old they are able to make underwater turns and stay under for five to 15 seconds. By eight days they make frequent dives, and by the time they are 12 days old, young loons can stay under for 30 seconds and make sharp underwater turns. By then they have become skilled divers, and come up in any possible direction from the angle at which they entered the water, even though they are still in downy plumage and are more buoyant than they will be when their juvenile feathers grow in.

Dives have specific characteristics according to the situation. Feeding dives are initiated by peering, often with the head moving from side to side. Then the loon focuses its head, aims and enters the water approximately at a 140 degree angle. Slide diving is a way of slipping quietly into the water from a nest, and it is preceded by the hangover incubating posture (Figure 2–4e). Loons do this in response to a threat or disturbance, and by so doing they make no ripples but swim underwater, unseen, to come up at a distance from the nest. Sink diving also produces no ripples, but it is done from the surface of the water rather than from the nest. It begins as the loon sinks deep into the water, with only its head and top of its back above water, then it quietly submerges. Sink diving is a way of slipping away from a threatening situation.

Jerk diving may be a visual display. It is used during courtship and social gatherings. The loon quickly extends its head forward, arches its back and enters the water abruptly. Loons, when together in a group, frequently engage in mutual jerk diving. Jerk diving is more aggressive than most other forms, but splash diving is the most aggressive of all diving postures. During splash diving, the entire body is lifted, then hurled down, to raise a stream of water as it breaks the surface at a shallow angle. This causes an auditory display, as well as a visual one, uses great speed, and may startle other loons or potential predators.

Time Budgets

Activity patterns have not been thoroughly described for loons during the breeding season. During that period, division of time is dependent on responsibilities and the breeding status of the bird. Nesting loons spend over 95 percent of the incubation phase taking turns sitting on eggs, and that immediately cuts in half the time available for feeding, comfort movements, and territorial defense. Adults caring for young spend most of their time feeding and defending them, and although carrying young on their backs would not seem to be an energy-expensive task, it cancels the opportunity for preening or feeding.

Christoff (1979) recorded feeding and resting activities of a pair and their two chicks between the time the chicks were 10 and 40 days old. In general, feeding was the major activity early in the morning and late in the afternoon, and drifting and sleeping occupied almost a third of the time during the late morning hours. Resting was resumed early in the evening. The schedule during cold, wet, stormy weather was somewhat different. Loons spent more time feeding and less time resting in inclement weather. A study is needed to see if there is a division of time during the breeding season which is similar to or different from that at other times of the year.

Time budgets have been described for the fall premigratory period and during the winter (McIntyre 1978, McIntyre and Barr 1983). Some similarities and differences exist in the partitioning of time during the fall and winter (Figure 5–4). Wintering loons that I studied off the Virginia coast did no flying; they spent all their time confined to a small bay. However, other wintering loons occasionally flew up and down the coast over offshore waters. Because adult loons are flightless from late January to the beginning of March, while they are molting, the schedule I recorded for this inshore population may well represent a generalized pattern for all adult loons at the time of their remigial molt.

Loons drift offshore at all times of the year. They tend to spend the night over the deepest part available to them, whether they are on a lake or in coastal waters. Small groups of loons raft together overnight on fall staging grounds. Early in the morning they fly inshore to begin feeding.

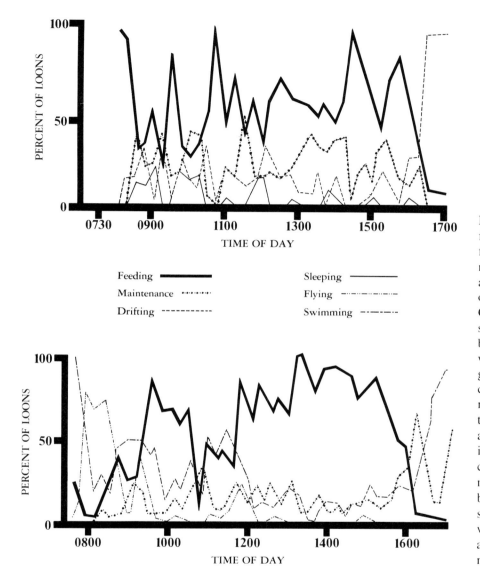

Figure 5-4. Activity times for Common Loons on the fall staging grounds in Minnesota at Mille Lacs lake and on wintering grounds off the coast of Virginia at Chincoteague and off Assateague Island. The activity budgets for loons during the winter, shown in the *upper* graph, are taken from data correlated with sun times, rather than with tidal times, to compare them with fall activity patterns as presented in the *lower* graph. In both cases, observations were made during daylight hours, but day length was not the same in the middle of the winter off the Virginia coast as it was in the fall in Minnesota.

During the winter, loons move to central feeding territories by swimming, rather than by flying. During both fall and winter, there is a concentration of time spent feeding early in the morning, but birds preparing for migration continue feeding longer in the morning than do wintering loons.

In winter, loons divide their time more evenly between feeding and maintenance activities than they do in the fall. This may be influenced partly by the winter molt. and a need for more preening as old feathers are removed and replaced by new ones. Loons concentrate on feeding as the tide goes out, and do not feed at high tide. During ebb tides, loons move closer to shore, apparently seeking optimal advantages for capturing prey that lags behind the receding tide, and that is likely to be concentrated at the edge of the outflowing waters.

Feeding times are correlated with light levels at all times of the year. During winter, loons stop feeding just before sunset, and in the fall, feeding ceases either just before or just after the sun sets. During both seasons loons gather in loose aggregations, and most are drifting alone, preening, and finally rafting within half an hour after they stop feeding. Because loons are visual predators, good light is needed for them to see and capture prey. There is no evidence that they feed at night, although during the breeding season their nocturnal calling indicates they are periodically active then.

During the day loons spend nearly equal time above and below water, with nearly 50 percent of their time foraging in the fall and winter. During the summer there are many underwater activities besides feeding, such as happens during the group gatherings discussed in the next chapter. As is known, underwater pursuits during the rest of the year are directed solely to chasing and capturing prey.

Time budgets are not completely worked out for loons, and this would be a worthy research project. In general it can be said that, except during the breeding season, loons spend most of the day eating and preening, interspersed with occasional periods of drifting and sleeping, and spend most of the night sleeping in rafts.

CHAPTER 6
Social Behavior

Behavior among social birds may call to mind a gull colony with dozens or hundreds of birds nesting side by side, a Purple Martin house bustling with its chattering inhabitants going to-and-fro, or a TV special with thousands of penguins marching across the screen en route to their Antarctic nesting grounds. Loons don't do any of those things, but they do engage in a number of social activities.

A mated pair is the smallest social unit, and a pair and its one or two chicks form a family. Nonrelated individuals become a functioning social organization when they are feeding together on a migratory staging ground, or late in the summer, when gathering at specific times and places, to hold ritualized ceremonies which we have come to call social gatherings. The call of one loon can elicit calling from all around, until a great chorus of loon music builds and blends and bounces from one shore to the other.

Some biologists claim that coincidental aggregation is not the same as social behavior. Others think that periodic feeding of flocks at sites of abundant food concentrations should not be called social. Nevertheless, some behavioral constraints must have evolved to permit the formation of associations even for short and irregular times. Signals must be either sent or withheld in order to prevent overt aggression when loons are together, engaged in feeding, preening, or sleeping. The extent of social behavior varies from one season to the next, is dependent on the stage in the breeding cycle, and is subject to some individual variability.

Loon Families and Juveniles Alone

Loon families spend most of the summer together. Males precede females to territories along the southern extent of the breeding range, but in the more northern parts, pairs arrive at the same time. Courtship is rather quiet, and is simple when compared to some of the more flamboyant displays of the bird world. Two loons are sometimes seen pursuing each other across the water, but these are not pair members with romantic passions aroused, they are a territorial loon and an intruder. Either sex can be the aggressor during territorial defense. I once witnessed a female attacking an intruder until the stranger loon was bloodied and dove into the depths of the lake, never to be seen again.

Pair members are together almost constantly from the time both are on territory in the spring. They do everything together, almost in synchrony, from swimming to feeding, from preening to sleeping, and even vocally, by duetting. Courtship begins as soon as both partners are on territory and continues until incubation begins, or from two to four weeks in most parts of the breeding range. All pairs do not stay together for the same length of time during the summer. If they are raising young, they are together most of the time, at least for eight weeks while young are dependent on them for food and protection, and they often stay together for five months or longer. Sometimes pairs are still together in the fall, nearly until freeze-up, in the winter.

If nesting is unsuccessful, the pair bond does not always last until fall, although some pairs stay together and on territory even if they have no young. In some cases, the female leaves the territory for longer and longer times if there are no young to be nurtured. Perhaps the duration of bonding is dependent on the quality of the territory. On small, marginal lakes, from which adults fly every day for part of their feeding, the pair bond disintegrates early; on territories with an abundant fish resource, pairs are often seen together well into the fall. Loons are not obviously paired when they leave during migration and there is no indication that they winter together.

The simplicity of courtship displays suggests that the same individuals may pair from year to year. If they have been successful in raising young, it is even more likely that individuals will repeat the same pair-bonding pattern the following year. It has been documented for members of other species, most recently for Florida Scrub Jays (Woolfenden and Fitzpatrick 1984), that annual pairing of the same individuals is common among monogamous birds.

Loon chicks are semiprecocial, but are dependent on parental feeding for several weeks. Juveniles maintain a submissive posture around their parents throughout the summer, and for the first two months they continue to hunch low in the water when begging food. Most loon chicks are members of a sibling pair, at least during part of their lives. A sampling of hundreds of broods indicates an average of 1.5 chicks per brood by the time of fledging (for example, McIntyre 1975, Yonge 1981), although Sutcliffe (1980) found that brood size averaged only 1.26 on his New Hampshire study site.

Petersen (1976) counted no more than one fledged young per brood during her studies of Arctic and Red-throated Loons in Alaska. She found a definite sibling rivalry and dominance of the first-hatched over its younger sibling. Until recently, Common Loon siblings were thought to display little competition between each other. Dulin (1988) studied parent-sibling and sibling-sibling interactions on Beaver Island in Lake Michigan as he floated in a muskrat-house blind, peering through observation holes, and watching what loon chicks were *really* doing.

Dulin found that siblings quickly established a dominance hierarchy. The older of the two was always dominant, and it maintained its dominance throughout the summer. It was the first to approach adults for feeding, and by a single look, a form of staring down, it could make its sibling back off and move away. If food was abundant, all was fine. The submissive chick eventually got fed and for the first two weeks there was plenty for both. Later, chicks were no longer satisfied with the same diet, and demanded more and larger FISH! This spelled disaster if there wasn't enough to go around, and the older sibling intimidated the younger until it moved as far as half a kilometer away from the family group, where it remained until nightfall, unfed and starving.

In 1985, two other studies conducted by graduate students reported similar results. Parker (1985) found that although young hatched on lakes in New York that had few fish, and although most chicks seemed to grow and appear healthy at first, some young died of starvation when they were three to four weeks old. Young loons have generally been considered survivors by that time, although they are not really fledged. Alvo (1985) found that more than half of the young on acidified lakes usually died within several weeks. He also found a shift in the food of chicks from a variety of invertebrates, vertebrates, and some plant material, to a demand for fish when chicks were older. Adults were successful only 10 percent of the time in finding food for their young on lakes with low alkalinity; on alkaline lakes, they were able to secure prey items on 23 percent of their dives. Alvo suggested that most brood mortality was the result of food shortages.

Overt fighting has only recently been reported between Common Loon chicks, although a dominance relationship is established early. Sadly, during the summer of 1986, Laurence Alexander, working on the Stillwater Reservoir in New York, collected ample evidence of physical aggression between young loons, resulting in starvation and death. Strong (pers. comm.) reported physical injuries during sibling rivalry resulting in the death of one chick on a Wisconsin lake. Such findings raise questions concerning recent habitat or pollutant changes which could be promoting mortality of young loons. Does only the dominant chick survive? Does reduction of food increase the level of aggression? We do not yet completely understand the relationship between recent changes and mortality.

Juveniles engage in no cooperative activities. After they are able to feed themselves, they occupy separate feeding arenas. Each moves to its own location during the day for feeding, even within the parental territory. If they move to a different lake when they can fly, each establishes its own feeding station. In both cases, young come together at night and raft side by side over the deepest part of their mutual holdings.

In 1973 I had the opportunity to follow a pair of marked siblings after they had fledged, until the day they migrated. They left their natal lake in September and flew to a larger lake where they occupied an area that had not been held by a territorial pair during the summer. They remained there for two months, until early November. Their feeding locations were always separate during the day, and each individual spent every day in the same site throughout the period (see Figure 6-1).

At dusk each night they came together and rafted side by side over the deepest part of their new residence. At dawn, they swam together toward shore, so close that, as I watched them each morning, I held my breath so they would not know I was just on the other side of shoreline vegetation. They pulled reeds, and fed on crayfish, bringing them to the surface before swallowing them. This was the only time each day when they fed together. After nearly an hour, one moved away to its feeding grounds on

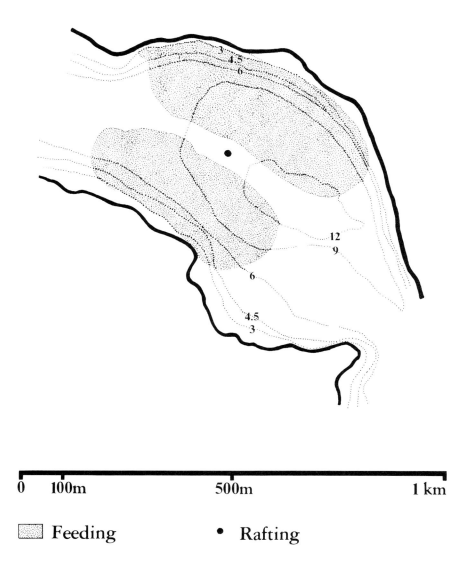

Figure 6-1. The channel occupied by the pair of siblings described in the text. Separate feeding locations are shown with stippling. The *dot* indicated as rafting is the place where the juveniles slept together every night.

| 0 | 100m | 500m | 1 km |

▨ **Feeding**   • **Rafting**

the opposite side of the channel, while the other remained on the side closer to me.

All day they stayed apart, and as the sun set, they moved quietly toward each other, preened, tucked their heads across their backs, and rafted side by side in the center of the channel. They stayed together all night, and through the mist of early morning each day I could once again follow them as they silently swam together shoreward for their morning crayfish.

I have never seen young loons engage in any activity that may be interpreted as play. Although they make small hoots, or contact calls, this is no different from hoots made by one adult to another, and certainly nothing in them indicates play. Even the pair of siblings I watched so carefully never conducted any activities together that could be considered play.

Juveniles leave natal lakes together in groups. Young from several lakes assemble on a single large body of water before beginning migration. I was lucky to be able to witness the departure of a group of them in 1973. It had snowed during the night of 2 November, and in the dim light of early morning I could make out three loons in the bay where the siblings lived. By 0745 it had grown light enough to see that one was an adult, and the other two were the marked young that I had been watching every morning. All were preening and occasionally swam in single file.

As they continued to swim and preen, I walked around the end of the point to see what might be farther out in the lake, for loons had been flying overhead and there were flight calls in the distance. Something was out there, and it was a flotilla of loons moving into the territory of the two siblings. The loons on parade did some preening en route, and a little feeding, but they continued to progress slowly into the bay.

By 0815 they were all together and spread out facing the open part of the lake. The adult moved away from the young, and the sibling pair joined the group of juveniles that had entered their holdings. All lined up side by side and reminded me of the Hell's Angels who had been at Itasca State Park a few weeks earlier. The motorcyclists lined up in the road, two by two, revved their motors, waited for a signal from their leader, and then took off together. The loons did the same thing. They lined up side by side across the bay, flapped their wings, and then at 0820 they took off, running across the water to become airborne. The last to run across was one of my marked birds, blue wing tag fluttering as the loon gained altitude and passed directly in front of me. I never saw that pair of siblings again. In spite of the appearance of an orderly departure, I had not seen juveniles engaged in social behavior until just before they left.

During the next two days I saw two unmarked juveniles at different locations, and I assumed they were not the same birds I had watched take flight together. Perhaps they were moving through from some more distant lake. By 5 November there were no loons on the lake, and on 6 November the lake began to freeze. A heavy snow later in the day confirmed that winter was approaching.

Banding recoveries from Minnesota loons have generally come from the gulf coast of Florida. Recent recoveries from other sites suggest where young may be spending the summer of their second year. One second-year loon died off the North Carolina coast in May, and two more were found off the coast of Nova Scotia, one in July and the other in October. While these recoveries were being reported, A. D. Smith of the Canadian Wildlife Service in New Brunswick wrote to say that immature loons appear every summer in waters between New Brunswick and Prince Edward Island. A few come in May, more arrive in June, and the rest appear in July.

In the summer of 1985 I went to New Brunswick to see young loons on the ocean. They were in small groups of seven to eight birds, and they moved together around the bay, feeding, preening, and sleeping The only calls I heard were tremolos rather than the hoot contact calls used by fall migrants. I made a wonderful tape recording one summer morning off New Brunswick on the shores of Baie Verte. It was a series of antiphonal calling bouts between young loons tremoloing on the water, together with dairy cows lowing from the shore.

Summer Groups

Adult loons begin to congregate from mid to late summer in groups, which may include from as few as three or four birds, to as many as 15, 20, or even more. I call these meetings social gatherings because birds gather together at specific times and places where they engage in behavior as stereotyped and ritualized as human social activities.

Most gatherings take place early in the morning or in late afternoon. Sometimes groups of loons congregate in a defended territory, but more often, meetings are held at a neutral site, a location not included in the territory of any one pair. On large lakes gatherings occur at boundaries between territories, and usually action is over deeper water, in particular at the edges of slopes. Both pair members frequently attend social gatherings together, but it is common for only one to be present if there are still small chicks to be cared for. One adult stays with the young while its mate interacts at the gathering site. If the meeting is held on a small lake, one occupied by a single pair using the entire lake as its territory, the resident pair leads the intruders into open water, away from nursery and young. Young hide quietly close to shore for the duration of the gathering, and will not appear again until the parents move toward them, calling as they approach.

Hoot calls signal the beginning of a gathering. Later, tremolo calls can be heard, together with an exhibition of vigorous running and defensive behavior. Yodels frequently are given after all intruders have left. A typical sequence includes bill dipping, head turning, pelican posturing, jerk swimming, and splash diving, all performed while loons are circling. Plate 6a shows loons during a social gathering. The wake that can be seen in the photograph clearly shows the circular pattern of their movements.

After all participants circle, one loon dives and the others remain on the surface, peering, for a few seconds, then dive while the initiator is still underwater. They emerge at a distance from where they originally dove, resulting in more loosely arranged spacing. Mutual divings are repeated many times, and the entire group may shift its position to move across the lake during the diving segment of the interaction.

It is not unusual for gatherings to include considerable combative activity early in the gathering season. Initially, the arrival of a stranger instigates aggressive activity. Nero (1963) described three-loon combats in early June involving side-by-side displays, two individuals nearly standing on the water with wings slightly raised, and chasing-running sequences in July involving two or three loons. The earlier account may have been more a description of territorial defense than of social behavior. Behavior observed in July included similar patterns, but led to a different outcome. Loons that Nero saw in July groups fed together at the end of the agonistic sequences, suggesting that ritualized social patterns may be derived from defense behavior, but include fewer aggressive components later in the summer.

Following the gathering, the territorial male surveys its holdings by swimming both on the surface and underwater. The female usually waits for her mate while he is checking their territory, and when both are reunited, they move together to retrieve hidden chicks, or if there are none, to resume other activities such as feeding and maintenance behavior.

The number of loons participating in each social gathering increases as the breeding season wanes. Early in the season, participants are primarily singles and unsuccessful breeders, but successful nesters join later. As their young grow older and become more independent, both pair members attend, leaving their offspring alone for longer and longer periods. This may well explain the increase in participants as summer approaches fall. Group size is smallest early in the summer, usually consisting of three, four, or five loons, but by August, large groups of 20 or more can often be seen together. The duration of each event also becomes longer late in the summer. By late July, gatherings may continue for one, two, or nearly three hours.

All evidence points to the likelihood that social gatherings function to reinforce cooperation among adults. They are a means of promoting familiarity among loons, and they also serve as practice sessions for skills used in flock feeding during migration. A waning of sex hormones late in the breeding season would also reduce levels of aggression and contribute to the increase of time spent in group activities. Ritualized behaviors prepare loons for cooperative feeding en route to the wintering grounds, unifying them as a cooperative feeding association.

Fall and Winter Groups

Migrating groups begin to form late in the summer. I have seen feeding aggregations in Saskatchewan, Manitoba, and Ontario in August, even occasionally as early as July. By September, group feeding is common. In Minnesota, where I studied loon behavior on the fall staging grounds, numbers en route and together in groups peaked from mid to late October (McIntyre and Barr 1983).

Some groups are loosely organized and large, and there may be 30, 40, or even more loons together. Most groups on the staging grounds include from 10 to 25 individuals. They stay together all the time, feeding during the day, moving to deeper waters at dusk, rafting offshore during the night, and flying to inshore foraging sites early in the morning. Group cohesion is maintained through nearly continual hooting.

Loon behavior during the winter is more variable than at other times of the year. Winter loon watchers have observed loons both inshore in groups, and as single birds offshore. I studied wintering loons off the coast of Virginia where a jigsaw shoreline and many islands provided numerous sheltered locations (McIntyre 1978). Loon groups were residents of one of these small bays. About 25 loons were in each of two groups, and each individual held a feeding territory during the day. Small, five- to eight-hectare locations were used exclusively by one loon, although I could not verify that the same site was occupied by the same individual day after day. It was rare to see conflict, but on a few occasions I witnessed agonistic or aggressive behavior (territorial defense?), and I heard a yodel during one of these encounters.

Loons stop feeding as light levels fall. A close correlation between sunset and cessation of feeding was noted from January through March. As day lengths increased, feeding times also increased and extended later and later into the day. Toward evening loons moved to the center of the bay, over the deepest water, where they rafted in a loose assemblage throughout the night. No aggression was seen within rafting groups.

There is little social activity among wintering loons, certainly not the kind found in summer social gatherings or in fall flock-feeding associations. The social behavior of loons is flexible and varies with the stage in the annual cycle. It is closely tied to the availability of resources, whether they be nest and nursery sites or a food resource. For much of the year loons are independent feeders and hold individual or pair territories. Only during migration do they feed together. This probably results more from lack of familiarity with new surroundings than from lack of food.

Lakes where staging is a tradition have an abundance of small fish, but loons visit them only during migration. Locating prey may be a problem. Thirty peering eyes and 15 diving bodies should reduce the time necessary to find food to the benefit of all loons participating in a feeding assocation. During winter and summer, when loons stay in one place for an extended period, they have time to learn where and how to find food.

It would be interesting to know if neighbors on the breeding grounds that join in social gatherings are the same individuals in fall feeding flocks and winter rafting groups. Are fall and winter groups all-male or all-female associations or are they mixed ? Do they include mated pairs? The answers to these questions are not yet available. We do know that loons form several kinds of social groups depending on the season and stage in their annual cycle. Stereotyped behavioral displays permit communication among group members. Description of, and explanation for, communicative forms are the subjects of the next chapter.

CHAPTER 7
Communication

Communication involves some degree of association between two or more individuals. A signal is sent by one animal or a group and received by others which then respond. Signals may be sent but not heard or responded to, but that is not communication. Communication by definition includes senders that signal and receivers that receive and then alter their behavior in some way.

Scent, touch, sound, and sight are channels that can be used to communicate. To the best of my knowledge, loons do not use chemical communication (scent), but all other modes are part of their communicative repertoire. Some tactile communication is used during parent-offspring interactions; visual displays span the range from subtle to spectacular, and loon vocalizations are used among loons themselves as well as directed to members of other species in conflict situations.

Tactile Communication

The only form of tactile communication between loons that I am aware of is begging by young loons. It is used when they want food or access to parental backs for riding. Signaling is simple, without stereotyped pat-

Figure 7-1. Posturings of Common Loons, in sequence from the least to the most aggressive. *a.* Hunched. Loon lies low on the water, partially submerged, and from this position is able to slide underwater at once. *b.* Head high. This is an alert posture; loon turns its head from side to side and looks around. *c.* Head straight. Used when two loons meet face to face. They do not look directly at each other, but pass going in different directions. This frequently ends with jerk diving. *d.* Circling. Several loons circle and alternately peer, bill-point, bill-dip, and raise their heads as the bird at *right* is

doing. After two or three circles, all birds dive, come up, and repeat the circling. *e.* Splash dive. A noisy dive, made frequently just before an aggressive attack. *f.* Rushing. Wings are held rigid and outstretched, and the head is straight with the bill pointing horizontally, a different posture from that used during preening and bathing, when loons hold their bills slightly uplifted as they shake their wings. Loons run along the water during this maneuver when charging an opponent. Figure 7-5a shows the highest level of aggressive visual display, the vulture posture.

terns, and persists as long as juveniles remain with the adults. Requests to back-ride include nudging the adult along its side and in front of the wrist. The parent responds by slightly raising its wing, just enough to permit chicks to climb on its back by crawling under the wing and up the side of the adult's body. Adults also shelter chicks by covering them with a wing. Chicks seeking either to back-ride or to be sheltered under a wing make identical requests.

Chicks peck adults on their heads, especially at the sides of the bill and face, when they want to be fed. Older juveniles include the entire head and neck surface as a pecking target. They rise up high out of the water to surround the older birds with a staccato of jabs. Adults respond by diving and searching underwater for food, returning with it to their young. These are straightforward pecking/begging signals, and they have not been ritualized and used as the basis for other displays. I know of no tactile signaling between pair members, and there is no mutual preening.

Visual Communication

Visual signals take a variety of forms. Some general principles apply to all animals, including loons. In submissive situations animals seek to make themselves appear smaller, and in aggressive displays they try to make themselves look larger. For loons, sinking low in the water in a hunched position makes them seem smaller, and becomes a signal of appeasement.

On the other hand, aggressive loons rise high out of the water, tread it to a swirling, frothing mass, and spread their wings. They point their bills directly ahead, so that they are looking into the eye of their opponent, their bill poised to attack. They look especially large in this pose, but somewhat vulnerable, too, with their white bellies exposed to a potential attack. True bravado! Just before attacking, loons may move into the vulture position (see Figure 7–5a). This places them slightly lower, and may put them in a better position to launch a physical attack. A sequence of these displays, from the most submissive to the most aggressive, is shown in Figure 7–1.

A loon's attack weapon is its bill. During physical encounters, loons either dive underwater and impale their victims through the abdomen, or chase them by running and raising themselves high in the water just before attacking them. This positions them for coming down on their opponent's back with their bills, and holding their victim underwater until it drowns. Since bills present a genuine threat, aggressive postures are not only

Table 7-1. Displays Used in Common Loon Courtship and
Relative Proportion of Time Spent on Each[a]

Display	Percentage[b]
Diving	
Short dive	70.8
Splash dive	16.7
Circle dive	8.4
Jerk dive	4.1
Head posturing	
Bill dip	45.1
Face away	38.7
Head throw	25.8
Bill flick	19.4
Head jerk	9.7
Pelican posture	6.5

[a]Data are combined from 31 courtship sequences.
[b]Figures indicate percentage of time spent in any dive form relative to all time spent diving. The percentage of time spent in any one head posture is relative to time spent in all head postures. Because more than one display can be used at one time, the total exceeds 100 percent.

stereotyped displays that send a message, they are also intention movements to attack.

Visual displays are also used among family members. When chicks beg, they rise higher and higher in the water as they peep for food, until they may be almost standing, with their tiny wings outstretched. As they grow older, their posture becomes more submissive, their heads are kept lowered, and they ride low in the water.

During courtship, bills are hidden as much as possible. Head turns, bill dips, head rubs, and pelican posture all serve to lower the visibility of the bill. Without these aversion displays, bills could point directly at the mate and send threat signals rather than sexual ones. Pair members perform display duets, during which they often swim side by side (Figure 7-2). There is not a specific sequence leading to copulation, but some display components are used more frequently than others (Table 7-1). Most dives are five to 10 seconds long, much shorter than dives used in other situations. Other types of dives are used during aggression, feeding, or escape.

The percentage of time spent in displays involving head postures adds up to more than 100 percent because more than one is frequently used at the same time. For example, facing away is often used with bill dipping, bill flicking, or pelican posturing. As with dives, the mildest displays are used the most frequently.

Figure 7-2. Courtship displays of Common Loons. *a.* Side-by-side swimming. *b.* Head turning. *c.* Bill dipping. *d.* Jerk diving. *e.* Male inviting female to land for copulation—the inviting display with a modified pelican posture.

Visual displays are also used during social gatherings, the composition of which changes during the summer. Initially they are composed primarily of unsuccessful breeders; later one member from pairs still engaged in some aspect of breeding joins; and later, both members of successful nesters are added to the group. There is no consistent sequence of displays during gatherings. Displays may take place within a defended territory as well as on neutral grounds. If a gathering is within a territory, heads are lowered to the pelican posture, especially by the pair leading the way to the specific place where the ritualized activity will take place, during the initial part of the ceremony. The lead pair is the territorial pair, and those following it are birds from adjacent territories and unmated individuals, meaning they are intruders with respect to the site of the ceremony.

During circling, loons avert their heads and engage in bill flicking and other displays that tend to hide their bills. They periodically dive, as described in the last chapter, and frequently after they surface, they shake their wings. Many years ago, when we were both graduate students, Joanna Burger and I spent a few days watching loons in social gatherings. We wanted to determine if loons turned away from each other when they shook their wings, thus reducing the potential threat that rising halfway out of the water and spreading wings might induce. We found no consistent pattern of turning away during wing shakes, but we also found there was a difference in the position of bills depending on whether loons were threatening each other or whether they were simply rearranging their feathers. Bills are held above the horizontal during wing flaps, a posture shown in Figure 5-1. Compare this with the position of the bill when loons are in an aggressive stance, such as in Figure 7-1f or 7-5a.

Visual displays dominate activity at the beginning of social gatherings, but in later stages, overt aggressive behavior replaces stereotyped displays. Early in the summer, when hormonal levels are still high, social gatherings usually end with running, chasing, and eventual departure by flying . Gatherings provide an opportunity for regular meetings of neighboring loons, and the displays promote synchronization of circling and diving activities while reducing the chance of physical combat.

Vocal Communication

Loons calls are distinctive, exciting, easily heard and recognized, and are given throughout most of the spring and summer. Loons use a variety of calls which can be placed in one of four categories: hoots, wails, tremolos, and yodels. Some are soft and carry for only a short distance. Others travel over the lakes for tremendous distances. These calls have become the symbol of wilderness, the positive affirmation of wild places, wild things, and wild sounds in the night. Examples of loon calls are given on the record at the back of the book, in the form of an acoustic glossary. Sonograms, or printed images of the sounds, are shown in Figure 7–3. Each category of calls will be discussed separately.

Hoots are short, single notes given among individuals in close proximity to one another. They are a form of contact call because they permit individuals to keep in touch with each other. Loons hoot during ritualized social gatherings and on the fall staging grounds. Hoots are also used by one loon as it approaches a group or enters the territory of another loon.

Wails are unmodulated pure tones, and may be given as one-note, two-note, or three-note calls. One-note wails consist of a single unbroken note, two-note wails begin on the same note but move quickly to a second note of higher frequency, and three-note wails add a third and higher frequency component to the two-note version. The note of highest frequency is held the longest, about two seconds, in all versions, although it can continue for as long as three seconds or be abbreviated to a single second.

One-note wails are a single note, but the frequency gradually increases to the middle of the call, and then just as gradually returns to its original pitch. There is not a break between one frequency and a shift to a higher or lower one, and the pitch is a little less than 1.0 kHz, although there is some individual variation.

Two-note wails have a first note like the one-note version, but it is shorter, and the second note is longer and at a higher frequency. In musical terms, there is commonly a major fourth between the first and second notes, although the exact interval may vary among individuals. As an example, if the first note is G in the second octave above middle C, the second note goes up to higher C. The call may end on the higher note, or it may return to the original. The average length of the call is two seconds, but this is far from uniform, and as with the one-note call, there are short two-note wails, as well as those which continue for nearly three seconds.

The first two notes of three-note wails are the same as the two-note version, and the third rises to a still higher pitch, usually an interval of a diminished fifth. For example, if the two-note wail just described begins the call, the third note rises to F#, so there is nearly a complete octave between the first and third notes, or almost a doubling of the frequency. There may be a return to the second note at the end of the call, or the wail may end on the highest frequency. An example of a two-note followed by a three-note wail is on the record. It was made by a mated pair calling on a moonlit night in early August.

Family members use several versions of wail calls. These are the "family wails." There is a soft one-note wail given between pair members, the "mew" or "ma" call. It is deliberate and soft, and rises to a perceptibly higher frequency in the middle than do other one-note wails, then falls to the lower pitch at the end. Its duration is one second.

Wails serve as mechanisms to reduce distance between loons. Loons move toward each other when they are wailing, and if one loon wails, its mate approaches, and may also begin to wail. Wails indicate a desire for closer contact, and the more intense the wail, the greater the urgency for contact and assistance. According to Barr (pers. comm.), wails develop from chick distress calls as there is a similarity in call types, including a change from a one-note to a two-note and finally to a three-note as the level of frustration increases. I agree this happens with chicks, but because during adult calling the responding individual also wails its answer, I wonder if wails would better be interpreted as indicating a willingness to interact, with all the range of messages and meanings which that definition could imply.

Parents use wails to call chicks off the nest, to signal when they have food for them, and to retrieve them from their hiding places. Males use the soft version to lure females ashore for copulation, pair members use it with each other when they are separated, and it is given by both pair members when they approach each other. Wails seems to be the loon versions of "come here" and "here I come."

These general statements are based on watching loons to see how they responded to hearing or giving a wail. I wanted to test a large number of loons in all stages of the breeding cycle so that I could measure their response to the three versions of the wail call. In 1981 a graduate student, John Brazner, and I broadcast wail calls to loons on Hanson Lake in northern Saskatchewan. We had the opportunity to work with 86 pairs of loons, so it was possible to secure data from a large number of loon pairs that were not in earshot of one another.

In these playback experiments, we transmitted one type of wail during each set of trials during 202 tests. Some loons were incubating, others were caring for chicks, and some either had not nested or had lost their nests. A large speaker mounted on the boat was connected to our tape recorder, and we played calls to the loons just outside their territorial boundary after we were sure they were not paying attention to us. We recorded their responses, which were termed positive if loons oriented to-

Table 7–2. Response to Wail Tests Played to Common Loons during June and July and Categorized by Call Type Presented

Response	One-Note (N=71)[a]	Two-Note (N=107)[a]	Three-Note (N=24)[a]
Vocal			
Wails			
One-note	1.4		
Two-note	5.6	6.5	16.7
Three-note	1.4	1.9	
Yodel		1.9	
Duet		1.0	4.2
Tremolo	4.2	21.5	
Tremolo-wail		1.0	
Hoot	4.2	8.4	8.3
Nonvocal			
Look around, alert	12.7	16.8	25.0
Orient to observers	7.0	17.8	20.8
Parallel/circle		1.0	
Direct approach	4.2	29.0	25.0
Fly to territory	1.4	2.8	
Swim to territory			4.2
Peer		2.8	16.7
Dive	25.4	8.4	12.5
Swim away	9.9	14.0	4.2
Fly away	1.4	1.0	
Nonvocal Response Summary			
Positive	12.6	50.5	50.0
Negative	11.3	15.0	4.2

[a]Figures indicate percentage of trials during which at least one response occurred.

ward us or approached directly. Movements away from us were categorized as negative.

Loons gave nonvocal positive responses after 12.7 percent of the one-note wail tests, and 50 percent of the time after two- and three-note versions were played (Table 7–2). Our tapes provoked more positive than negative responses and we concluded that wail calls serve to bring loons together. Our tests indicate that wails are graded, meaning versions of the same call correspond to changes in intensity of the motivation, but there is less difference between the two- and three-note versions than between the one-note wail and either of the others. On the other hand, wail responses were greatest following the playing of three-note versions. Two-note wails elicited a large percentage of tremolo answers.

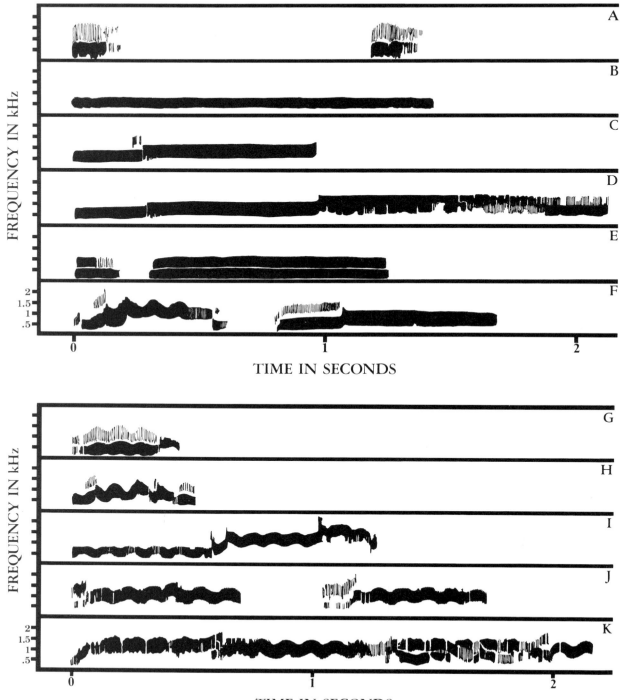

When pair members wail at each other they usually begin with a one-note call, then go to a two-note version, and may continue to a three-note wail if the mate does not respond. I have often wondered if wails that initiate nocturnal choruses might be given as a loon seeks its mate. Perhaps sleeping loons tend to drift apart, and from time to time awaken and vocally search for each other.

Tremolos, or laughing calls, have been studied and described by Barklow (1979). He recorded and analyzed nearly 3,000 tremolo calls from loons in northern Maine. He described tremolos as frequency-modulated calls of variable length, lasting from 0.15 to more than one second, and including between 1.5 and seven modulations, a modulation being one rise and fall in pitch.

Tremolos are transmitted in three versions which Barklow calls graded signals, or variations on a theme. They provide the same information, but the intensity of each differs. A Type 1 tremolo is from 600 to 800 Hz on a single fundamental frequency. A Type 2 begins like a Type 1, then moves to a higher frequency, about a third of an octave higher in most cases, up to about 1.2 kHz. A Type 3 begins like a Type 2, then moves to a yet higher frequency, to nearly 1.5 kHz. These values are for Maine loons; in Minnesota loons have higher voices, and their tremolo calls sometimes exceed 2.0 kHz.

There is some temporal overlap in the two notes of a Type 2 tremolo and in the three notes of a Type 3. Barklow (1979) believes this may indicate that the notes are made from separate sources, an example of the two-voice phenomenon in birds, by which the two parts of the syrinx, or sound-producing structure in birds, are capable of producing separate sounds.

Males call at a lower frequency than their mates do. If the pitch of a call is a reflection of body size, then, since males are larger than their

Figure 7-3. Sonograms of Common Loon vocalizations. The horizontal axis is time, in seconds; the vertical axis is the frequency, or pitch, of the sound, in kilohertz (kHz). For reference, middle C on the piano is 262 cycles per second, or 0.262 kHz, and with each octave the frequency doubles. Common Loon calls have as a midpoint a frequency of about 1.0 kHz, or about 2 octaves above middle C, 1.046 kHz. For sonograms of the yodel, please see Figures 7-4 and 7-6. Calls shown in this figure are: *A.* Hoot. *B.* One-note wail. *C.* Two-note wail. *D.* Three-note wail. *E.* Ma or mew call. *F.* Tremolo-wail. *G.* Type 1 tremolo. *H.* Type 2 tremolo. *I.* Type 3 tremolo. *J.* Flight call. *K.* Duet between pair members.

mates (Barr 1973), it would be expected that their voices would also be lower. Barklow analyzed numerous calls from the same individuals and he found that all tremolos, irrespective of what type they were, changed pitch as a correlate of the length of the call. Short tremolos were given on a lower pitch than were higher ones. For example, if a particular loon gave a tremolo with a fundamental frequency of 1.0 kHz, and it lasted half a second, then a shorter tremolo, perhaps one lasting only half as long, would have a fundamental frequency of 0.9 or 0.95 kHz.

Barklow (1979a) describes tremolos as alarm calls, given during threatening situations. This means it is often given when people approach nest or chicks. It is no wonder tremolos are more often identified as "loon" than other calls are; people frequently, albeit unintentionally, intrude on loon family life.

As the intensity of a threat increases, the tremolo is likely to change from a Type 1 to a Type 2, and finally to a Type 3 as shown in Figure 7-3. In a segment on the record a tremolo is given by a parent with chicks—as we moved closer, we became an increasingly greater threat to them. The Type 1 tremolo changed first to a Type 2, then to a Type 3. It can be heard on the record, together with the patter of feet as the loon raced across the water. Type 3 tremolos are frequently accompanied by water-treading displays.

Barklow noted a tendency to flee that accompanied the tremolo; the higher the frequency the greater the chance the bird would leave. Loons seem more reluctant to attack as frequency increases, but Barklow did not link this directly to whether the bird was giving a Type 1, 2, or 3 call. Calls progress from one to the next as a conflict situation continues or increases in intensity.

Some versions of the tremolo are given special names to indicate their special status. *Flight calls* are tremolos given by loons when they are flying. They are short, of constant length, with four to five modulations, and I believe they are timed to coincide with the flapping rate of flying loons. There are four flaps per call segment, and this may be linked to inhalation and exhalation, although the respiratory rate for loons in flight has not been confirmed. Flight calls are given by loons over occupied territories. They may or may not be answered by the territorial birds. Barklow also found that flight calls were primarily given over occupied territories; if loons flew over unclaimed lakes, they rarely gave a flight call.

Duets are antiphonal tremolos given by pair members. During calling, pair members alternate their signals, each given in different frequencies from that of its mate. Barklow found that pair members frequently used different call types, and this, too, would serve to exaggerate or maximize the pitch differences between the two birds.

Pairs use duets during nocturnal chorusing when it is difficult for observers to ascertain the exact context in which they are given. The loons are always too far away to see using any form of night scope I have tried. Nocturnal choruses include yodels as well as wails and tremolos. *Yodels*, discussed later in this chapter, are individually recognizable calls, and are given at night together or alternating with duets by members of a pair other than the yodeling bird. They emanate from territorial boundaries, suggesting that they are used to defend territories. Does the use of duets together with yodels suggest that duets are also used in territorial defense or proclamation? Duets are not thought to be used in loon pair bonding, as they are for several other species of birds.

Duets are also used in flight, especially when loons leave their territories during conflict situations. As a pair takes flight, it circles its territory, duetting as it goes. Surely there is an agonistic element in this behavior — components of both fear and defense are apparent. Nevertheless, I think it is safe to say a duet is a territorial statement.

There have been no playback experiments for any form of tremolo. Interpretation follows observations of behavior associated with tremolo calling. Tremoloing birds are defensive, yet also have a tendency to flee. During high-intensity calling, loons run across the water, alternately approaching and retreating. Flight calls are given by birds passing over a territory, not by those landing. Birds leaving interactions on lakes other than their own give tremolos as they move away. A loon being chased is much more likely to tremolo than is the loon doing the chasing. Finally, a loon tremolos while defending its young from human intruders, runs across the water toward the disturbance, then turns and just as quickly runs the other way, or dives and comes up at a distance. These examples strongly suggest that tremolos are agonistic calls.

Yodels are male calls, perhaps the counterpart to male song in most other bird species. They seem to remain identical from year to year for any one loon (see Figure 7–4), but so far no one has marked loons with colored wing tags or leg bands and then recorded their yodels from one year to the next. Since marked and banded loons return over and over to the same territory and individuals occupying the same territory also have the same yodel from one year to the next, as discussed in Chapter 1, it is highly probable that yodels are providing information on individual identity for other loons just as they are for biologists.

A special posture is assumed during yodeling (Figure 7–5b). Rummel

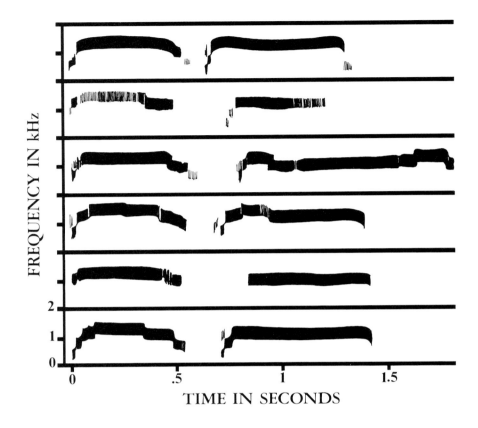

Figure 7-4. Drawings made directly from the sonograms of yodels from six male Common Loons occupying neighboring territories. The portions represented are the redundant motifs; the first part is *Figure 1*, the second is *Figure 2*. See Figure 7-6 for explanation of the divisions of the yodel.

FREQUENCY IN kHz

TIME IN SECONDS

and Goetzinger (1975) called this the crouch and yodel display because the yodeling male lies flat across the water, neck extended, and lower mandible just above the water. Males usually do not remain in one position, but pivot, or swivel, sending the sound spraying out around the lake in a giant semicircle. Presumably this acts to broadcast the sound over a wider area than it would if the bird transmitted its call in a single direction.

I have often wondered if loons extend heads and necks to maximize their ability to project yodels over long distances. I have seen loons yodel from other positions only a few times, and then only when they were engaged in close face-to-face combat with another loon. They stood high in the water, wings extended, head straight ahead or slightly lowered. Rummel and Goetzinger (1978) termed this the vulture posture (Figure 7–5) and claimed it to be hostile and a higher intensity than the typical yodel posture. Perhaps, as Barr has suggested (pers. comm.), the combination of vocal and visual signals acts synergistically to amplify an aggressive message.

Figure 7-5. Postures assumed by male Common Loons while yodeling. *a.* Loon in the vulture posture. *b.* Loon in the crouch and yodel posture.

There is some geographic variation among yodel calls. I recorded males in Minnesota, Saskatchewan and New York, then prepared contour sonograms of the calls (Figure 7-6). Frequency, amplitude, and time were quantified and coded so the frequency with the greatest energy concentration could be identified using the methods developed by Bowman (1979). Figure 7-7 presents the results as histograms showing amplitude relationships of the two parts of the redundant motif for loons recorded in each of the three populations.

Minnesota birds have the highest voices, New York loons the lowest, and Saskatchewan loons are in between, although they are very close to

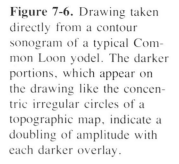

Figure 7-6. Drawing taken directly from a contour sonogram of a typical Common Loon yodel. The darker portions, which appear on the drawing like the concentric irregular circles of a topographic map, indicate a doubling of amplitude with each darker overlay.

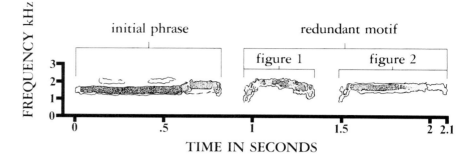

the Minnesota birds. In general, small animals have higher voices than do large ones (Morton 1977). I suspect the difference in frequency of Common Loon calls results from body size differences, as differences in voice correlate with differences in body sizes of each population. If so, then Icelandic and Baffin Island loons must be the real basso profundos of the loon world!

The function of yodels has been described as territorial marking (Sjølander and Ågren 1972) and territorial defense or a ritualized aggressive display (Rummel and Goetzinger 1975). Young (1983) examined the entire vocal repertoire of Common Loons and recorded shifts and changes in the relative proportion of call types throughout the breeding season. She predicted that yodels should be most common before nesting began if they were used primarily to attract a mate; if they served their major role in territorial acquisition or defense, they should be used most extensively at times when territories were being attained, expanded, or defended.

Young found that yodels were given primarily during nesting, twice as frequently as they were before incubation began, and six times as often as when adults were caring for chicks (Figure 7–8). She also found that adults were highly defensive of their territories just before hatching, more so than at other times, and they expanded their boundaries just before and during hatching at the expense of neighboring pairs that had nested unsuccessfully.

This same kind of territorial expansion was noted by Rummel and Goetzinger (1975) just after hatching, but not when chicks were older. I have seen both New York and Saskatchewan loons expand their territories at the time of hatching. Adults with brand-new chicks push their boundaries farther and farther into territories of pairs that are unsuccessful. Young concluded that yodels definitely were territorial calls, serving as aggressive proclamations of territorial ownership.

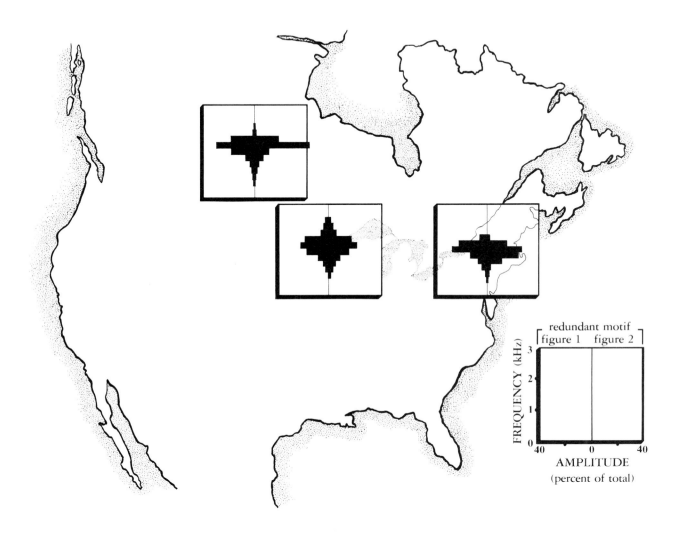

Figure 7-7. Histograms of the two figures of the redundant motif in Common Loon yodels for each of three populations. These illustrate energy concentrations, or the relative amplitude (dB) at each frequency. The major concentration for the first figure is at 1.67 kHz for Minnesota loons, 1.61 kHz for Saskatchewan birds, and 1.46 for New York loons. In the second histogram, the averages are 1.65 kHz, 1.65 kHz, and 1.41 kHz, respectively. The box at the *lower right* labels the axes for the boxes containing the histograms.

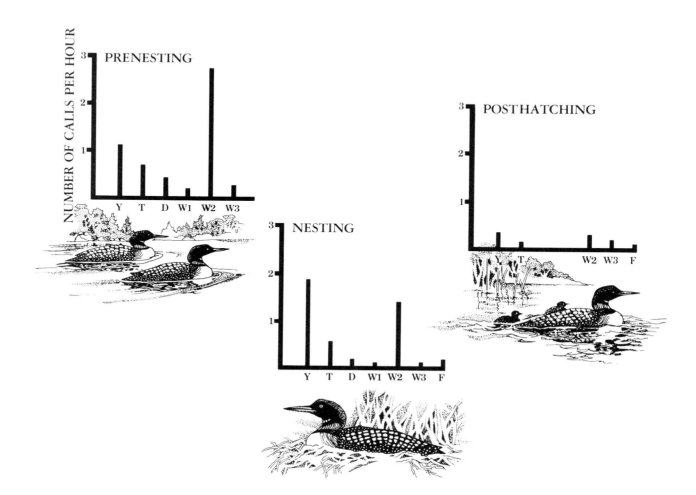

Figure 7-8. Summary of the relative proportion of Common Loon calls given during each stage of the breeding cycle, from data on loons of Adirondack lakes in New York. (From Young 1983.)

In 1981 John Brazner and I played yodels to nearly 80 pairs of loons on Hanson Lake and monitored the responses in a series of playback experiments. We used a yodel from the same individual for all tests, a yodel given by a loon outside the population with which we were working. Incubating loons were most likely to respond to a strange yodel by yodeling, wailing, or duetting. Loons with young in tow tremoloed a reply and

Table 7–3. Responses to Normal Yodels Played to Loons during
Different Stages of the Breeding Cycle

Response	No Nest (N=26)[a]	Incubating (N=16)[a]	Young (N=35)[a]
Vocal			
Wail	15.4	25.0	14.3
Yodel[b]	19.2	37.5	2.9
Duet[b]	3.8	25.0	
Tremolo	3.8		22.9
Hoot	3.8	6.3	
Nonvocal			
Alert, look around	7.7		14.3
Orient to observers			11.4
Swim parallel or toward boat			8.6
Approach directly			25.7
Fly to territory		6.3	
Peer	7.7		8.6
Dive	3.8		11.4
Swim away	3.8		8.6
Fly away		6.3	

[a]Figures indicate percentage of trials during which at least one response occurred. *No nest* refers to loons tested before egg-laying or with unsuccessful nests, and include results from all three series of tests during June, July, and August. *Incubating* loons are sitting on eggs. The *with young* category includes both those with small chicks and those with older young.
[b]Yodels and duets are both assumed to be used in territorial defense.

oriented toward or approached directly the speaker. Loon pairs with neither nests nor young were far less likely to give any response (Tables 7–3 and 7–4).

In addition to the normal yodel, we played modified versions. The amplitude was changed in the altered variations so that it was either increased by 10 dB in the first figure of the redundant motif and the second figure decreased by 10 dB (shown as Yodel type 2 in Table 7–5), or the first figure was decreased by 10 dB and the second figure increased by 10 dB (Yodel type 3, Table 7–5). The introductory portion remained unaltered. We played the three variations on a theme to 37 pairs of loons in all kinds of weather, at eight different times over 24-hour periods, during all stages of the breeding cycle (nesting, rearing of young, and nonnesting) and throughout the breeding season, from early June through August.

I was asking the question, "If the entire yodel provides a message such

Table 7-4. Responses to Normal Yodels Played to Common Loons during the Summer and Categorized by Month in Which Tests Were Given

Response	June (N=24)[a]	July (N-32)[a]	August (N=21)[a]
Vocal			
Wail	25.0	18.8	4.8
Yodel[b]	33.3	12.5	
Duet[b]	8.3	9.4	
Tremolo		15.6	19.0
Hoot	4.2	3.1	
Nonvocal			
Look around, alert	4.2	9.4	14.3
Orient to us		9.4	4.8
Swim parallel or Circle boat		3.1	9.5
Direct approach		18.8	19.0
Fly to territory	4.2		
Peer	4.2	12.5	4.8
Dive		3.1	23.8
Swim away			19.0
Fly away	4.2		

[a]Figures indicate percentage of trials during which at least one response occurred.
[b]Yodels and duets are both assumed to be used in territorial defense.

as, 'I am a male loon, I am on my territory, and I am prepared to defend it,' and if some parts are louder than others, so that they will fade out or be lost as the receiver is farther and farther away from the source, will the part of the call which can still be heard far away provide slightly different information than the entire call does?" For example, if the unattenuated call says, "I am a MALE LOON, on TERRITORY and prepared to DEFEND it," would this be heard far away as "male loon territory defend," or still farther away simply as "loon," or "male," or "territory"?

Information contained in bird calls includes species, sex, and individual identification, as well as location and motivational states of the signaler (Smith 1977). This information may be encoded in a number of ways. Among those shown to be important are frequency, or pitch of the signal; syntax, or the order in which parts are arranged; and timing or temporal patterning of call components (Emlen 1972, Brooks and Falls 1975, Brown and Lemon 1979). Amplitude modulation has been considered unimportant as a species-specific factor because it is so easily lost or altered over distance by wind or thermal gradients (Becker 1982). It is

Table 7–5. Responses to Normal (1) and Altered (2 and 3) Yodels Played to Loons during Different Stages of the Breeding Cycle

Response	No Nest			Incubating			With Young		
	1 (N = 26)	2 (N = 24)	3 (N = 19)	1 (N = 16)	2 (N = 21)	3 (N = 23)	1 (N = 33)	2 (N = 35)	3 (N = 35)
Vocal									
Wail	15.4%	12.5%	15.8%	25.0%	19.0%	8.7%	14.3%	21.2%	17.1%
Yodel	19.2	4.2	10.5	37.5	23.8	13.0	2.9		
Duet	3.8	4.2		25.0	19.0				
Tremolo	3.8	12.5			9.5	4.3	22.9	15.2	25.7
Tremolo-Wail								3.0	2.9
Hoot	3.8		5.3	6.3					
Nonvocal									
Alert, look around	7.7	25.0				14.3	18.2	25.7	
Orient to observers		4.2					11.4	6.1	5.7
Parallel circle		4.2					8.6	9.1	5.7
Approach		4.2			4.8	8.7	25.7	12.1	17.1
Fly to territory				6.3					
Swim to territory					4.8			3.0	
Peer	7.7	4.2				4.3	8.6	3.0	20.0
Dive	3.8	8.3	15.8				11.4	18.2	11.4
Swim away	3.8	4.2	5.3		4.8		8.6	12.1	20.0
Fly away		4.2		6.3					

[a]Figures indicate percentage of trials during which at least one response occurred. See text for explanation of artifically altered yodel tapes. Status of loons is same as in Table 7-3.

thought to provide only information about distance (ranging) as shown by the work of Wiley and Richards (1978) and King et al. (1981).

If any bird is going to use amplitude differences to send information, loons should be the most likely candidates. They call primarily at night when wind speed is low or nonexistent. Measurements of attenuation, or loss of intensity over distance, of pure tones over water show that sounds in the frequency at which loons call become degraded at a uniform rate, especially at night. Time after time, irrespective of temperature or moisture in the air, the loss of sound, or attenuation, was nearly the same. Wind speed was the single factor that caused fluctuation in attenuation at any time of the day or night, and since wind speed is exceedingly low on most nights, it is unimportant as a factor affecting sound transmission.

All three variations of the yodel were played to loon pairs. Altered calls became altered signals, and there were some differences in the ways loons responded to them. Version 3 seemed to elicit less vocal response for most pairs, unless the pairs had young with them. In that case, they were more likely to call, and almost twice as likely to lift their heads and look around, but they were also less likely to move toward the speaker and approach it, and nearly three times as likely to dive.

How did the message differ? Was it the increase in volume at the end of version 3 which provided a false signal, interpreted as the caller's moving closer and becoming a threat? Birds at other stages of the breeding cycle may have interpreted the message in the same way, but having no chicks to defend, gave different responses. More refined experiments must be done using playbacks of all calls in the loon's repertoire. Understanding of loon calls is still limited. Wails serve to reduce distance between or among loons, tremolos indicate conflict, pairs duet in defense of territory, yodels identify individual males and are used in territorial defense, and hoots are contact calls.

Young loons have calls with some characteristics of adult vocalizations; other calls are limited to chicks. *Peeping* is used to keep in touch with the parent birds, is used for begging, and resembles the peeping of chicks of other species. Increased intensity of begging results in an increase in the speed with which peeping is given, and peeps are often interspersed with pecks delivered near the bill of the adult. Chicks begin to peep before hatching. *Yelping* is used from the first day after hatching. It too is a single note call, but there is a drop in frequency during its delivery. It is used in begging, and is a higher intensity call than peeping.

Wails are given by chicks beginning when they are one week old. They are used in begging, and are more intense than peeping or yelping. Chicks progress from peeping to yelping to wailing as they beg food from the adults. Wails are also given as distress signals, for example, by chicks that have become separated from their parents. They have the same gradations as adult wail calls, with an increase in the frequency of sequential notes suggesting increasing intensity.

By fall, when juveniles are three to four months old, they give wails and tremolos that are indistinguishable from adult calls. They have ceased peeps and yelps, but have added the hoot to their repertoire. Only adult males yodel, and it is not known how old loons are before they are competent to yodel.

Daily patterns of loon calls were studied by Young (1983). She found that loons call primarily at night, with a peak intensity during the hour just before midnight. In fact, when loons called during the day, she reported they almost always tremoloed, usually in response to human disturbance.

Her conclusion was that there was little intraspecific vocal communication during the day relative to the extent of nocturnal signaling.

Loons have large territories, and pairs are spaced far apart, so it is expected that their calls would be given at times when they would carry the farthest. A number of recent studies have shown that birds call at times when the likelihood of their being heard is greatest (Morton 1975, Marten and Marler 1977, Marten et al. 1977). These studies and others tested the physical features of the environment in vegetated habitat, where the attenuation of sound is determined primarily by features such as absorption by the surrounding vegetation. Loons call over water where other factors, primarily micrometeorological conditions — such as temperature, humidity, and wind — play the major role in determining if sound will attenuate less at one time than at another.

Young (1983) studied the shifts and changes in composition of loon repertoires during the breeding season. A definition of repertoire generally used for the study of avian vocalizations is "the total number of versions of song which any one male sings" — in other words, the number of variations on a song theme. Songs are specific vocalizations, and by definition they are used to declare territorial ownership, and for some species, they are also used to attract mates. Birds give other calls, but they are not called songs.

Young defined a repertoire in the same way it is defined for concert performers, that is, the entire listing of compositions rehearsed and ready to be performed. For loons, that includes all their calls — tremolos, wails, yodels, hoots — which they are ready to give. It includes calls given by both males and females, as opposed to song, or the yodel, which is not performed by females. Young listened to loon calls at night, during bouts of intraspecific calling, to examine only those being used among loons themselves, and to avoid counting calls directed to people, boats, airplanes, and other human-related disturbance factors. She found a difference in the relative proportion of each call type during the breeding season, but not a change in call types included in the repertoire per se. Throughout the season, loons wail, tremolo, hoot, and yodel, but before nesting begins, yodels are used more than other calls. All call types decrease after chicks hatch, until there are just infrequent yodels and wails and an occasional tremolo.

Hoots are about the only call used during the winter, but tremolos and yodels can be heard infrequently. Loons apparently are *competent* to perform all calls in their repertoire at any time of the year, but are not in physiological condition to do so. There is no information on the hormonal levels of loons at varying times of the year and how they might correlate with vocalizing, but gonadal hormones probably play a role in the timing of loon calls as they do for other species that have been studied.

Loon communication, for all its flashy visual components and its haunting vocal messages, has received less serious scientific attention than it warrants. Perhaps the discussion given in this chapter will whet the appetites of other biologists, sending them scurrying to investigate loon communication.

Plate 1. Copulation by Common Loons. The male is on the top. (Photograph: Peter Roberts.)

Plate 2. Predator experiments. *a.* Man-made loon nest with a double-yolk turkey egg dyed to resemble a loon egg. A mixture of wet sand and clay is placed around the nest. (Photograph: Judy McIntyre.) *b.* Raccoon footprint identifies the predator that ate the egg. (Photograph: Judy McIntyre.)

Plate 3. Common Loon eggs. *a.* A two-egg clutch in a nest on a Minnesota lake. (Photograph: Peter Roberts.) *b.* A loon nest with muddied eggs on a Canadian lake. Water levels had dropped, yet adults continued to crawl overland on their breasts to reach nearly stranded nests. The picture attests to parental perseverance and to the loon's inability to walk upright. (Photograph: Judy McIntyre.)

Plate 4. Incubating Common Loon, showing location of eggs under the bird's abdomen. (Photograph: Judy McIntyre.)

Plate 5. Parental care of the young by Common Loons. *a.* Male of the same pair shown in *c* giving an upright defense display while calling with Type 3 tremolos. The calls in *a* and *c*, plus the patter of this loon's feet as he runs across the water in *a*, are in the acoustic glossary. (Photograph: Pat McIntyre.) *b.* Adult feeding its chick by passing a fish from bill to bill. (Photograph: Tom Martinson.) *c.* Pair swimming with their day-old chick. The male leads and is giving Type 1 and Type 2 tremolos. (Photograph: Pat McIntyre.) *d.* Back-riding, a technique by which loon chicks are kept warm and safe from underwater predators such as fish and turtles. (Photograph: Tom Martinson.) *e.* Newly hatched chick being wing-brooded on the nest by its parent. Later, when chicks have left the nest, they are sheltered from time to time under a parental wing while swimming or loafing on the water. (Photograph: Tom Martinson.)

Plate 6. Social gatherings of Common Loons. *a.* Adults peering and about to dive during a social gathering. Note the movement of the water showing the circled configuration of their activity. (Photograph: Judy McIntyre.) *b.* One loon, probably the territory holder, leading the visitor loons to the location where a ritualized display will take place. This is usually over a slope or a deeper part of the lake. (Photograph: Peter Roberts.)

Plate 7. Four of the five species of loons, family *Gaviidae*, in the alternate plumage worn during the breeding season. *a.* Red-throated Loon on its nest in the Shetlands Islands. (Photograph: Robert Furness.) *b.* Pacific Loon. This North American loon shows little plumage difference from its European and Asian counterpart, the Arctic Loon. (Photograph: Grimes/Cornell Laboratory of Ornithology.) *c.* Common Loon in a hangover posture on its nest in New Hampshire. (Photograph: Judy McIntyre.) *d.* A swimming Yellow-billed Loon. (Photograph: K. Wilson/Cornell Laboratory of Ornithology.)

Plate 8. Some physical features of Common Loons.
a. Common Loon chick in its first downy plumage. (Photograph: Pat McIntyre.) *b.* Juvenile Common Loon in its juvenal plumage. Note the scalloped appearance of the contour feathers. (Photograph: Tom Martinson.) *c.* Supraorbital, or salt glands. Skull on the left has glands removed, showing depressions in the skull. Glands are intact in the skull on the right. (Photograph: Judy McIntyre.) *d.* Ventral aspect of Common Loon during February off the coast of Florida. Note the missing flight feathers characteristic of complete remigial molt. (Photograph: Judy McIntyre.)

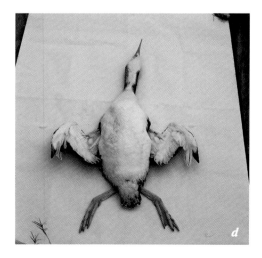

Plate 9. Capture and marking of Common Loons. *a.* Juvenile loon wearing a bright orange wing tag. A unique color-making scheme for each individual permits recognition and identification at a later time. (Photograph: Judy McIntyre.) *b.* Pat McIntyre sitting over the bow of the pursuit boat wearing an airplane landing light mounted on his helmet and carrying a long-handled dip net for picking up loons during capture. (Photograph: Judy McIntyre.)

Plate 10. Artificial nesting islands. *a.* Artificial island made from sedge mat (Minnesota). (Photograph: Pat McIntyre.) *b.* Artificial island made from logs and wire, filled with vegetation (New York). (Photograph: Judy McIntyre.) *c.* Loon nesting on an artificial island in Minnesota. This pair hatched, and successfully reared, two young. (Photograph: Craig Borck.)

CHAPTER 8

Evolution and Classification of Loons

Loons are a small and closely related family of diving birds (Plate 7). They are sufficiently different from all other birds to form an entire order by themselves. Separated evolutionarily by about 50 million years from their closest relatives, their ancestors may have been the same as those of penguins, albatrosses, or gulls. Loons may sound primitive when they wail their lonely calls across a lake on a summer night, but they are highly advanced, or specialized, birds and are no older than many other groups, such as ducks, storks, cranes, or grebes.

Modern forms emerged about 10 million years ago, at the same time most living nonpasserine, or nonsong birds, first appeared. The divergence of Yellow-billed Loons from Common Loons happened no earlier than a million years ago. When the last glaciers were retreating and melting, Common Loons gradually followed behind to take up summer residence on the newly made, glorious, cold, clear northern lakes.

Loons can be introduced by scientific or common names. They are called loons in North America, but in Great Britain they are known as divers. In France they are referred to as plongeons, and in French-speaking

Table 8–1. Common Names for Loons and for Common Loons from Several Languages

Generic Name	Language/ Ethnic Group	Meaning
Loon	American	clumsy, awkward
Lom	Danish, Swedish, Norwegain	clumsy
Buvar	Hungarian	diver
Diver	English	diver
Duiker	Dutch	diver
Plongeon	French	diver
Seetaucher	German	diver
Gagara	Russian	sounds like call
Huart	French-Canadian	sounds like call
Kuikka	Finnish	sounds like call
Himbrimi	Icelandic	surf-bird

Name for *Gavia immer*	Language/Ethnic Group
Common Loon	American
Amerikan Jaakuikka	Finnish
Colimbo grande	Spanish
Eistaucher	German
Great Northern Diver	British
Himbrimi	Icelandic
Ijsduiker	Dutch
Islom	Danish, Norwegian, Swedish
Mergulhao	Portuguese
Nur Lodowiec	Polish
Plongeon imbrim	French
Shioeri ohamu	Japanese
Strolaga maggiore	Italian
Temnokluqaja poljarnaja gagar	Russian

Indian or Inuit Names	Language/Ethnic Group
Hukweem	Milicete
Kwee-Moo	Passamaquodie, MicMac, Algonkin
Mahng	Ojibway
Moke	Barren Ground and Davis Inlet Inuit
Too-lik	Hooper Bay Inuit
Tood-lik	Perry River Inuit
Tuhlik	Mackenzie Delta Inuit
Tullik	Leaf Bay and Baffin Island Inuit
Tuu'lik	Keewatin, NWT Inuit

Canada they are called huarts. Their common names can be assigned to one of several categories. For example, *diver* and *plongeon* refer to diving ability. *Loon* and *lom* are derived from an old Scandinavian word meaning clumsy, and both call attention to the loon's inability to walk gracefully. *Huart*, *kuikka*, and *gagara* all sound like loon calls when they are pronounced properly, and the Inuit names, *too-lik*, and *tullik*, literally mean "having a tusk," in reference to the loon's long bill (Table 8–1).

Over the years loons have been assigned to a succession of families and orders. They have been known at one time or another as Pygopodes (the rump feet), Urinators (tail swimmers), or Cecomorphs (shaped like a seabird). In other classification schemes they have been assigned to groups shared by birds now considered to be unrelated, in orders such as the Colymbiforms or the Anseriformes. An excellent review of their taxonomic placement and scientific names since 1840 has been given by Sibley and Ahlquist (1972). The most recent American Ornithologists' checklist (AOU 1983), together with the 1985 supplement (AOU 1985), offer the currently accepted scientific name for the order (Gaviiformes) and for each of the five loon species.

Superficial resemblances arising from convergence between two groups of aquatic birds prompted early taxonomists to link loons with an ancient group of birds, *Hesperornis*, large diving birds with reduced wings, large feet, and teeth. The earliest fossil discoveries of *Hesperornis* were made in 1870 by O. C. Marsh in the Niobrara Formation of western Kansas. Later he found more hesperornithine fossils in the same locality, and over the past century this region has continued to provide an impressive array of fossil material.

In the last 100 years, fossils of this ancient group of divers have been unearthed in several sites in Kansas, Nebraska, Montana, South Dakota, Canada at both the arctic edge and inland, as well as in both South America and Europe (Martin 1980). Thirteen species have been described and an excellent discussion about these extinct birds was given by Feduccia (1980) in his book, *The Age of Birds*.

Heilman's *Origin of Birds*, written in 1927, was the first book published specifically on avian evolution. Heilman thought there was a direct *Hesperornis*-Loon phylogenetic relationship and his arguments influenced thinking on loon affinities for several decades. The recent paperback of his work (1972) will doubtless continue to influence public understanding of evolutionary relationships for some time to come. This may be unfortunate, because the book is only a reprint of the 1927 work rather than a revision, and includes no recently discovered findings.

Table 8-2. Comparisons between *Gavia* and *Hesperornis*

Differences	*Hesperornis*	*Gavia*
Teeth	present, conical, set in grooves in both upper and lower jaws	absent
Olfactory bulb	large	small
Wing	vestigial humerus	normal for flying birds
Caudal vertebrae	expanded and flattened transverse processes	no specializations
Sternum	no keel	prominent keel
Clavicles	weak and unfused	fused to a furcula
Pygostyle	derived from two caudal vertebrae	derived from many caudal vertebrae
Cnemial crest	formed solely from patella	formed solely from tibiotarsus
Toes	specialized articulations of 4th toe permitting rotation between recovery and power strokes	no specializations
	4th toe longest	3rd toe longest

Similarities	*Hesperonis* and *Gavia*	
Tarsometatarsus	laterally compressed	
Skeletal structure	non-pneumatic	
Leg musculature	lies within the body as far as the tarsus	
Femur	short and broad; reduces walking mobility	
Synsacrum	long and extended posteriorly	
Tibia	elongate and parallel to ilium	

There are some similarities between loons and hesperornithine birds. That is to be expected between groups that are aquatic, piscivorous, foot-propelled divers, for both are the end products of selection for characters which must function efficiently in the same kind of habitat. Marsh himself considered that loons and hesperornithines were convergent, that they shared many similar characters, but were not closely related. Comparisons between the two groups are summarized in Table 8-2. All foot-propelled diving birds share some features, but that does not mean they share the same ancestors. Phylogenetic relationships are not disproved because of differences, and similarities among some characters cannot automatically be assumed to indicate convergence if other characters differ.

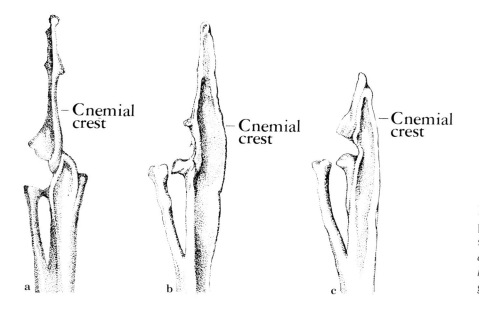

Figure 8-1. The proximal portion of the tibiotarsi showing the cnemial crest. *a. Hesperornis. b. Gavia immer. c.* A representative grebe.

However, two differences stand out and indicate it is unlikely that loons are closely related to the hesperornithine birds.

First, the wing of *Hesperornis* has been reduced to one bone, the humerus, and neither ulna nor radius has been retained. *Hesperornis* evolved a highly specialized and superbly adapted structure for a diving bird long before the earliest "true loons" had come into existence. The probability of reevolving a multiple-boned wing from a vestigial structure, one identical in its components to that of other birds, is close to zero.

Second, though both *Hesperonis* and loons have elongated tibiotarsi, the bone between the thigh and foot, with an extension called the cnemial crest (see Figure 8–1), the way in which each developed is quite different. In both cases, the cnemial crest provides for the extensive muscle attachment necessary for power strokes used in diving. However, the cnemial crest of loons is derived solely from the tibiotarsus and the patella, or kneecap, has been reduced to a tiny remnant of bone; in *Hesperornis* the cnemial crest evolved from the development and expansion of the patella. If these birds were closely related, it is unlikely that the formation of this structure would have evolved along such very different pathways.

Recently, Cracraft (1982) has once again championed the *Hesperornis*-loon relationship. He placed loons, grebes, and *Hesperornis* together in a group he labeled the Gaviomorphs, one he said was most closely related to the penguins. On the basis of a cladistic analysis of skeletal material, or examination of the pattern of evolutionary branching, he stated that loons, grebes, and *Hesperornis* shared a common swimming ancestor. However, Martin (1983) reminds us that hesperornithines lived during the Cretaceous era, or about 30 million years before the earliest evidence of loons, first identified from the Eocene epoch some 40 million years ago. The earliest fossil loons were relatively unspecialized divers, as described by Storer (1956), and are another indication that the split was very early, long before both groups could have claimed the same swimming ancestor.

Loons and grebes have been linked together, too. In 1840 Nitzch first put loons, grebes, auks, and penguins together in a group he called the Pygopodes, based on similarities he saw in the pattern of their pterylosis, or feather arrangement. For a long time grebes and loons were linked together, or with other species, and continued to be called Pygopodes (Sclater 1880, Seebohm 1890, Shufeldt 1892, Ogilvie-Grant 1899). Shufeldt (1904) stated that loons and grebes were subfamilies under the family *Podicipidae* within the Pygopodiformes, and were probably derived from a hesperornithine relative. Pycraft (1909) thought that the dried skins Nitzch was working from led him to erroneous description, and, using fresh material, Pycraft presented contradictory information. However, the American Ornithologists' Union committee on nomenclature continued to classify grebes, loons, and alcids in the same order, Pygopodes, until 1931.

Huxley (1867) placed loons and grebes into a family he called the *Colymbidae*. He said he suspected both were most closely related to gulls and a little more distantly related to rails. Coues (1866) based his conclusion that loons were most closely related to the grebes on similarities of their bones and muscles. Stolpe (1935) made an extensive comparison of anatomical characters of grebes and loons, compared them with the characteristics of *Hesperornis*, and outlined major differences among them. Following his paper, which promoted the idea of convergence rather than monophyly among the three, other researchers continued to substantiate his conclusion by adding supportive evidence from a variety of sources. A summary of similarities and differences between loons and grebes is presented in Table 8–3.

Storer (1956) presented a number of differences between loons and grebes, including feather structure and nesting differences. He compared not only modern grebe and loon material, but he compared both with the fossil *Colymboides*. He found no evidence that grebes and loons shared a common swimming ancestor and he suggested that loons may have been derived from larid stock (gulls and terns are larids) between 50 and 60 million years ago. His statement more than 20 years later was even stronger: "Ideally they should be placed next to or near the Charadriiformes" (Storer 1978).

Tyler (1969) conducted extensive tests comparing eggshells of many avian groups, including comparisons of grebe, loon, pelican, and tubenosed swimmers. All four groups have true shells formed with large crystals, but Tyler considered that the lack of pigmentation and the presence of a shell cover on grebe eggs differentiates them from loon eggs. Evidence substantiating separate evolution of grebes and loons is given when nitrogen content is measured. The proportion of soluble to insoluble nitrogen is reversed between the two groups. Grebe shells have a high soluble and low insoluble nitrogen content; loon eggshells contain low soluble and high insoluble nitrogen.

Martin (pers. comm.) pointed out several major differences between grebes and loons involving the articulation of bones of the lower extremity. Each has evolved mechanisms for efficient diving, but in very different ways, indicating separate evolutionary lines. One interesting difference is that the bones of grebe feet are grooved on the lateral side so that, during the recovery stroke, the toes fold into each other. Loon toe bones are not grooved.

In a recent Swedish study, Midtgård (1981) compared counter-current heat exchange systems in birds. Grebes have a complex system of pathways between arteries and veins, a tibiotarsal rete system between numerous peroneal arteries and veins. Loons, as well as gulls, terns, guillemots, and shorebirds, have a *venae comitantes* system (literally "companion veins") surrounding the major, or tibial, artery. Both systems provide for reduction of heat loss by cooling blood going to the feet. However, if loons and grebes shared a recent common ancestor that was a diving bird, a heat-conserving mechanism in the legs would probably have already evolved and loons and grebes would share the same mechanism.

Sibley and Ahlquist (1983) have used the techniques of DNA-DNA hybridization to compare the single-copy genomes of many groups of birds. From unpublished DNA comparisons, Sibley and Ahlquist (pers. comm.) note that the loons are apparently the sister group of a clade, or branch, which includes, in addition to loons, the tubenosed swimmers (Procellariidae), penguins (Spheniscidae), and frigatebirds (Frigatidae). The grebes are not members of this cluster, and they seem to have no close living relatives.

Olson (1985), in his exhaustive nexus on fossil birds, believes that evi-

Table 8–3. Comparisons between the Loons and the Grebes

Differences	Grebe	Loon
Geographic distribution	world-wide	Holarctic, no tropical species
Karyotype	2n=78, 2n=80	2n=88
Coracoid	relatively long and narrow	broad and stout
Dermotemporal muscle	none	well-developed
Tongue	patch of spinous processes at the back	single posterior row of spinous processes
Cecum	rudimentary	short but well developed
Nasal gland	lies within orbit on dorsal side	lies in supraorbital groove
Rete system in legs	present	absent
Toes	lobed	webbed
Lores	bare	feathered
Feathers	chick plumage striped, definitive plumage directly from single downy plumage	chick plumage solid, two downy plumages before juvenal plumage
	12 primaries	11 primaries
	rudimentary tail	well-developed tail
Eggshell	true shell covered with calcareous cover	true shell covered with cuticle
	high soluble and low insoluble nitrogen	low soluble and high insoluble nitrogen
	unpigmented	pigmented
Feather-eating	yes	no
Pellet casting	yes	no
Territories	colonial or semi-colonial for several species	individual pairs hold large territories
Nest	over water or on floating structure	on land
Clutch size	3 to 9	usually 2
Incubation	cover nest when leaving	do not cover nest when leaving
Age at maturity	1 to 2 years	at least 3 years
Courtship displays	elaborate	simple
Back-riding of young	chicks climb on by crawling over rear and up the leg	chicks climb on back under wing; less frequently by crawling over rear

Table 8–3 – *Continued*

Differences	Grebe	Loon
Sleeping posture	head with bill pointed forward lying under neck	head laid over back with bill pointed caudally, tucked under scapulars
Swimming	toes rotate 90° prior to recovery stroke	no rotation
Flight	several flightless species; uncommon except during migration	no flightless species
Migration	nocturnal	diurnal

Similarities	Grebe and Loon
Bone structure	non-pneumatic
Tarsometatarsi	laterally compressed
Skull	schizognathus, holorhinal, perforate nostrils
Sternum	low keel, rounded sternal notches formed by processes that curve medially and coracoidal sulci that are deep and continuous across the midline
Femur	anterioposteriorly compressed
Vertebrae	caudal vertebrae lateromedially compressed
Pelvis	extremely elongate with post-acetabular portion of ilium much longer than anterior portion
M. sartorius	single insertion on medial side of head of the tibia
M. gastrocnemius	bicipital pars interna with origin from proximal half of tibia
Leg musculature	lies within skin of body as far as the ankle
Uropygial gland	feathered
Shell structure	true shell (but see differences)
Back-riding	chicks ride parents' backs (but see differences)
Mating system	monogamous
Incubation	both sexes share incubation duties
Young	nidifugous and semi-precocial

dence leads to suggestions that the closest relatives of loons are the Procellariiformes and the Spheniscitformes. All three groups, and no others, have chicks with two true successive, downy plumages before the juvenal feathers erupt. It is generally agreed that the earliest loons evolved during the Eocene epoch, or about 40 to 50 million years ago (Martin 1983). Brodkorb (1963) indicated that two Cretaceous fossils, *Lonchodytes* and *Enaliornis* were Gaviiformes, but most now agree that similarities they share with loons are results of convergence (Storer 1978, Olson and Feduccia 1980).

The earliest loon is thought to be *Colymboides anglicus*, a bird partially specialized for diving, which lived during the late Eocene in England. The next oldest fossil is a small one found in France, in Aquitanian deposits, indicating it lived during the late Oligocene or early Miocene. This was *Colymboides minutus*, now considered a side branch and not on the direct line leading to modern loons. It was specialized for diving, though not as much as modern loons are, and was well described by Storer (1956), who considered it to be a true loon.

Birds of another genus, *Gaviella*, described from the Oligocene (Wetmore 1940), have been called loons, but Storer (1978) finds that this group differs in several respects from other loons and is probably not closely related to them. Olson (1985) believes the whole group was more likely part of an extinct diving group related to the pelicans, the *Plotopteridae*.

Several loons have been described from the Miocene in addition to *Colymboides minutus*. Wetmore (1941) described one found in Maryland, and placed it in the modern genus, *Gavia*, although Olson (1985) now believes that Wetmore erred. Olson examined the upper layers of deposits, and consequently believes Wetmore must have found a Pleistocene fossil. Howard (1978) described a fossil from deposits in California from the upper Miocene, and placed it in the genus *Gavia*, as she did another larger fossil that she found in late Miocene deposits. Recently, a new species was described from the lower Miocene of Czechoslovakia (Svĕc 1982) and placed, once more, with other *Gavia*. It was a small loon, and similar to, but not as advanced as, Red-throated Loons.

Several species have been described from the Pliocene, or from about two to six million years ago. Pliocene loons of four species have been found in deposits in Italy, Florida, and California, and all have been assigned to the genus *Gavia* (Regalia 1902, Wetmore 1940, 1943, Brodkorb 1953). Brodkorb has reviewed them and noted that the North American representatives fell into three size classes: (1) a very small loon, smaller than Red-throated Loons, yet most closely related to Arctic Loons; (2) a

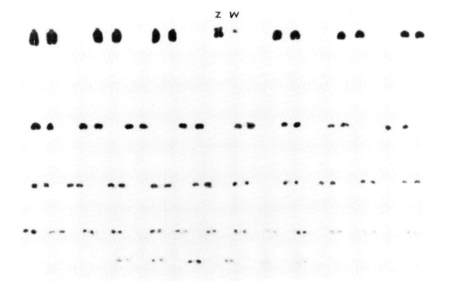

Figure 8-2. Karyotype of the Common Loon. Example is from a female. Note that the fourth chromosome is the Z, or sex, chromosome, the only large submetacentric chromosome, which makes it easily distinguishable from the others (2n = 88).

slightly larger species related most closely to Red-throated Loons; and (3) a large loon, nearly the size of Common Loons, but showing most affinity to Arctic Loons.

The most recent published description of a new fossil was of a *Gavia* from early to middle Pliocene Italian deposits (Delle Cave et al. 1984). It was large, and the authors suggest it occupied a position between the larger Common Loon and the smaller Arctic and Red-throated Loons. In their paper, Delle Cave and her colleagues also cite correspondence concerning the finding of a fossil loon in Germany from middle Eocene deposits, and it appears to be a good *Gavia*. To the best of my knowledge, this is still unpublished work, and has not been formally described. If its identification is verified, it would indicate an earlier differentiation between *Gavia* and the *Colymboides* than is currently recognized.

There are fossils from the Pleistocene of all contemporary species from sites throughout the present range of loons (Brodkorb 1953). Recent speciation occurred as late as the last glacial period. It is likely that Common Loon populations became separated during the onset of the last glacial period, with some "stranded" in Arctic refugia, while others were held to the south of the ice fields. This may have permitted sufficient diver-

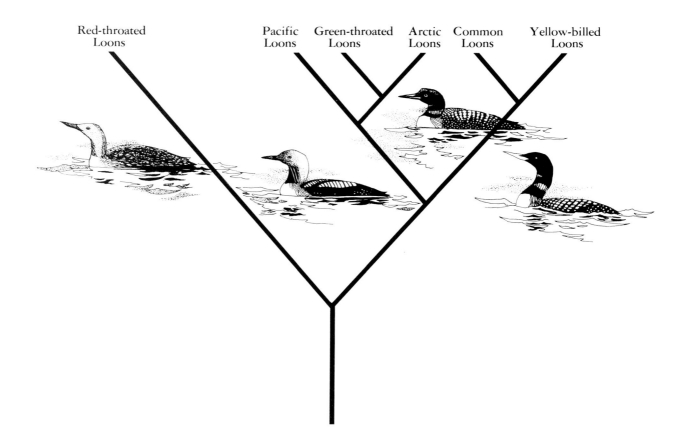

Figure 8-3. Phylogenetic tree of extant members of the family *Gaviidae* as suggested by R. W. Storer.

gence to have given rise to Common Loons and Yellow-billed Loons. Yellow-billed Loons remained as breeders in the tundra and adjacent Arctic coasts. Common Loons moved slowly northward as glaciers melted and new lakes became available, but in general followed the forested regions. Storer (1978) suggests that the Yukon-Bering Sea refugia became the geographical limit for the evolving Yellow-billed Loon.

The five modern loon species are very closely related. Sibley has looked at the results of DNA-DNA hybridization experiments for three of the five species (*Gavia immer*, *G. arctica*, and *G. stellata*) and finds they are nearly indistinguishable and constitute a very homogeneous group (Sibley, pers. comm.). Karyotypes have been done for Red-throated Loons and Common Loons (Hammar 1970, McIntyre 1975). Both species have a diploid complement of $2n = 88$, and the Z-chromosome (sex chromosome in birds) is #4, a large, submetacentric, easily distinguished chromosome. The karyotype of Common Loons is shown in Figure 8–2.

Storer thinks the relationship among the species can be described graphically as shown in the phylogenetic tree in Figure 8–3. He considers Red-throated Loons the least specialized species because their adaptations for diving are less well developed than for the other four species (Storer 1978). Red-throated Loons have the largest wing area relative to body size, and can make the most efficient takeoff for flight. Some reports have noted they can, at times, take off directly from land (Barr, pers. comm.). Storer also considers their plumage the least modified. Breeding plumage lacks features that other species share, such as iridescent head feathers, stripes on the neck and back of the head, and large spots on the dorsal contour feathers.

Two records of hybridization between Arctic or Pacific and Common Loons suggest an extremely close relationship (Hunter and Dennis 1972, Robertson and Fraker 1974). Recently diverged Common and Yellow-billed Loons share similarities and are still designated as separate species, but constitute a superspecies, or very closely related pair. For that reason, they are placed next to each other in phylogenetic listings.

Arctic and Pacific Loons breed in a continuum around the arctic and subarctic, except for Iceland and Greenland. They were formerly designated as three subspecies of Arctic Loons: *Gavia arctica arctica* breeding across Europe, *G. a. viridigularis* in Siberia, and *G. a. pacifica* in North America. There is some overlap of *G. a. viridigularis* to Alaska, and of *Gavia pacifica* to Siberia, but north of the Green-throated population. Based on field studies, Soviet biologists presented the strongest argument for considering Pacific Loons as a separate species. To the best of my knowledge, no field work has been done on this continent seeking evidence for full species status.

The recent decision by the AOU to accept the Pacific Loon as a distinct species (AOU 1985) now provides for the following arrangement of loons, indicating the degree of relatedness between any two species as well as the assumed sequence of evolution within the group:

Common Name	Scientific Name
Red-throated Loon	*Gavia stellata*
Arctic Loon	*Gavia arctica arctica*
	G. a. viridigularis
Pacific Loon	*Gavia pacifica*
Common Loon	*Gavia immer*
Yellow-billed Loon	*Gavia adamsii*

This listing does not completely agree with the tree suggested by Storer (presented in Figure 8–3), which places the Pacific Loon closest to the Red-throated Loon. The tree illustrates an earlier split between the North American Pacific Loon and its Eurasian counterparts than the one between the Green-throated and Arctic subspecies. Until field work is done in sectors where overlaps occur, it is unlikely everyone will agree on the exact format used to show phylogenetic relationships. What is generally agreed is that loons are a unique group.

CHAPTER 9
The Look of a Loon: Anatomy and Plumage

John James Audubon once painted two Common Loons, a portrait that has become familiar to thousands during the last century and a half. One black and white bird is standing on a nest, with bill open, calling, while the other, a gray one, is nearby in the water. Audubon painted the black and white adult on July 9 and 10 in 1833 while watching loons in Labrador, "in rain that wouldn't stop!" The gray loon is a winter-plumaged bird, a specimen he shot in October 1819. The painting, with its graceful flow of line and pattern is delightful, but I have often wondered how many people think this shows a pair of loons, a black and white male with its mousy, little gray mate.

The following descriptions of anatomy, plumage, and molt are limited to Common Loons, although all loons have many of the same characteristics. Loons are heavy-bodied diving birds and their primary modifications adapt them for an aquatic life. All loons have grayish feathers in the winter and a more striking plumage in the summer. Juveniles and adults look different, although the plumage of immature birds is similar to that of wintering adults.

Loon Anatomy

Common Loon males are generally larger than their mates, but this doesn't mean that all males are larger than all females. Some size overlap exists between the sexes when measurements are compared without regard to age or geographical differences. Because heads are readily visible to an observer, and because head sizes of males always *appear* larger than those of females, I compared bill and skull sizes on more than 100 museum specimens (McIntyre 1975). Male bills were significantly longer than those of females, and averaged 77.3 mm for males compared to 74.8 mm for females (t=2.64, P < .01). Skulls, on the other hand, showed no significant difference between the sexes, averaging 47.8 mm for males, and 46.3 mm for females (t=1.09, P > 0.2). There was, however, a very broad size range between the sexes for both characters, so much so that even bill size alone cannot be used with certainty to determine the sex of individuals in the field. Storer (1988) compared males and females from the same populations and found a consistent, but small, degree of dimorphism. The greatest difference was between the depth of the bills (those of males were larger) and between bill lengths (those of males were longer).

The only way I initially felt confident in sexing loons was to verify the sex of each pair member by watching the female lay eggs. Later I found that only the male of these pairs yodeled, and more recently I have been using both characteristics for sexing loons in the field. Every male that I have been reliably able to sex has been larger than its mate. Barr (pers. comm.) told me that males of all pairs that he has measured and weighed have been larger than their mates, and he also described some interesting size differences in their digestive tracts (Barr 1973). He found in males a more extensive surface area in the proventriculus, or glandular stomach, as well as significantly larger digestive glands than in females. This suggests food partitioning, or the selection of prey items of different sizes, by pair members.

Adult Common Loons weigh from 2.7 to over 6.3 kilograms, and are nearly a meter long from bill tip to outstretched feet. Weight varies among individuals and from one population to another. At one time, regional size differences led to division of Common Loons into two subspecies, the larger *Gavia immer immer* and the smaller *Gavia immer elasson*. This classification is no longer accepted, and they are now considered to have no subspecific designations (AOU 1985). Information is not available on seasonal weight changes of individuals, and it is not known if adults increase body fat or pectoral muscle mass before they migrate. If seasonal weight differences do occur, it may be necessary to reanalyze museum data, to take seasonal fluctuations into account.

Rand (1947) compared bill length and wing chord, the measurement of a folded wing, for 50 specimens from the National Museum of Canada. All were adults taken on their breeding grounds, and included specimens from throughout the breeding range. Wing length was smallest on loons from Manitoba and North Dakota, in the central part of the range, as well as from the most northerly sites in the MacKenzie Delta. Lengths on loons from the east through Ontario, Quebec, Greenland, and Baffin Island, and to the west, specifically in British Columbia and the Yukon, were longer. These measurements indicate a double size gradient, with the smallest loons in central populations, and larger ones both to the east and the west. Measurements of bill length did not provide exactly the same conclusions, although loons with the smallest bills were in the center of the range (Manitoba and North Dakota) and the MacKenzie Delta. Rand found larger bills in loons from Greenland, Baffin Island, British Columbia, and the Yukon, and the largest bills of all in those from Ontario and Quebec.

In the most recent analysis, Storer (1988) discerned some variation, with the smallest loons in North Dakota and adjacent parts of South Dakota and larger specimens from eastern Canada and the western states and provinces. However, he cautions that differences are small and overlap great.

Anderson, Lumsden, and Hickey (1970) measured eggs from several museum collections, and in most cases found that egg size corresponds with body size from population to population. The smallest eggs had been laid by birds breeding in North Dakota, Manitoba, Saskatchewan, and Alberta; larger eggs, in the northeastern states and Canadian provinces eastward to Greenland; and the largest eggs, in Iceland. There is a geographical cline, with the smallest loons and the smallest eggs from the south-central part of the breeding range, and larger ones in the northwest and northeast sectors.

The digestive tract of loons has no unique modifications for eating fish and is a very typical avian system. In general, grain- and seed-eating birds have the largest and strongest gizzards; many carnivorous species have only a glandular stomach or proventriculus. Some fish-eating birds have a simplified digestive tract with no gizzard and only a proventriculus between esophagus and small intestine. Instead of passing fish bones, spines, and other hard material through the gut, they regurgitate indigestible material directly, casting it as pellets. Loons, on the other hand, pass all food

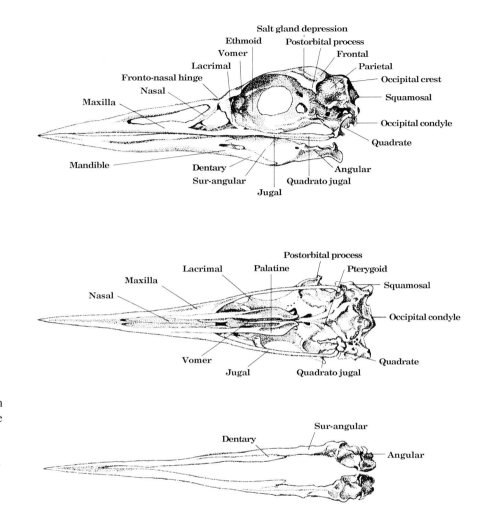

Figure 9-1. Common Loon skull. *Upper* drawing is the lateral aspect from the left side, *middle* shows the inferior perspective, and *bottom* defines the lower mandible.

through the intestinal tract. They have a powerful, keratin-lined gizzard, and use small stones for grit to grind their food before it passes into the intestines.

Salivary glands lubricate food and provide digestive enzymes. Loons seem to lack taste buds, and they probably sense their food only tactilely (Barr 1973). They ingest saltwater on their marine wintering grounds, and salt is excreted as a concentrated solution through large glands above the eyes. These lie in deep, supraorbital grooves in the skull, and the bony depressions are shown, both with the salt glands, and with them removed,

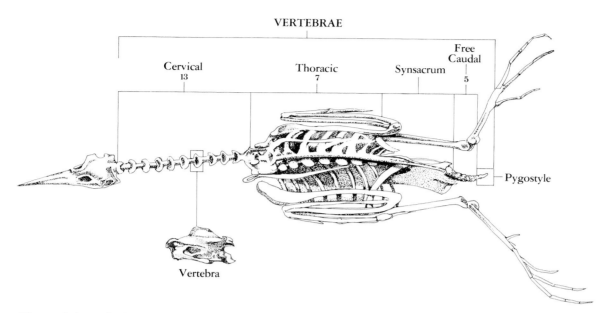

Figure 9-2. Articulated skeleton of a Common Loon showing size relationships among components. *Insert* provides details of a cervical vertebra.

in Plate 8c. Secretion of excess salt is stimulated quickly, and I found that even young chicks, no more than two weeks old, are competent to remove salt if they are fed saline solutions.

Most skeletal and muscular modifications relate to swimming and diving (Figures 9-1 to 9-6). The entire skull is unusually thick and heavy for a bird. The foramen magnum, or opening at the base of the skull through which the spinal cord passes, is oriented perpendicular to the longitudinal axis of the skull. According to Barr (1973), this permits the head to be held directly in line with the neck during diving in order to reduce drag, while still permitting the maximum extension of the head and neck during strikes at prey. At this angle the loon becomes a highly streamlined and efficient underwater predator.

The bill is laterally compressed, and the tomia, or inner edges, are sharp, but not serrated. The nostrils have an unusual flap or valve on the upper rim which is unique to loons and is thought to close during dives. As in most birds, the base of the upper mandible is kinetic, or slightly movable. Barr (1973) noted that upper and lower mandibles are mobile and used simultaneously to grasp prey.

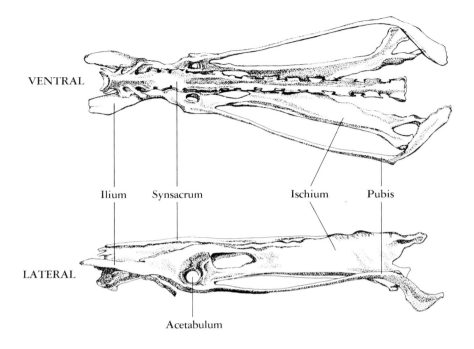

VENTRAL

Ilium Synsacrum Ischium Pubis

LATERAL

Acetabulum

Figure 9-3. Pelvic girdle of a Common Loon. Note the elongation of the synsacrum.

Loons are foot-propelled divers and do not "fly" underwater like some birds, such as penguins and auks. The synsacrum is long and narrow. The tibiotarsus has a long cnemial process that functions primarily for the attachment of the gastrocnemius, the major extensor of the foot, and the power muscle in swimming. Both it and the femur, which is short and aligned at right angles to the body, are displaced to the caudal end, fixed in a horizontal plane, and completely enclosed within the skin. The pelvic muscles are thoroughly described by Wilcox (1952) and are modified to permit powerful extension for diving and swimming.

Although positioning of the legs far back on the body permits superb diving, it causes loons to be clumsy on land. Loons cannot walk in the same way as ducks and geese do, and when they try, they move one foot at a time, shuffling along, breast held close to the ground. They seem better able to cope when moving fast and for short distances; with wings flapping, they can run quickly. If frightened while on land, they scamper at a rapid clip to reach the water.

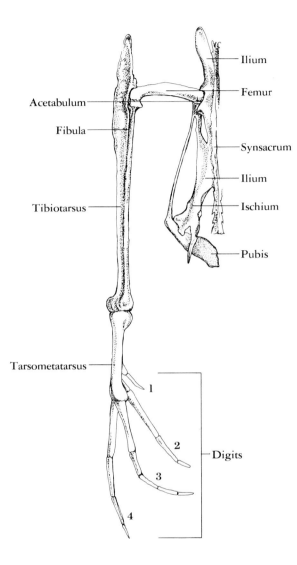

Acetabulum

Fibula

Tibiotarsus

Tarsometatarsus

Ilium

Femur

Synsacrum

Ilium

Ischium

Pubis

1

2

3

4

Digits

Figure 9-4. Skeleton of the lower extremity of a Common Loon. The femur is short and extends perpendicular to the pelvic girdle, and the cnemial crest is the extension above the knee on the tibiotarsus.

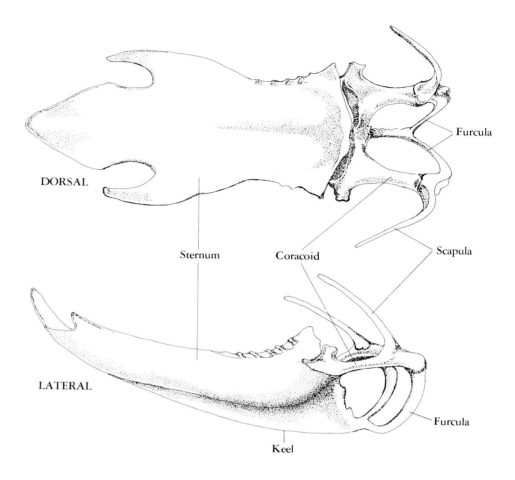

DORSAL

Furcula

Sternum   Coracoid   Scapula

LATERAL

Furcula

Keel

Figure 9-5. Pectoral girdle of a Common Loon from the dorsal and lateral aspects; note depth of the keel.

Many years ago I found that loons were quite capable of running on land, especially if the run was uphill. One winter I kept a loon in a small pool in my basement, a pool with running water and live fish and even a tiny islet in the middle. Every day I carried the loon down the hill behind my house for a swim in the creek that ran along the back of the property. With a bright-red dog harness put on upside down and attached to a long rope, this loon-on-a-leash could swim up and down the creek and still be retrieved. When it was time to go, I picked her up, held her under my arm,

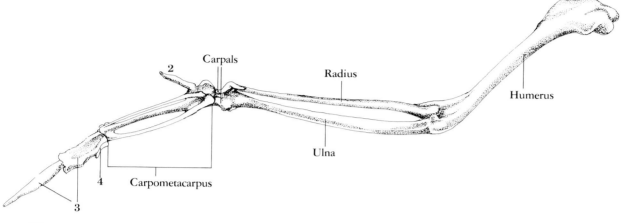

Digits

Figure 9-6. Skeletal components of the loon wing. Digits *2*, *3*, and *4* remain and support the primary flight feathers and the alula. There are two carpal bones, and the metacarpals are modified, forming the carpometacarpus, which is the usual arrangement in birds.

and back up the hill we went. From time to time she squirmed free from my grasp, and there was a lively chase as she outran me up the hill and back to her pool. Walking may not be an adult loon's forte, but as long as it can keep its wings flapping and its body weight forward, running is definitely something a loon does well. Young chicks, on the other hand, can walk upright much better than adults.

Loons also run across the water when taking flight. They run into the wind, and the distance needed before they can take to the air depends on windspeed. With a brisk wind, loons can become airborne quickly, but, in a calm, loons may run as far as several hundred meters before they have gained sufficient speed to take off.

The sternum (see Figure 9–5) is wide with a deep keel to accommodate substantial flight muscles, but it is also somewhat elongate and contributes to the streamlining of body shape important to a diving bird. Loon wings are each 55 to 65 cm long from body to tip and are narrow, being no more than 16 cm at the widest point, the wrist. The span from wing tip to wing tip is about 130 to 140 cm when wings are fully outstretched. Wings are set about half way along the body, making loons look like flying crosses when they are overhead. Skeletal wing components are not highly modified (Figure 9–6).

Loons have small wings relative to their body weight. *Wing loading* is a term used to indicate the weight carried per square unit of wing area, and it is usually calculated as grams per square centimeter (g/cm^2) . It is a way of looking at the flight potential of a bird. I weighed Common Loons from Minnesota and New York breeding populations, photographed their outstretched wings, then calculated the surface area and compared it with the weight of each bird. They had an average wing loading of 2.45 g/cm^2. For comparison, wing loading is reported to be 1.0 for Canada Geese, 1.36 for Mallards, and 0.41 for crows, while hummingbirds, the lightest of all, have only a tenth as much weight to carry relative to their wing size as loons do, or 0.24 g/cm^2.

Air sacs are extensions of the respiratory system in birds, and loons have fewer of them than most other birds. Most species have nine, four pairs along each side and a single one between the clavicles. Loons do not have cervical air sacs, but their single interclavicular has two extensions that continue anteriorly and perhaps should be considered homologous to the cervical sacs (Gier 1952).

Most birds also have spaces within their bones, small extensions of the air sacs. Loon bones are nonpneumatic, so are rather more solid than hollow, and this makes them heavier for their size than bones of most birds, increasing specific gravity. That helps loons carry their bodies low in the water and expend less energy swimming underwater.

Much of the body weight is in the two great muscle masses of breast and thigh, those used in flying and swimming. The pectoralis muscle is large relative to the supracoracoideus because it provides for the power, or downstroke, in a wingbeat, and in that way is similar to that of most flying birds. The pelvic musculature as described by Wilcox (1952) provides for powerful swimming ability. Loon modifications in these muscles, their attachments and points of origin and insertion, have been selected for their role in swimming, thus limiting the mobility of hip and knee joints. Ability to walk has been sacrificed for power of the leg and thigh in swimming.

To compensate for the high ratio of weight- to-wing area, loon wings have much camber, or curvature, which provides lift. Loons also fly with a rapid wing beat, from 260 to 270 beats per minute. This is a fast flap rate, but not unusual for heavy-bodied birds, because speed is needed in order to achieve sufficient lift to stay airborne.

Kerlinger (1982) radar-monitored loon migration flights over Albany, New York, and found the average ground speed to be more than 160 kilometers per hour (kmph). Speeds were faster in the fall than in the spring, because autumn winds are stronger, and their prevailing direction is the same as the loons' flight path. Ground speed varied somewhat during Kerlinger's study, but airspeed did not, and was stable at 121 kmph, or about 75 mph. Loons fly between 1,500 and 2,700 meters above sea level during long migratory flights. Kerlinger offered several suggestions regarding advantages of flying this high. For example, the lower air density adds about 10 percent to the flight speed, and lower temperatures minimize heat stress. Most important, air turbulence is lower at high altitudes, and has a laminar, or smooth and stratified, air flow at about 2,000 meters.

Plumage and Molting

Efficient swimming and flying necessitate streamlined contour feathers, and loons have no crests, plumes, or other accessories. But they do have a striking color pattern on their alternate plumage, or summer, feathers. Arrangement and terminology of these feathers are shown in Figure 9–7. Loons have 11 primaries, 22–23 secondaries and 16–20 rectrices, or tail feathers. The uropygial gland, or preen gland, is also feathered and can be seen as it is squeezed to secure oil for preening.

Adult loons have one plumage during the winter, the *basic* plumage, and another, the *alternate* or *nuptial* plumage, which they keep from spring until the fall molt. The basic gray contour feathers of wintering adults are much like juvenal feathers, but a few black and white feathers are retained and can be used to age loons. Contour feathers of adults are slightly more square on the ends than are juvenal ones, and young loon backs have a scalloped appearance derived from the wide light edge on their feathers. A sampling of juvenal feathers is shown in Figure 9–8. Both juveniles and wintering adults have some white feathers just in front of and above the eyes (McIntyre and McIntyre 1974). Feathers of the belly and wing lining are white all year long. Feather shafts are dark, and this is a character used to distinguish between Common and Yellow-billed loons, the latter having white shafts on primaries and secondaries (Burn and Mather 1974).

A complete molt begins in late January and lasts until the beginning of March, resulting in new black and white coverts, the back and scapular feathers of adults. Loons are flightless during the winter molt (Plate 8d). They have only this single remigial molt, although other feathers are

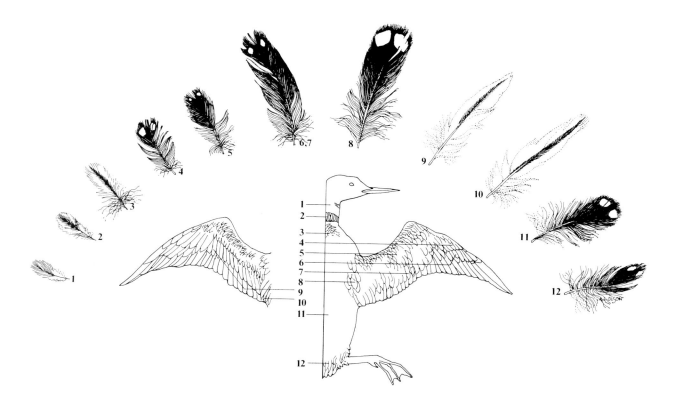

Figure 9-7. Feathers and feather arrangement on adult Common Loons in alternate plumage. All patterns, including spots and stripes, except the throat striping and the necklace, are from contour feathers on the back and scapula. Both rectrices and remiges are solid black and breast feathers are white. All feathers shown are contour feathers, and do not include flight feathers. *1.* Head and neck feather. *2.* Necklace feather. *3.* Striping between back and breast. *4.* Median wing covert. *5.* Lesser wing covert. *6* and *7.* Primary and secondary greater wing coverts. *8.* Scapular feather. *9* and *10.* Lining of the wing. *11.* Back feather. *12.* Upper tail covert.

molted twice. Spring migration commences shortly after the winter molt has been completed. The fall molt begins at the end of the breeding season. It starts earlier for unsuccessful nesters. The difference in hormone levels between unsuccessful loons and those which continue the breeding pattern through the chick-caring period probably causes the difference in timing of this molt, though no one has measured hormone levels in any species of loons during the breeding season.

Figure 9-8. Examples of contour feathers from juvenile Common Loons. Back and scapular feathers are shown. The lighter coloring on the edges gives a soft gray edging or scalloping, but is not sufficient contrast to the rest of the feather to provide for spots. The border on adult basic contour feathers is narrower.

When molt begins, loons appear to be growing white mustaches, because the first feathers to be replaced are facial ones, especially those surrounding the bill. Replacement of contour feathers continues for a prolonged period, and people frequenting the Great Lakes in the fall report finding great numbers of molted feathers washed to shore in late fall and even early in the winter (Hamas, pers. comm.). Some scapular feathers are retained far into the winter, and may be the last to molt, although a complete molt cycle has never been documented for loons.

Flight feathers are kept, worn as they are. Woolfenden (1967) noted that among loons, only Red-throated Loons have retained a typical avian molt pattern. Many other water birds, including most ducks, molt during the summer. Why, if ducks molt in July, and endure a flightless period, don't loons do the same? Ducklings feed themselves, and the period of intense parental care is shorter for them than for loons. Loon chicks require nearly constant parental attention during the summer, and loonlings must be fed by their parents for nearly three months. Is it possible that the extended care period has influenced timing of the molt? Perhaps loons would not be able to provide for young and still fulfill their own metabolic requirements during molting. Storer (pers. comm.) suggested that a contributing factor may be the additional time required to grow Common Loon remigial feathers, which are longer than the flight feathers of ducks. The oligotrophic lakes, habitat for most Common Loons, may not provide a sufficient abundance of food to permit rapid growth of new feathers.

Immature loons have a different molting schedule. Young chicks have two downy plumages. Newly hatched chicks are primarily black except for their white bellies (Plate 8a). Black feathers are pushed out by the secondary brownish-gray down feathers when chicks are between 10 days and two weeks old. These, in turn, are replaced by juvenal contour feathers (Plate 8b). These begin to erupt when young are about a month old. By the time young are 10 to 11 weeks old, their juvenal plumage is nearly complete, and flight feathers have erupted sufficiently to permit some flight. Primaries continue to grow for another two to three weeks. These feathers are retained until the following summer, when a complete molt replaces all juvenal feathers with another basic plumage . . . more gray feathers!

Loss of primary and secondary feathers at the time when adults are beginning to nest may prevent the young from returning to their natal lake. It may be a strong selective force acting to prohibit young loons from moving to inland lakes during the breeding season, particularly if they return to the lakes where they were hatched. Competition for resources is reduced for the breeding pair if the previous year's young are not feeding in the same lake. When young are molting, they are forced to remain on the coastal waters, and this in turn maximizes the benefits of freshwater lakes to the new offspring of the parent birds. Genes are shared by parents, juveniles , and the new chicks, so it is possible that kin selection could explain why second year loons do not migrate.

However, migratory flights also entail a cost and it is expensive for immatures to fly back to natal lakes and not breed. A price is also paid for acquiring and maintaining a summer territory on freshwater lakes in competition with older and more experienced birds. These costs may be greater than benefits juveniles gain by forsaking the ocean for freshwater lakes.

Second-year loons are occasionally found on the breeding grounds, and when they are, it is usually on lakes close to the wintering grounds. For example, three to five are regularly reported in New Hampshire each summer. Occasionally, young from the previous year are found farther inland, even in Minnesota. In 1973 I watched an immature loon in Lake Calhoun, a lake in the heart of the city of Minneapolis. Because it spent midsummer molting and was flightless, it could be easily observed. It is not difficult

Table 9–1. Evidence for Time of Molt in Subadult Common Loons

Museum and Specimen #	Collection		Condition of Primaries
	Date	Location	
American Museum of Natural History, New York			
435836	6/3/04	Long Island, N.Y.	worn
90018	5/11/1883	Swan Pt, Md.	badly worn
300410	3/11/34	Montauk, Long Island, N.Y.	in molt
79209	5/20/1892	Crawford County, Pa.	worn
National Museum of Natural History, Washington, D.C.			
207980	5/23/11	Grand Batture Island, Ala.	worn
298955	4/16/26	Santa Rosa Sound, Fla.	only a few alternate plumage feathers
Sutton Collection, Delaware Museum of Natural History, Greenville, Del.			
3282	6/11/50	Grand Lake, Delaware County, Okla.	in full molt
Museum of Natural History, University of Kansas			
6868	5/14/1896	Jefferson County, Kans.	worn
3168	5/23/1898	Douglas County, Kans.	frayed
67585[a]	5/8/72	Douglas County, Kans.	new flight feathers, contour feathers almost complete
National Museum, Ottawa, Canada			
8390	6/18/15	New Brunswick	in molt
22803	6/8/28	Labrador	worn
19633	summer 1924	Cape Dorset	in molt
64520	6/18/75	New Brunswick	in molt
Liverpool Museum, England			
(no number)	7/14/30	Hoy, North Orkneys	growing primaries

[a]This specimen was completing its molt to alternate plumage in May, which indicates it may have been one of the young adults that can be seen arriving on the breeding grounds a month or so after breeding pairs have established territories.

to determine whether or not a loon has fully developed flight feathers because loons flap their wings at the end of maintenance sessions. When wings are outstretched, it can be seen if they are the abbreviated wings of a molting bird or the full wings of a loon with all its flight feathers. The Lake Calhoun juvenile molted during July, and by early August new flight feathers were partly in. By late August the molt was complete and the bird could fly. More recently, Eberhardt (1984) reported that a few northern Minnesota two-year-olds, identified because they were banded as juveniles, reappeared on their natal lakes the following summer.

Some juveniles and subadults in museum collections also provide evidence for the later molt of young loons (Table 9–1). Several in this table were collected in May and early June and had very frayed flight feathers, obviously old feathers from the previous summer. The specimens were collected from places as far apart as New York, Oklahoma, Labrador, and Florida. A juvenile was collected 11 June 1950 and had recently shed its primaries and secondaries. Other specimens were either in molt or still had frayed, old flight feathers in May and June.

Several good specimens housed at the Museum of Natural History at the University of Kansas were collected in May, too late to be adults migrating northward to nest, and none were young of the year. They seem to be young adults, perhaps undergoing their first alternate molt.

The molt pattern for loons has not been completely worked out, but evidence shows that second-year birds undergo a remigial molt in the summer, that they molt earlier in subsequent years, and that adults are flightless in February. We still do not know when loons first breed, but confirmation of the molt schedule would provide helpful clues for solving this puzzle.

CHAPTER 10
Where Are Loons?
Distribution and Migratory
Routes

Depending on age, breeding condition, molt condition, and time of
year, any individual loon might be in one of several places: its breeding
range, staging ground, migratory route, or wintering site. The distribution of Common Loons is primarily Nearctic. The New World population
is distributed throughout Canada and the northern United States, and there
is a smaller Old World population breeding in Iceland and Greenland and
wintering along European coasts.

Loons are aquatic birds, migrants that divide their time between marine
waters and freshwater lakes. During their first fall, immatures move from
the inland lakes where they hatched and were reared to coastal sites, and
they remain on saltwater until they reach maturity three or four years
later. During migration loons aggregate in large numbers on traditional
staging grounds, large lakes and reservoirs. Because it is not easy to capture loons, few have been banded compared to other waterbirds for which
major banding programs have been initiated. For that reason, much of the

information presented in this chapter is based on a small sample size.

Most of the banding I have done, as well as that of Minnesota's Department of Natural Resources for the past five years, has involved capture by night-lighting on shallow lakes. Some loons have been caught and marked on deeper lakes, and recent attempts have succeeded using modified Bailey beaver traps with decoy lures. Gill netting has not been effective, and though funnel fish traps would seem to be a feasible way to capture numbers of loons, equipment costs have prevented test runs. There is a real need for an efficient and cost-effective capture procedure.

Banded loons wear U.S. Fish and Wildlife Service leg bands. I also tag the wings of those I capture with colored plastic markers to identify individuals. The tag goes around the wing next to the fourth secondary feather, but is not fastened through the patagial skin. Plate 9 shows banding operations and a wing-tagged loon. The longest interval between marking and sighting a loon I have banded is seven years, when a blue-tagged loon from Minnesota was observed swimming on Chickamauga Lake, a Tennessee reservoir, during fall migration.

Unfortunately, young loons must be at least five to six weeks old before their legs are large enough to hold adult-sized bands, and by that time they are expert divers and difficult to capture. We have banded the toes of small, easily captured chicks (McIntyre 1977), but this has not been as rewarding as leg banding in providing recovery data. It also makes chicks vulnerable to predation by gulls during the interval between their release (by us) and being reunited with their parents.

Breeding Range

The breeding range of Common Loons includes a narrow band across the northern tier of the contiguous United States, most of Canada and Alaska except the high arctic, the western side of Greenland, and Iceland. It has shrunk northward during the last century, and the southern boundary has probably changed greatly over time, more so than indicated by the map (Figure 10–1). Common Loons probably followed the retreat of the glaciers to the north over several thousand years, expanding their range as new habitat became available. A northward population shrinkage has continued within historical times. This is shown by the white area between the dotted line and the stippled area on the map. Most of the shift has occurred within the last 100 to 150 years.

Direct competition for habitat between humans and loons is thought to figure prominently in this northward shift. There is much concern about

Summer Range
Winter Range
Former Southern Limit

Figure 10-1. Geographical range of the Common Loon. Stippled areas represent winter and summer ranges, while the dotted line represents the former southern limit as determined from historical records. There are no historical records for the region between California and Iowa, hence the break in the dotted line.

the effects of recent human disturbance on declining loon populations, particularly with respect to recreational use of loon habitat, shoreline development, and the growing numbers of predators such as raccoons, crows, and gulls, animals known to follow human settlements (Vermeer 1973b, McIntyre 1975, Wood 1979, Titus and Van Druff 1981, Heimberger et al. 1983).

Disturbance is probably not as recent a factor as we once thought. Development and the increasing human-related pressures associated with it have occurred for a long time. Examples appear in the history of New York. Settlements there began more than 300 years ago, and by 1786 even the western part of the state was settled. The Finger Lakes formerly had nesting loons, but were bustling with steamboat traffic as early as 1810 (Cooper 1810). Father Joques discovered Lake George in 1642, which was even earlier, and the battle of Lake Champlain between the Iroquois and Algonquins occurred in 1609. This must surely have been a disturbance factor to resident loons!

Although lack of breeding success for one year does not necessarily cause a population to decline, examples point out that loon disturbance goes back much further than the last 20 or 30 years. Even so, a comparison of present populations with an earlier report (Arbib 1963) suggests a substantial decline even in those two to three decades. The Adirondacks, a holdout of pristine wilderness in New York, and now part of the largest park within the United States outside of Alaska, were being explored by surveying parties by 1799. An influx of fishing parties followed. The procession of "sports," as city men were called, and their Adirondack guides, to remote lakes must have drastically changed the primitive character of the loons' homes (Wallace 1899).

Recreational use and disturbance began long ago, but something else happened that was not so benign, and which may have had an even greater and more devastating impact on loon populations. Sport shooting was very popular around the turn of the century. Loons are quick divers and fast fliers, and they became the challenge to which men with guns responded. Who would win, shotgun or loon?

Unfortunately, as guns improved, loons lost. Forbush (1912) described the mass slaughter along spring flyways. Men lined both sides of Buzzards and Manomet bays on the coast of Massachusetts, and on good days, when winds stirred migrants to fly low, hunters considered it a test of their skill to hit the fast-moving targets. Because these were spring shoots, the loss was very great for the breeding population — adults were killed before they could reproduce.

Inland, something similar was happening. Lake Umbagog, a large lake on the border of Maine and New Hampshire, relied on steamboats as the primary transportation to move people and goods from one side to the other. Brewster (1924) described an all too frequent scenario during these boat trips when he wrote, "Often the progress of the steamer up the lake was indicated and proclaimed by the frequent popping of guns fired from her decks at loons and other waterfowl." He suggested that loons offered "conspicuous and attractive targets for rifle practice."

Not all shooting was done for personal challenge and a test of skill. Sometimes loons were intentionally killed because of the belief they were eating game fish. Eaton (1910) noted, "loons, among other fish-eating birds, were most injurious to fish and frog populations, particularly voracious, and particularly destructive to large numbers of small fish."

This kind of pressure surely contributed to a population decline 75 to 100 years ago. Loons once bred on many lakes in Connecticut and Massachusetts, then for nearly a century there were no confirmed breeding records in either state. Slowly, very slowly, they are making a comeback. Breeding was suspected in 1943 in Massachusetts, but it wasn't until 1975 that well-documented records were presented (Clark 1975). A single pair bred that year, and by 1984 there were six territorial pairs on Massachusetts' largest reservoir and one pair on a smaller one. Newly available habitat with islands and fish apparently provided exactly what was needed to beckon the loons to return. At this time their comeback is tenuous, but it is very, very exciting, and it is hoped the population will continue to expand. By summer 1987, loons were breeding on eight bodies of water in Massachusetts. The most recent numbers from states and provinces where they have been reported are given in Table 10–1.

Historical records are more difficult to secure than those of the past 20 years, yet all across the United States a retreat line can be verified. Loons once bred in Pennsylvania, and in 1908 a pair and their nest were reported from Bushkill, in Monroe County. Chicks did hatch, although they did not survive (Harlow 1908), and breeding was not confirmed again until the 1980s, when a pair with flightless young were seen at Penn Forest Reservoir in 1981 and 1983 (Street and Wiltraut 1985). Loons formerly nested in northern Indiana (1891 is the most recent record); in Illinois in the 1800s (but uncommon even by the 1870s, Ridgway 1895); and on large lakes in northern Iowa until the turn of the century (Dinsmore et al. 1984). When Newberry (1857) submitted his report on railroad surveys of the Cascades in northern California and Oregon, he wrote that loons were everywhere.

Table 10-1. Estimated Numbers of Common Loon Populations during the Summer in States and Provinces Where Surveys Have Been Conducted within the Last 10 Years

State/Province	Number of Adults	Source
Maine	3,500	Lee and Arbuckle 1988
New Hampshire	350	Wood et al. 1985
Vermont	69	Rimmer 1988
New York	804	Parker and Miller 1988
Massachusetts	14	Blodget and Lyons 1988
Michigan	600	Hess, 1986 NALF report
Wisconsin	2200	Anon. 1985
Minnesota	10,000	Henderson, pers. comm.
Montana	60	Skaar, 1986 NALF report
Idaho	at least 16	Fitch, 1985 NALF report
Washington	4	Richards and Musche 1985
Wyoming	20	McEneaney 1988
Quebec	35,000	Desgranges/Laporte 1979
	200,000	McNicoll 1988
Ontario	200,000	Ashender 1988

California's nesting records go back to 1887 (Grinnell et al. 1930) from several lakes to the east of Lassen Volcanic National Park, all at about 40° north latitude. During 1982, Ron LeValley, regional editor for *American Birds* in northern California, asked his reporters to pay particular attention to whether or not there were any loons breeding in California. All reports were negative; loons no longer breed there. It is interesting, as he noted, that the only loon legends from Indians in California are from the northern part of the state, suggesting that northern California may have been the southernmost limit of breeding range for a very long time.

There have been no confirmed reports of nesting in Oregon, though paired adults were seen throughout several summers in the 1930s (Gabrielson and Jewett 1940). Earlier, loons were common breeders in many parts of Washington, both east and west of the Cascades (Jewett et al. 1953). Even in the early part of this century, loons summered just "sparingly" on secluded lakes in the mountains and foothills of Washington and were becoming rare (Dawson and Bowles 1909). A typical *American Birds* seasonal report for the northern Pacific coast, including coastal portions of British Columbia, Washington, and Oregon, says that the only nesting report came "as usual" from Vancouver Island. Now there is recent evidence that loons are breeding in Washington, in the northeast corner of the state; a 1985 report confirmed the presence of two pairs with young (Richards and Musche 1985). A new survey project will clarify the extent to which there is a viable Washington population.

The Coeur d'Alene region of Idaho claims to have loons each summer in the same sector where they were recorded as breeders in the last century (Burleigh 1972). As recently as 1963 two pairs and their young were seen at Crane Falls Lake (Larrison and Sonnenberg 1968), but a study of the size of this population and their breeding success is just beginning. A survey during summer 1985 found only one successful nesting pair, though 33 loons were sighted, according to a report Tom Fitch gave at a 1985 meeting of the North American Loon Fund.

Northwestern Montana's loon population has been documented in recent years by several people. The lakes in the Fortine area are reported to have some breeding loons, but Weydemeyer (1975) indicated their numbers were declining. P. D. Skaar initiated a survey over a large part of northwestern Montana by checking lakes larger than four to eight hectares and below 1,538 meters elevation. He found 50 pairs and 23 single birds in 1982 on the 234 lakes he checked. After his death, his son took over the survey work and reported 25 to 30 nesting pairs in 1986 (Skaar 1986).

In 1925, Skinner reported that loons moved through Wyoming only during migration, though from time to time, people suspected that a few bred there. Indeed, breeding has been confirmed on lakes along the corridor between Yellowstone and Grand Teton national parks (Bert Raynes, pers. comm.), in the state's northwest corner. The only successful pair reported from Idaho was actually using a lake shared with Wyoming, and most of the lake could be designated as being in Wyoming rather than in Idaho. Western loons may be in trouble if it is necessary to share credit for one pair between two neighboring states!

Loons breed in North Dakota, though no numbers are available. East of North Dakota, loons breed in every state along the northern tier, as well as throughout Canada with the exception of the most northerly rim and the high Arctic. The loon population in Minnesota appears nearly stable (McIntyre 1988), and there are breeding pairs as far south as the six counties surrounding Minneapolis and St. Paul. In Wisconsin, almost all loons nest only in the northern counties. Surveys by Wisconsin's Project Loon Watch have provided many years of records on the state's loon population (Anon. 1985). In 1987 Terry McEneaney reported at the North American Loon Conference that 10 pairs were confirmed to be breeding in Yellowstone National Park (McEneaney 1988).

Michigan's declining loon population is a cause for concern. However, the most southerly record of breeding loons anywhere in the United States is that of the pair nesting near Kalamazoo, at about 42° north latitude. A pair summered on a lake near the Indiana border for two years in a row, but breeding was not confirmed. Each year several observers check for evidence that loons have returned to stay and raise young. With cooperative effort among independent researchers and the Michigan Department of Natural Resources, the U.S. Forest Service, and the Michigan chapter of The Nature Conservancy, the geographical distribution of Michigan loons may soon be known.

Concerns have been voiced for years about faltering loon populations in the northeastern United States. New York, Vermont, New Hampshire, and Maine all have loon populations, in addition to Massachusetts' seven pairs. Most of Maine's loons are concentrated in the northern part of the state; a smaller population resides in the south (Arbuckle and Lee 1985). In Vermont, only 15 lakes scattered throughout the state had breeding pairs in 1986 (Anon. 1986).

A decline of 53 percent was estimated in New Hampshire in 1978 (Sutcliffe 1978), but loon populations have been on the upswing since then. In New York, about 35 percent fewer lakes have territorial loons now than at the turn of the century (McIntyre 1979). Most of the present population is concentrated in Adirondack Park, with a few pairs still nesting on islands in the St. Lawrence River and along the northwestern edge of the state (Parker 1986). The southern limit of breeding has not shifted in either New Hampshire or New York, but some lakes have lost their resident loons.

There have been concerns about populations in Canada, too, even in the heart of the Common Loons' breeding range, where loon populations were estimated by McNicoll (1988) to be about half a million. Habitat has changed in many places, and it is thought that some decline may result in regions where summer recreational pressures are the greatest (Heimberger et al. 1983). However, the boundaries of Canada's population remain essentially unchanged since Common Loon population boundaries were first mapped. Most of the country is included except for the southern parts of Saskatchewan and Alberta, and the northern portions of the Northwest Territories (Godfrey 1979).

In Alaska the Common Loon breeding range aproaches the southern border of the Brooks Mountains (Gabrielson and Lincoln 1959) and is replaced by habitat of the Yellow-billed Loon in treeless regions to the north. Common Loons have also been reported breeding in Labrador north of 60° north latitude (Gross 1937) and in Baffin Island at 63°45' north latitude (Sutton and Parmelee 1956).

The easternmost extent of the Common Loon's breeding range is in Greenland and Iceland, at about 66° north latitude. Vagrants have been reported from Komandorskiye Islands in the Soviet Union, but no breeding has been confirmed (Flint et al. 1984). There are two questionable specimens, an adult and a juvenile, in the Zoological Museum of Moscow, and they were said to have been collected from the northern Soviet Union (Dement'ev 1968). In 1970 one pair of Common Loons nested in Scotland (British Ornithological Union records, from Cramp 1977), but this was an isolated event and has not happened since. From time to time Common Loons may be reported from places outside their normal range, but this does not indicate a range expansion, only some lost loons. The Common Loon should continue to be regarded primarily as a bird of the Western Hemisphere.

Wintering Range

Most Common Loons winter along the coasts, including the periphery of North America along the Atlantic coast from Newfoundland south to Florida, around the northern side of the Gulf of Mexico, and along the Pacific coast from California to Alaska. Band recoveries show the southern limit to be off the Florida Keys, and there have been additional sightings near Sonora, Mexico (Zimmerman 1967).

Some Common Loons are reported wintering off the eastern Atlantic coast. Most European loons are reported offshore from Great Britain, but others use waters from Norway to southern France, with an occasional report of a loon off the coast of Algeria (Etchécopar and Hüe 1964). These birds have been assumed to be Icelandic nesters, but wintering distribution may be more complex than that. It was also thought that loons wintering off the coast of Iceland were probably Icelandic nesters until gizzard stones removed from recovered loons were identified as metamorphic material, in particular, granite. Granite is not found in Iceland, so Iceland's wintering loons had to be coming from somewhere else (Gudmundsson 1972). Birds wintering off English or Norwegian shores may also come from somewhere other than Iceland or Greenland, and their identity continues to be a puzzle. Some loons winter inland, on the Great Lakes when they stay ice-free, or on reservoirs and larger lakes in the south. The extent to which loons use freshwater habitat during the winter is not completely known, but seasonal reports in *American Birds* indicate it happens in some places every year.

Figure 10-2. Migratory routes of Common Loons as constructed from band-recovery data. *Solid lines* indicate banding to recovery points, and are either from birds banded as adults and later recovered, or from juveniles recovered during their first winter. *Dotted lines* are recoveries of second-year birds. *a.* Juvenile banded in Minnesota and recovered in May off the North Carolina coast during an oil spill. *b.* Location off the coast of Nova Scotia where two immatures banded in northwestern Minnesota were recovered in July and October.

Breeding populations from specific regions may winter together in the same geographical area, but data are few. Those taken from banding records indicate that at least some wintering populations may be composed of individuals from specific breeding populations. Birds wintering along Florida's gulf coast are thought to be midwestern birds. Those banded in Minnesota are most frequently recovered along Florida's west coast during the winter, and indications are that the body size of recovered loons agrees most favorably with breeding populations from the Midwest. Recoveries from Lake Michigan and sighting of a Minnesota wing-tagged individual on a Tennessee reservoir add credence to a suspected flight path between Minnesota and the gulf coast of Florida.

Other information secured from recovered birds and summarized in the migration map in Figure 10–2 suggests that loons breeding in central Canada are the same ones that winter along the Atlantic coast from Maryland through the Carolinas and perhaps down to the east coast of Florida, while the most northeastern breeding populations winter at nearby offshore locations along Canadian and New England shores. In the West, two banding records suggest that loons wintering on the Pacific coast are those which breed west of the Rocky Mountains. More banding needs to be done before winter–summer relationships can be made with confidence, but already there are some signs that wintering distribution is not random.

Most winter mapping has been based on Christmas Bird Count records provided in *American Birds*, with only little input from band recoveries. This restricts the time from which information can be secured to a few weeks between late December and early January. Adult loons stay in marine waters for five to six months each year. Are they mobile? Do they move up and down the coast as weather and food supply permit? Information from *American Birds* suggests weather-related distribution patterns. When weather is mild in the early part of the winter, loons either stay inland on migratory stopping points longer, or in large numbers on the northern part of the Atlantic coast. When weather is unusually cold, few loons stay inland, fewer than usual are recorded from northern sites, and large gatherings can be counted along southern coasts.

Three examples from *American Birds* seasonal reports provide evidence that weather influences the location of loons in winter. There was a late freeze during the winter of 1978–1979, followed by very cold weather in mid-February. More than 100 loons stayed on a single inland lake during the early part of that mild winter, which was unusual, but by late February following the cold snap, all but three had moved on. Similar reports came from other reservoirs in the South, indicating loons may stay on and on until cold weather forces them to the coast. The winter of 1982–1983 was also mild. Reports noted "lots of inland winterers." On the other hand, another Texas report, from 1981–1982, stated that under pressure from high winds and choppy waves, loons tend to move back in toward shore and concentrate near dikes.

In 1980–1981, the weather turned unusually cold by mid-December and fewer loons were reported from locations such as along the coasts of the Delmarva Peninsula, New Jersey, and New York. At the same time, a record number of 2,503 Common Loons were counted farther south, off Morehead, North Carolina, and over the winter an exceedingly high number (more than 10,000) were counted at Pamlico Sound. Both places are south of concentrations usually reported during Christmas Bird Counts.

Another example supports suspicions that wintering movements may be influenced by temperature. During 1981–1983, large concentrations of loons were found inland in Tennessee, Illinois, Oklahoma, Texas, southern California, Washington, British Columbia, and even South Dakota, where there was a first winter record. Even rivers and reservoirs in New Jersey were host to wintering loons that year. Oceanic waters were warmer than usual, which kept large populations of baitfish offshore. This resulted in many of Florida's loons staying farther out than they usually do, some over 32 kilometers offshore from Cape Canaveral (Hoffman 1983).

I examined Christmas Bird Count records over the past 15 years to see if there was a tendency for loons to concentrate off the northern Atlantic coast when fall had been long and mild, and winter slow in arriving, and to move southward when weather turned cold early in the year. To achieve as much uniformity of sampling as possible, I compared records from locations where an annual count had been made every year since 1970. Loons tended to be in northern waters during mild years and along the southern coast when weather turned cold by the time of the Christmas Bird Count.

However, there was no way I could be sure how much variability may have existed among counts from year to year, and there were few locations where an annual count had been made in exactly the same site over many years. It would be worthwhile to organize an annual survey with counts taken once a month, in order to secure long-term information on loon locations and weather factors. We conducted a winter watch as a pilot study along the Atlantic coast during 1984 (McIntyre and Smith 1984) and we hope someone will continue this work. The Maine Audubon Society and the Maine Cooperative Fish and Wildlife Research Unit continue to conduct winter counts off the coast of Maine and it would be beneficial to expand this work to other states.

Large numbers winter along the Pacific coast, and there are indications that some sites act as concentration sites just before spring migration (Corkran 1988). There are places along the Atlantic coast where loons concentrate, too, for example around Chincoteague, Virginia; North Carolina's Outer Banks; and Litchfield-Pawleys Island, South Carolina. Factors such as food resource availability may be important predictors of loon wintering sites, but no work has been done on this.

Loons are generally considered coastal, not pelagic. I studied the wintering behavior of Common Loons off Assateague/Chincoteague islands, Virginia, and concentrated on following the behavior of inshore birds (McIntyre 1978). Two groups of 20 to 25 loons occupied the same feeding locations every day within a small cove no deeper than four meters, and at night they moved to the center of the same bay. I mapped the locations that each bird occupied daily, and the sites were remarkably stable throughout the winter. Yet, when I had a chance to go offshore on a local fishing vessel and spend all the daylight hours moving between one and two kilometers out, I found loons there, too. Common Loons were flying up and down the coast, as well as swimming and feeding alongside the boat. Following these findings, several questions arose. Do individual loons have wintering site preferences? Are loons mobile and do the same birds move in and out, up and down, back and forth? Are there sex differences in site preference? Are there age differences?

Most loons reported during Christmas Bird Counts are close to shore, or observers walking along beaches wouldn't be able to see them. Recently, however, there have been simultaneous offshore counts. Common Loons have been counted both inshore and offshore in surveys done the same day at the same latitude. Perhaps loons occupy a wider strip of coastal waters than has been realized.

Until more banding data are available, it is difficult to form conclusions about wintering populations. An intense banding effort by the Department of Natural Resources in Minnesota has recently been launched, and has resulted in a meaningful number of loon bandings in the last few years. Recoveries of these birds over time will show if migration data support the concept of discrete wintering sites. At this time it can be said that Common Loons winter off most North American and western European coasts, are generally found inshore but do utilize offshore water, and may be mobile as influenced by food availability and weather factors.

Migratory Movements

The routes and pathways loons follow during migration across North America are numerous and broad. Their flights cover an extended period in the fall, beginning in September and continuing into December. Routes between Iceland and Greenland to wintering destinations are unknown.

Timing of spring movements is dependent on the speed with which lakes become free of ice. Records come from diverse sources, such as monitoring from bird observatories, reports from hawk lookout stations, correspondence from individuals, and banding recoveries and sightings of marked loons. If these records are put together with data from studies specifically addressing loon migration, some generalizations can be made.

Loons move along several routes (Figure 10-2). One Atlantic pathway is offshore, following the continental shelf from Nova Scotia to the Carolinas, and another is farther inshore, following the coastline and crossing Cape Cod (Powers and Cherry 1983). Inland, a broad southeast/northwest path goes between the Atlantic coast and central Canada, funneling through one of two parts of the Great Lakes, Georgian Bay in Lake Huron or Lake Michigan.

Another route lies in a north/south line through the central part of the United States to and from the Gulf of Mexico. The route has been documented by collected specimens and records from observers in Oklahoma, Kansas, and Texas, though no banded birds have been recovered so far along this flyway. Loons flying along this route may be breeders from the west-central portion of the northern tier of states, and may include some Canadian breeders. Finally, there is a movement along the western edge of the Rocky Mountains between Alaska or western Canada and the Pacific coast.

Several birds banded in Minnesota have been recovered from Lake Michigan and the Gulf coast of Florida, as well as from Mille Lacs lake in the central part of Minnesota. The recovery from Mille Lacs, together with a more extensive study of loons using this large, shallow walleye lake before fall migration, suggest that after the breeding season both adults and juveniles aggregate on large lakes with an abundant fish resource (McIntyre and Barr 1983). Staging grounds on other large lakes have also been reported from Manitoba and Saskatchewan (Nero 1972,1974, Predy 1972, Lysack 1985) and from New York (Bull 1974).

There are large numbers of loons in the fall on both Lake Michigan and Lake Huron. A ship captain who kept records of all the birds he encountered as he plied his route along the Great Lakes shipping lanes wrote of a sighting in November 1944, "As far as we could see there were loons on the calm waters of Lake Michigan." He continued by saying that there was "a concentration of divers for miles" (Perkins 1965).

The cause and extent of periodic die-offs of water birds on Lake Michigan are discussed in Chapter 4. Locations where loons are found during these epidemics have provided information about migratory movements on the lake. In October, loons concentrate along the north shore, and in November and December they congregate along the south end of the lake. This suggests a migratory route through the lake from north to south, progressing with the onset of winter (Fay 1969).

Loons also use the other Great Lakes during migration. Mortalities from commercial fishing operations have been the source of evidence of regular buildups of loons in Georgian Bay at the northeast side of Lake Huron. Lake Superior also has numbers of loons, especially along the southeast shore. There is concern about loon mortality there, too, because of the prevalence of commercial fishing entrapment. Migrating loons also use Lake Erie, and they feed around the south shore of Lake Ontario in the spring. Records from both the Christmas Bird Counts and the seasonal reports in *American Birds* indicate that loons tend to linger at inland waters in the fall until just before lakes freeze. When mild weather continues unusually late, loons remain longer on freshwater, but as soon as a cold snap occurs, they move to maritime sites.

Spring migratory behavior is different from that in fall. Flight to the breeding grounds is direct, unless weather factors necessitate lingering stopovers. The timing of spring thaw controls the movements of loons, and if territorial lakes stay frozen longer than normal, loons may concentrate wherever open water is available. As soon as possible they move on, but if lakes open late, there may be a considerable backup of migrants on small open-water sites.

For the past several years, Whitefish Point Bird Observatory in Michigan, located on a point jutting into Lake Superior, has been the site of a count of migrant birds. In 1982 nearly 5,000 Common Loons flew over, 3,000 between May 7 and 10. During a single hour, from 0630 to 0730 on May 8, 738 loons moved northward (Ewert 1982). April had been unusually cold and the mass movement may have been in response to a buildup of loons waiting to proceed.

Groups of two to 15 individuals moving northward have been reported to leave Florida's gulf coast from shortly after sunrise until about 0930 (Williams 1973). Migratory flights along the Atlantic coast were monitored by Powers and Cherry (1983), who tallied the largest counts of migrants between 0500 and 0800. All accounts, whether from Michigan, Florida, or the Northeast, indicate that loons are diurnal migrants and begin their flights early in the morning.

Migratory movements continue over a prolonged period, and loons form packs along the way if frozen water impedes their progress. Numbers peak as loons reach the Great Lakes in both spring and fall. Throughout the fall they stage on the Great Lakes and feed in flocks. In the spring there are indications that loons stay on the Great Lakes only until they can move to their breeding territories.

Kerlinger (1982) radar-tracked loons migrating over central New York and found that flights continued throughout the day. He was monitoring loons at a far greater altitude than previously had been done, as other reports had been offered by observers using only binoculars or spotting scopes. Numbers peaked across central New York in the morning, several hours past sunrise in the spring and a little earlier in the fall. Birds moving between Lake Ontario and the Atlantic coast had ground speeds averaging 147 kmph in the spring and more than 170 kmph in the fall. This means that the time spent between the coastal departure point and Kerlinger's tracking station was between two to three hours, which supports the early-morning flight hypothesis.

Other overland flights have been regularly reported from Tennessee, Appalachia, Oklahoma, Nevada, Idaho, and the Salton Sea in California. Large numbers of migrants cross Pennsylvania, and at Hawk Mountain hundreds of flying loons are counted during the fall. In their reports, Boyle et al. (1979, 1980, 1982) frequently refer to the loons counted at Hawk Mountain. During these seasonal counts, there is intensive monitoring of migratory hawks, but other species are counted too, and this provides valuable information on the timing of loon migration. For example, on 13 November 1977, 488 Common Loons were counted in a single day, and on 22 November 1981, 456 flew over.

Boyle et al. (1979) wrote that Common Loons were generally overland migrants. On the other hand, Powers and Cherry (1983) noted that substantial coastal migrations of Common Loons occurred in spring and fall and that there were inshore and offshore routes. If both reports are accepted, it appears that Common Loons may have various migratory routes, depending on which population is being considered. They may fly overland from interior breeding grounds, and inshore and offshore from the most easterly populations. Powers and Cherry (1983) suggested offshore Common Loons may be from Nova Scotia, and because Nova Scotia has more than 5,000 lakes, and a healthy population of breeding loons, this is certainly a possibility. Offshore migrants may also be immature birds. Recent information on the movements of nonbreeders during their second year may help to identify individuals using coastal routes.

Common Loons also winter along the Pacific coast, and large aggregations of loons are reported along the California coast preceding spring migration. In 1977 tremendous numbers of loons were counted off Pigeon Point. Most were Arctic and Red-throated loons, nearly half a million, but there were also over 6,000 Common Loons at the same site. On 16 April, 537 Common Loons moved through in a single day (Winter and Morlan 1977). Common Loons are also regularly seen migrating through Washington, and some rafting is reported along the coast and in the bays. Records up the coast to Alaska are sparse at this time.

Movements of Juveniles

There is only a vague understanding about the whereabouts of the young until they become adults and return to the breeding grounds, but sightings and a few banding records are helping to clarify the picture of juvenile movements. In Figure 10–2, banding/recovery locations are shown for three immatures that died during their second summer. They were banded in Minnesota on the territory where they were hatched. One was found off the coast of North Carolina in May and the other two off the Nova Scotian coast in July and October. Does this mean they were moving northward in the spring, to remain there while molting their flight feathers? Were they following fish movements en route?

Every year large numbers of juveniles appear off the coast of New Brunswick. A. D. Smith of the Canadian Wildlife Service has recorded numbers of immature loons in Baie Verte for many years. The first arrivals come in May, and more continue to arrive until July. They stay throughout the summer in small groups of five to a dozen individuals. Those I watched were in groups of sevens and eights, and they stayed together to feed, preen, and apparently to spend the nights rafting over deeper water. They moved inshore early in the morning, and followed the tidal cycle during the daylight hours.

In 1977 and 1978 more than 100 could be counted at any one time on Baie Verte, but there have been fewer during the 1980s. Are these individuals the same ones that spend their first winter off the southern coasts, perhaps off the gulf coast of Florida, then move together northward at the beginning of their second summer? Do they stay together throughout the first two or three years, and do they represent the young from a geographically well-defined breeding population? Could they be the loons that Cherry and Powers reported as offshore fall migrants? This would be a fertile area for new research.

Loons are found in different places at different times. In late spring and summer, adult Common Loons are on northern lakes of the boreal region across North America, in Iceland, and in Greenland. They spend the winter as coastal inhabitants along North America and western Europe, and in between they move along several routes, following major waterways. And the juveniles? Like juveniles everywhere, they are puzzling.

CHAPTER 11
Human Impact on Loons

The impact of people on loons takes many forms. It includes disturbance from recreational activities, habitat loss from lakeshore development, entanglement of birds in fishing nets and aquatic debris, toxic chemicals, oil spills, and direct killing. On the plus side, new habitat has been created for loons by the formation of many new reservoirs through dam impoundments. Loons use reservoirs during the breeding season and as migratory stops.

Recreational Pressures

People and loons are alike in some ways. Both prefer the same kinds of large, clear northern lakes, with islands and plenty of fish. People are drawn to lakes like these to relax and enjoy summer holidays — theirs is a migration for pleasure. For loons, it is a migration to breed and raise young.

The overlap resulting from similar preferences causes some problems for loons, but the evidence on how serious these problems are, and which intrusions are the most damaging, is conflicting. People use lakes for many kinds of recreation: camping, canoeing, family outings, fishing,

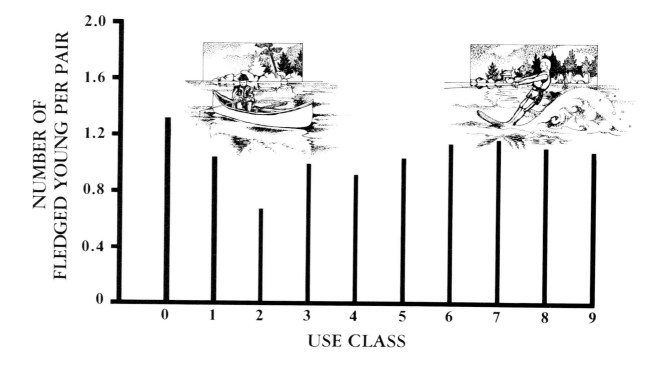

Figure 11-1. Productivity expressed as number of juveniles fledged per pair, classified by the extent of recreational use of the lake. Data were reported by volunteers in the Minnesota and New York Project Loon Watch programs. Use classifications are: *0.* No use. *1.* No boating. *2.* Occasional boating or canoeing. *3.* One or two boats a day, maximum. *4.* Daily use of boats, canoes, or sailboats; no motors. *5.* Occasional use of boats with motors. *6.* Daily use of one or two boats with motors. *7.* Motor boats used frequently; a fishing lake. *8.* Occasional waterskiing or boat racing. *9.* Heavy lake traffic, including waterskiing or boat racing.

water skiing and motorboating. Each activity has the potential to cause a different kind of disturbance and each has a greater or lesser effect depending on what stage of the breeding season the loons are in when the conflicts occur.

Do recreational pressures have any relationship to the loons' ability to produce fledged young? Several studies have examined this question. Two questions answered by volunteers in the Minnesota Project Loon Watch program refer to the extent of recreational pressure on each lake, and how many young each pair raised to fledging. Figure 11–1 provides information gathered from nearly 600 responses. These data indicate no significant difference in the loons' productivity if they are nesting on a busy lake or on one with little activity. In fact, some loons on lakes with a high level of human activity have greater success than those on lakes with less boating, fishing, and other recreational activities.

Two studies addressing the effects of recreation on loon productivity were done on canoe routes in the United States. A route in the Kenai National Wildlife Refuge of Alaska was established in 1965–1966. In 1979 and 1980, Liz Smith, then a graduate student at Colorado State University, surveyed 10 lakes on the canoe route and 10 lakes with no human traffic and compared the ability of loons to nest successfully on both. She found productivity identical on both sets of lakes. In 1979 she reported 0.67 young per pair on the canoe-route lakes and 0.64 young per pair on the lakes used as a control group (those with no human traffic). In 1980 she found 0.33 young on canoe lakes, and 0.30 on lakes in the other group (Smith 1981).

Another canoe route, the well-known Boundary Waters Canoe Area (BWCA) in northern Minnesota, provided the locale for another recent study of loons and recreational pressure. Titus and Van Druff (1981) reported that in 1975 productivity on lakes subjected to the heaviest traffic was identical to that on more remote lakes where little canoeing and camping occurred, but in 1976 low-use lakes had 80 percent more young fledged per pair than the high-use lakes did. Recreational effect was examined in Canada along Big Rideau Lake, in the heart of Ontario's cottage country. Productivity was reported to be 0.70 chicks fledged per pair, and that is as high or higher than productivity on most wilderness lakes (Price and Keith 1975).

It seems as though loons do just as well on busy lakes as they do on quiet ones, so why all the fuss in the popular press? Articles have cried out concerning loon problems and the conflict between loons and people. Has this been crying wolf? Loons have been placed on threatened-species lists and on lists of species of special concern in several states. Many individual researchers have entered pleas of concern for loons, especially in heavily populated areas.

We know from historical records that loons have declined in many sectors. In New York, for example, indications are that there are about 35 percent fewer loons now than there were 25 to 50 years ago (McIntyre 1979), although Parker and Miller (1988) present a more hopeful outlook. New Hampshire's loon population is thought to have declined approximately 53 percent during the last 50 years (Sutcliffe 1981).

Perhaps these declines are a result of heavy recreational pressure on lakes where loons have traditionally nested. Although each of the remaining pairs may be able to raise young, there may be fewer young in all as some pairs move away and seek more private quarters. Vermeer (1973a) found a significant inverse correlation between the extent of disturbance and the numbers of breeding loon pairs on lakes in northern Alberta. Smith (1981) found only six territorial pairs on canoe-route lakes in Alaska, but 11 territorial pairs on more remote lakes. The St. Regis Canoe Area in New York's Adirondack Park was established in 1982. Fifteen years earlier, in 1967, there were six pairs, which Taylor (pers. comm.) had been photographing for several years. Suddenly he found fewer and fewer loons, until only seven years after the onset of the new canoe area, he could count only an occasional loon.

Hanson Lake in northern Saskatchewan has little traffic, and much of the lake rarely sees a human intruder. This can be considered undeveloped, pristine habitat, and there is one loon on Hanson Lake for every 21.7 hectares of water surface, which is considered a dense population. The Stillwater Reservoir is another large lake, and also has many bays and islands, much like Hanson Lake. However, it is located in the Adirondack Park, close to the southern limit of the breeding range, and has heavy boating traffic and other intensive recreational use. Because most of the lakeshore is owned by the state, the area is undeveloped, except for a few cabins clustered at one end along a short stretch of shoreline. The largest concentration of breeding loons in New York is found there, but each loon has 96.9 hectares, scarcely a match for Hanson Lake. This may not be caused solely by the influence of human recreation; other factors such as food supply may also be important. However, recreational pursuits must be considered when these differences in loon populations are being investigated.

Squam Lake in New Hampshire is the same size as the Stillwater Reservoir, and it, too, has many islands and bays. It also has heavy recreational use, and its shoreline is highly developed, with cabins surrounding its perimeter. Squam Lake has 124.5 hectares of water surface for each loon. The three lakes offer an excellent opportunity to compare the effects of shoreline development and recreational use. I have not worked on other lakes of similar size and configuration with a highly developed shoreline and no recreational use. It would be wonderful to know where one could be found to contrast with the other three.

The portion of the Boundary Waters Canoe Area in Minnesota where Jim Titus conducted his doctoral research in the mid-1970s included the same lakes as the earlier survey by Sigurd T. Olson in 1949 (Olson and Marshall 1952, Titus and Van Druff 1981). Titus found more territorial pairs in 1975 and 1976 than Olson had found almost 30 years earlier, yet the human disturbance factor had increased exponentially.

Titus found that territories were not the same as they had been in 1949. Originally loons had positioned their territories around islands, usually those on which they nested. Islands had been taken over more and more by campers on the canoe route, and by noncampers stopping for a lunch on shore. This resulted in the loons' moving back into the quiet bays and along the shoreline. Many nests were not on islands at the time Titus studied the area; many were placed directly on the mainland. Apparently loons were able to shift their nest sites when suitable alternatives were available.

Summer homes are built along the shoreline on some lakes, others attract fishermen who anchor along the shore and in quiet bays. On these lakes, the alternative shoreline sites that loons find in the Boundary Waters are not available. With nowhere to nest, either productivity falls or the loons shift their territories to other lakes.

If loons are flexible enough to select alternative nest sites, perhaps they also exhibit other behavioral shifts in response to continued human recreational pressures. Do they acclimate themselves to human presence? Disturbance distance measures how close an intruder can approach a nest before a loon flushes. This was measured on canoe routes in Alaska and Minnesota. Smith (1981) found in Alaska that loons on canoe routes had a short disturbance distance and stayed on their nests longer than those on undisturbed lakes. On canoe lakes, intruders could approach to an average of 8.5 meters from the nest before the incubating loons would slide into the water. Disturbance distance was much greater on remote lakes, where loons left their nests when people were 112.6 meters away. Smith also found other behavioral differences. For example, loons along the canoe route waited until she was very close before they began penguin dancing (16.2 meters, as compared to 63.6 meters for noncanoe lakes) and they engaged in splash diving when she was about 12 meters away, as opposed to 64.8 meters on more remote lakes.

Titus and Van Druff (1981) found that loons on busy lakes sat quietly, and Titus named them "stickers." If they did not stay on the nest, and some did not, they slid quietly into the water and surfaced far away, giving no vocalizations, making no sound. On the other hand, loons on lakes visited only rarely by canoeists, flushed off their nests at human approach. They splashed, ran, and made a noisy and hasty exit, and continued to display with calls and postures after they were in the water. Does this mean loons adapt to people? Or does it mean there are individual differences? Are some stickers by nature, continuing to nest on high use lakes, while others, not responding in the same way, leave for quieter places?

Titus and Van Druff (1981) also found that sticker birds were reproductively more successful than others. They found that 14 pairs of stickers produced 22 young; two nests were washed out when water levels rose, and two nests produced one young each. This productivity was three times greater than overall on their study area.

I monitored the success of 51 pairs on Hanson Lake in Saskatchewan and found opposite results. Seventeen pairs sat tight, and though they hung low over the nest in the posture so typical of disturbed and frightened loons, they let us pass without leaving their nests. Some quietly left after we had gone by, but they did not exhibit excitement or overt defensive posturing or calls. However, only 58.8 percent of these loons hatched chicks; 79.4 percent of those exhibiting agitation were successful.

Traffic anywhere on Hanson Lake is slight when compared to the busyness of the Boundary Waters. As far back as 1966, Ream (1976) reported that some major canoe routes in the Boundary Waters had more than 14,000 people traveling through them during a summer. By the mid-1970s, estimated recreational use for a single season had increased to more than 175,000 people. It not only takes time for loons to acclimatize to canoes and boats and increased people pressure, but the full effect of getting used to may not be expected until the generation of loons which has been reared on a busy lake returns to breed. Juveniles raised around people show less fear, and they approach closer to boats than those that grow up not seeing humans.

A question frequently asked is: Which has a more negative effect on loons, canoes or motorboats? The answer is that it depends on the stage in the breeding cycle. Loons on nests tend to stay on them if boats continue along established routes and keep moving. They are more inclined to leave nests when boats stop to fish or when canoes slowly drift by and poke along the shoreline. When loons leave their nests, the eggs become vulnerable to a host of predators.

On BWCA lakes, motorboat use is heavy from the opening of the fishing season for two to three weeks, generally starting around May 17. Canoe traffic is heaviest in August, long after loons have completed nesting. Titus and Van Druff (1981) reported lower productivity on lakes where motors are permitted than on canoe-only lakes, 0.52 young per pair compared to 0.71 young per pair. They made more than 100 sightings of fishermen stopping near loon nests and staying there for between 30 minutes and an hour, causing loons to leave their nests. On the other hand, when boats move along, loons stay on their nests. I have followed loons both in New York and in Saskatchewan, both populations nesting on large lakes that have established boat routes. In general, loons do not leave their nests when the traffic flow of boats continues along these established pathways.

Motorboats may cause another form of disturbance, even if they move right along. After chicks hatch, they remain with the adults, and this is important for them because if they stray, they are subject to predation by a variety of underwater predators as well as being vulnerable to a host of avian threats, principally gulls. If they accidentally wander into an adjacent territory, they are likely to be killed by the resident loon. Even if chicks are not directly killed, they are vulnerable to disturbance by boats which can prevent adults from feeding and brooding their offspring. Canoes are less of a threat at this time. Canoes move slowly, and adults and chicks can move out of the way, unless the canoeist is intent on trying to capture a chick. If canoes are numerous and become a nearly continual parade, they can prevent adults from feeding chicks as often as they do when undisturbed.

Motorboats present a different problem. Loons keep their young in nurseries most of the time until they are two to three weeks old, and at that time they move them farther and farther out into the main body of the territory. Motorboats sometimes run between young and adults when they are in open water, and although it may be unintentional on the part of the boaters, the separation of chicks from their parents can cause their death. Adults with one chick in tow will not wait for a second chick to catch up. They will leave should danger be present, and the second chick, the one left behind, is deserted. If it is lucky, it is eventually reunited with its parents, but frequently it is lost.

The timing of holidays presents other problems. Memorial Day means heavy use of lake country in the United States. Another heavy-use holiday is the May 24 weekend in Canada, the celebration of the Queen's Birthday. Earlier in the year, there is some fishing use, but even nonanglers are likely to "go to the lake" over the May weekend holidays. This is soon after most nests have become established, at a time when adults are most likely to desert them if they are disturbed. If they do leave, and the nest is lost to predators, a waiting period of about a week and a half must pass before adults are ready to nest again. Initiation of the second nest during the second week in June coincides with the end of school and beginning of lake holidays for families with school-age children. Even if nesting is established at that time, it means that hatching would not be possible before 8–10 July, just after the second big American holiday takes place, the Fourth of July or Canada Day on July 1. Again, this is one of the busiest weekends at most lakes, and the threat to nest loss occurs at a critical time.

Recreational use probably has contributed to a decline in loon populations in parts of the country where there are high levels of lake activity. Whether or not a specific activity is disruptive depends on the time of that activity. Steady motorized traffic poses little disturbance to nesting loons, but may be a major factor in chick mortality. Slower, nonmotorized boats frequently contribute to nest loss, but in general do not interfere with the rearing of chicks. Camping has influenced loons to shift nesting sites on almost all lakes where island camping is prevalent. If alternative sites are not available, the loons' ability to nest will be restricted.

Shoreline Development

Development of the shoreline with rock fill or retaining walls prohibits loons from nesting, and this kind of development may occur on some lakes. More commonly, development means building cottages or summer homes near the lake; radical alteration of the shoreline itself is less frequent. The buildings themselves appear to have little effect on loon choice of a nest site, but human activity around the buildings does.

In New Hampshire, some concerned citizens have chosen to postpone use of their summer cottages until nesting is over if a traditional nest site is nearby. Among cottages, those on islands are the ones most likely to be near loon nests because islands offer optimal nest sites. The New Hampshire Loon Preservation Committee reported that productivity increased when owners of vulnerable sites delayed their summer arrival until loon chicks had hatched.

It is difficult to obtain direct measures of the effect development has on loon productivity, but extent of cottages, resorts, and campgrounds can be correlated with presence or absence of loons and their reproductive success. Reports from Minnesota Project Loon Watch include information on development and reproductive success. Figure 11–2 suggests that development does not seem to be a deterrent to hatching or fledging success. In fact, a look at the solid line across the graph shows that more chicks fledged per pair on lakes with intensive development than on some lakes with more intact shorelines. This seems contrary to what would be expected if development had a negative effect on loons. It could be that fewer loons occupy lakes with shoreline development, and those that do

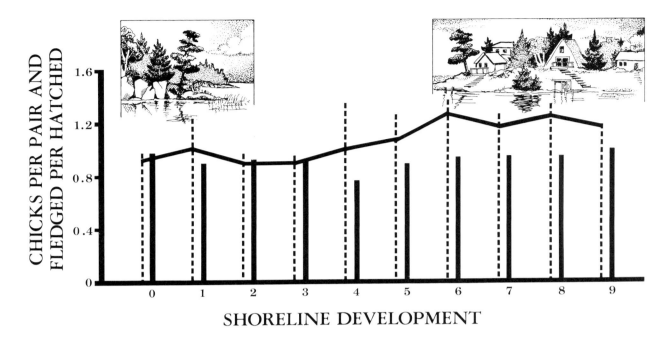

Figure 11-2. Relationship of shoreline development to hatching and fledging success presented as number of young per nesting pair. *Dotted lines* represent hatched chicks per pair, *solid vertical lines* represent number of fledged young per chick hatched, *solid horizontal line* represents number of fledged young per pair. Data are from Minnesota and New York Project Loon Watch reports. Shoreline classifications are: *0.* No development. *1.* One home. *2.* Two or more homes. *3.* Resort only. *4.* Campground only. *5.* Resort and campground. *6.* Private home(s) plus resort. *7.* Private home(s) plus campground. *8.* Homes, resort, and campground. *9.* Unknown.

are successful because they are using the optimal habitat still available.

From 1977 to 1979, between 37 and 40 lakes in the cottage district of southern Ontario were monitored. Loons did not seem to "prefer" developed or undeveloped habitat, but their reproductive success seemed to be related to the proximity of cottages. Reproductive success was compared to the distance cottages were located from nest sites. There was a great difference in hatching rates between loons nesting close to cottages and those nesting at some distance, but once the eggs hatched, survival of chicks was the same whether they were close to the bustle of people, boats, and cottages, or whether they were far away (Heimberger et al.

1983). When cottages were located within 4,000 meters of a nest, chances of success were less than half (45 percent); if cottages were farther away, nearly three-fourths of the nests were successful (74 percent). In Alberta, Vermeer (1973b) used shoreline development and a ranking of campsites, resorts, homes, and summer cottages as disturbance factors. He compared these factors with territorial selection and breeding success and concluded that loons prefer to nest on lakes where there is a minimum of human disturbance.

On the Stillwater Reservoir in New York, there is an expanding population of territorial loons and a good rate of success. Boating and canoeing are popular sports, with armadas of canoes on some days. However, only a few homes are clustered together along a short part of the mainland shore, and on only three of the lake's 42 islands. Evidence at this time indicates that both shoreline development and recreational use can have detrimental effects on loons, but it seems that the way in which development causes disturbance is through its use by people, rather than by structures themselves.

Predators/Scavengers

The major predators on loon nests and chicks include scavengers such as American Crows, Common Ravens, Herring Gulls, and raccoons. All have grown in numbers because of an increase in garbage dumps and the availability of free meals. Several published accounts report that Herring Gulls are also a major problem for other species of birds, among them Common Terns, whose nesting habitat is usurped by the larger and more aggressive gulls.

Loons do not face the same kind of threat from gulls. Theirs is a different problem, for gulls do not take over loon nesting sites, but they eat loon eggs and chicks. I have seen them attempt to take eggs, and be repelled by loons, and I have found half-eaten eggs with bill holes in them in habitat where gulls are the only potential avian predators. I have seen gulls swoop down on lone chicks and take them off the water. They fight over small chicks while airborne, and the tiny loonlings may be pulled this way and that by a flock of gulls. A wandering chick, or one left alone, even briefly, on the surface of the water while parents hunt for food or defend their territory, is fair game for the voracious gulls.

Crows were the major avian predator in my Minnesota study, and I have watched them as they watched loon nests, biding their time until they could move in to take the eggs. Disturbance that drives the adults off the nest means the ever watchful crows can swoop down and destroy the eggs. Ravens have also been thought to be nest robbers, but it wasn't until 1976 that it was confirmed. At that time, a biologist studying ravens in northern Minnesota and going to the nesting ledges to check on young, found loon eggs in the raven nests. Ravens, with their large bills, obviously were capable of carrying off whole loon eggs, leaving empty loon nests a mystery to Jim Titus during his BWCA study before the discovery that the eggs from his study were being eaten by the ravens in his colleague's study!

Raccoon populations have expanded in some places, New Hampshire and Minnesota among them. I was able to identify raccoons as the most likely predator on loon nests through experimental testing as described in Chapter 5. Raccoons in New Hampshire have caused the destruction of many loon nests. Sutcliffe (1980) credited them with destroying between 75 and 80 percent of all nests lost on the state's two largest lakes in 1977. An outbreak of canine distemper, to which raccoons are susceptible, resulted in high raccoon mortality later that year, resulting in destruction of fewer loon nests. Bald Eagles have occasionally been mentioned as loon predators. Paul Strong, from the Wisconsin Project Loon Watch, wrote to say that a fair number of reports are submitted every year in Wisconsin, noting that Bald Eagles have either harassed or, in some cases, carried off loon chicks.

There are many other predators, among them northern pike and muskellunge, fox, mink, and occasionally other mammalian carnivores. However, ravens, crows, raccoons, and gulls have been increasing in numbers as a direct result of the availability of human refuse. All are avid scavengers at garbage dumps, and can find enough food there to allow large numbers of offspring to survive, accounting for their mushrooming populations. Loons have evolved together with modest numbers of predators, but may be finding it difficult to cope with the recent population boom of these four species.

Direct Killing by Humans

Loons have been considered a threat by many fishermen. I remember an angry comment following a lecture I gave recently, as a young man stood up and accused loons of taking more than $50,000 in trout that his club had stocked in its private lakes. He was not suggesting loons be shot; rather he suggested they might like to pay dues! Unfortunately others feel that loons are in direct competition with fishermen, and many advocate eradication through whatever means is necessary. As recently as 1970, nine loons were killed in New York by irate fishermen who claimed their leased ponds had no trout because loons ate them all. They were asked not to do it again, but were never prosecuted.

At the turn of the century, loons were commonly shot for sport. Attitudes changed during the early part of the 20th century. In 1910, Eaton, writing about the birds of New York, stated that loons were the most injurious to fish and frog populations, destroying great numbers of the food base for game fish. By 1925, Forbush, writing about the birds of Massachusetts, said that loons may be beneficial to fish by helping to maintain healthy populations. He asked that a study be undertaken to look into this possibility. By then there were no loons breeding in Massachusetts; they had not bred there since before 1900, and did not return until the early 1970s.

Occasionally some loons are still shot for sport. Many of the loons that are prepared as museum specimens contain shot imbedded in muscles of their necks. The imbedded buckshot is not the cause of death, but it indicates that loons present such a good target that it is tempting for some people with guns to shoot them.

The most gruesome evidence for intentional killing of loons comes from Redondo Beach, California, in an incident that happened several years ago. Common Loons were not the victims, but it is worth mentioning here because the thinking that resulted in such cruel and wanton destruction could just as readily have been directed at Common Loons, if they had been "in the way." Pacific Loons were found washed up on shore, their bills tightly tied together with red rubber bands. The conclusion was that commercial fishermen had caught them in their nets, considered them to be detrimental to their business, and made sure it didn't happen again by binding their bills. They starved to death, and became a grim reminder, as they washed ashore, that ignorance, combined with anger, can be dangerous and destructive. No one knows how many loons were killed this way. The culprits were never found, though the practice did stop after a journalist directed public attention to the atrocities (Elliott 1978).

Loons are still being taken for food by Indians and Inuits, who have eaten them for thousands of years. It is difficult to secure absolute figures, but a study in northern Quebec a few years ago revealed that Cree communities from northern Quebec have an annual harvest of between 2,500 and 6,500 loons, primarily Common Loons (Desgranges and Laporte 1979). The study found that 90 percent were killed in the spring, generally during hunting expeditions for seal and waterfowl. Hunting at this time of year is doubly hard on loon populations since it kills adults that have successfully wintered just as they are about to breed.

The Canadian Wildlife Service team that conducted this study estimated that Cree harvest about 20 percent of the total population each year. They fear loon populations will not be able to sustain such a high level of hunting pressure and remain stable. They calculate the present population of the region to be about 12,000 pairs. If 20 percent are taken before breeding and the annual population increase is 25 percent, there would be a loss of about 4,800 adults and a gain of about 4,800 juveniles by fall. This seems to balance, and so not be reducing the population, but it does not take normal mortality into account. It does not include losses from oil spills, parasite burdens, old age, winter storms, toxic pollutants, and so forth. A population of 12,000 pairs in equilibrium would be expected to have an annual natural mortality rate of about 6,000 individuals, given a reproductive rate of 0.50 chicks per pair per year. It is easy to see that the loon population of the northern Quebec-James Bay region cannot remain stable under present hunting conditions.

Similar data are not available on the extent of hunting pressure in other parts of Canada. However, Cree across central Canada take loons. Inuits of northern Canada also hunt loons, though they take primarily Arctic, Yellow-billed, and Red-throated loons. There certainly is abundant evidence that loons are still intentionally killed, both for food and because they are considered a threat to fishermen. However, the impact of this form of mortality may be small when compared to other causes of people-related hazards.

Fishing and Loons

Loons get tangled in nets and monofilament line, and caught in fish traps. The number of water birds caught in discarded fishing gear will probably never be known. There have been several articles in the popular press implicating pelagic debris as a cause of death both for marine mammals and for birds. In the oceans it is considered a serious threat.

Such problems are not confined to the oceans. On lakes where commercial fishing occurs, loons are known to be captured and unable to free themselves from nets and traps. They also become entangled in the monofilament line used by sport fishermen, but the extent of mortality is difficult to assess because accidental drowning of individuals cannot be checked in the same way counts can be made from mortalities related to commercial fishing operations.

Serious threats to loons exist on the Great Lakes. Fish traps are set in Lake Superior and Lake Michigan, funnel traps into which loons are readily attracted by the fish that are already captured, but which they are unable to leave. Deep-set traps keep loons underwater, and they quickly drown. If traps are set near the surface, captured loons will continue to remain alive for a while, but traps are not checked every day. If loons are lucky enough to enter just before a check, they can be rescued; otherwise they eventually die.

Some progress is being made with commercial fishermen. Some have been cooperative with biologists seeking to monitor the nets and traps for entangled and captured loons, but many more are unwilling to engage in joint efforts or even to report numbers of loons caught and drowned. The problem is that loons cannot be easily freed, and to do so necessitates cutting the trap, causing expense to the fishermen.

Gill nets also pose a hazard. A count was taken between the last half of May and the first half of June in 1960 and 1961 for nets set in the Northwest Territories. Dead loons were tallied from nets near Big Island in Great Slave Lake. In just a few weeks, and in sets made near only one island, 5,662 loons were reported to have perished (Vermeer 1973a). They were primarily Red-throated and Yellow-billed loons, but all four North American species were included. There are similar fishing operations all across the loons' breeding range, and unreported and unpublished mortality can be assumed to occur over and over again. For example, Bartonek (1965) noted that Common Loons were among species lost to fishing nets on Lake Winnipegosis in southern Manitoba. On how many other lakes is this happening, but is never reported?

Loons are also caught in nets used during coastal fishing operations. Watermen from Chincoteague, Virginia, told me that from time to time, primarily on windy March days, they catch loons in their fishing nets. I asked them to notify me if they caught any loons so I could band and release them. If they were dead, I asked them to turn them over to me so they could be prepared as museum specimens. One day I returned to my apartment to find 13 dead loons on my doorstep, one Common and 12 Red-throated Loons.

Oil Spills

Damage to birds from oil spills throughout the world is enormous. It is estimated that avian mortality may run as high as 100,000 each year. The wreck of the oil tanker Torrey Canyon off the coast of Great Britain in 1967 caused the death of 40,000 seabirds (Dolensek and Bell 1977). This one accident brought the problem to the attention of the public, but 40,000 deaths is a high price to pay for notoriety. It spurred the establishment of private organizations seeking to rescue and rehabilitate oiled birds. This work continues and birds are released each year, but the success rate is extremely low. Oil continues to enter the oceans through tanker spills and offshore drilling accidents. Treatment methods have improved since the spills of the late 1960s and early 1970s, but oil still claims many waterbirds every year.

Oil spills are not a new problem. Reports of oiled birds and warnings about tankers and their impact on waterbirds were published over 60 years ago when oil tankers became common in a world quickly shifting to an oil-fueled economy. Hadley (1930) tells of oil so thick on coastal waters around Massachusetts that on a summer day in 1929 "they had to post a man at the Yacht Club landing to keep people from throwing lighted cigarettes and matches into the waters." A sampling of mortality in 1930 includes figures such as a "beach covered with dead and dying birds, more than 1000" on 25 February, and a report from another beach of 512 dead and oiled birds on 27 February (Hadley 1930). All accounts noted that a sizable number of victims were loons.

Oil spills have probably been happening for a long, long time. Dolensek and Bell (1977) remind us that between 2,000 and 3,000 years ago, Phoenician ships engaged in the transport of olive oil were often shipwrecked. The wooden Phoenician ships were fragile and vulnerable to heavy storms, and as they crashed against the rocks, their hulls split and their cargo, carried in pottery jars, oozed out across the Mediterranean.

Spills can also happen on inland waters. A coastal or marine situation isn't a requirement for oil problems. In 1977 a spill on the Hudson River caused the oiling of several thousand birds. Only 35 were saved following rehabilitation attempts. The St. Lawrence disaster of 1976 left an oil line along shoreline rocks which is still visible today; it caused the death of many birds and aquatic organisms. Both are river systems. The St. Lawrence is a shipping lane for oceanic vessels and the Hudson is partially a tidal river. In 1973 a pipeline break in Wyoming, far from the coast, sent oily water flowing into a nearby lake, causing the death of 5,000 to 10,000 waterfowl. No loons were involved, but the event demonstrates that the potential for spills is widespread. At some other time of year or in some other place, it could have been a loon disaster. Loons congregate at specific stopping places during migration, and an oil spill on one of their staging grounds could be disastrous.

Loons are particularly vulnerable to oil spills because their immediate reaction to danger is to dive. If warnings can be sounded in time, many other species of birds will respond by flying up and away from the potential oil threat. So far a method by which loons can be encouraged to fly away, rather than dive, has not been developed.

Environmental Pollutants

The tragic effects to wildlife resulting from toxic chemicals and heavy metals are amply documented and widely known. Populations of many top-of-the-chain predators have plummeted. The plight of Peregrine Falcons, Bald Eagles, Osprey, and Brown Pelicans has been the focus of hundreds of scientific papers as well as the mass media. Some of these species have been completely eradicated in parts of their former ranges and nearly wiped out in others. All were declared Endangered Species at one time or another.

Loons are also at the top of their food chain. Yet, little direct experimental testing has been done concerning the effects of pollutants on loons. Do chemicals that are the most threatening to eagles, osprey, and pelicans not affect loons in the same way? Or has there been too little research to determine how pollutants may affect loons?

Environmental pollutants can be assigned to one of several categories. Organochlorines, such as the DDT complex, are one form; heavy metals, such as lead, mercury, and selenium are another; and acid rain resulting from atmospheric pollution is a third. Chlorinated hydrocarbons, and particularly DDT, became widely used to control agricultural pests following World War II. Early indications of its effects on wildlife were noticed soon afterward. Robins began dying in Michigan after a DDT control program aimed at Dutch elm disease was put into effect, and George Wallace of Michigan State University was quick to monitor and report on the probable cause. Rachel Carson brought the problem to public attention with the publication of her book *Silent Spring* in 1962. By the late 1960s there was broad concern for what pesticides were doing to the environment. DDT and its metabolites are persistent in the environment, soluble in fat, and can be disseminated through both air and water.

Eggshell thinning was linked to DDT in England by Ratcliffe (1967) and in North America by Hickey et al. (1966). Eggshell thinning was shown to be responsible for declines in Peregrine Falcon, Osprey, Bald Eagle, and Brown Pelican populations, numbers of all dropping so rapidly there was concern they might become extinct.

Loon tissue was first examined in 1962 when Walter Breckenridge, then director of the Bell Museum of Natural History at the University of Minnesota, sent livers from two loons to the Wildlife Research Center in Denver. Levels of DDE, a product of DDT decomposition, were 12.5 ppm for one bird and 6.1 ppm for the other, not high enough to have caused the death of the birds. This seems low in comparison with levels averaging 75 ppm in Brown Pelican eggs (Lamont et al. 1970), 369 ppm in fat deposits of Peregrine Falcons in the Northwest Territories (Enderson and Berger 1968), and the exceedingly high levels found in Herring Gulls from Lake Michigan (1925 ppm from healthy adults collected in 1963–1964; Hickey et al. 1966).

Just because levels in loon tissue were lower than levels in other birds does not mean they could not have had adverse effects. Keith and Gruchy (1972) pointed out during the meeting of the 15th International Ornithological Congress that species do not all have the same response to equal levels of pollutant residues. For example, a 20-percent reduction in eggshell thickness occurs in American White Pelican eggs when DDE levels are about 12 ppm, but it must be 162 ppm before Herring Gull eggshells thin by 20 percent. Twenty percent is used as a critical point because when eggshells thin beyond that, incubating birds are likely to break them.

Examination of shell-thinning and pesticide levels in loon eggs suggested that a DDE level of about 47 ppm would induce 20-percent thinning. Tables 11-1 and 11-2 summarize the results of pollutant assays and shell measurements for more than 200 loons, and provide evidence they carried relatively low levels through the 1970s. Compared with shell thickness before the use of DDT (Anderson et al. 1970), there was an average thinning of less than 10 percent. This was a statistically significant value, but should not be considered biologically significant, since it did not reach the 20-percent critical point, and there was no evidence of shell breakage.

Several studies compared shell thinning with pesticide level. There is reason to believe that a negative relationship exists between DDE levels and eggshell thickness, although not all studies showed a significant correlation. Eggs with higher levels of DDE residues had thinner shells than did eggs with lower amounts of the DDT metabolites in most cases (Vermeer 1973b, McIntyre 1975, Sutcliffe 1978, Fox et al. 1980, Frank et al. 1983).

Chlorinated hydrocarbons produce other adverse effects on birds. The DDT complex has been implicated in reduced productivity through infertility and altered breeding behavior of the adults, and recently Fry and

Table 11–1. Pollutant Levels and Eggshell Thickness in the Eggs of
Common Loons across the Breeding Range

Study Area	N	Date	Pollutant Levels $\bar{x} \pm$ (SE), ppm			Source
			DDE	PCB	Hg	
New Hampshire	14	1975 1976	5.88(1.73)	18.3(4.8)		Sutcliffe 1978
	3	1974	4.76(0.14)	20.39(12.4)		McIntyre 1975
Ontario	4	1968	41.4			All data: Frank et al. 1983
	14	1969	8.6			
	34	1970	33.6	33.	0.92	
	15	1972	24.8	65.	1.11	
	12	1978	6.6	10.5	0.81	
	19	1979, 1980	3.98	6.1		
Minnesota	9	1970 1971 1972	4.99(0.8)	12.7(1.2)		McIntyre 1975
	5	1967	18.2(1.1)			Ream 1976
Saskatchewan	5	1969- 1973	10.88	17.58		Gilbertson and Reynolds 1974
	7	1974	6.28(1.6)	14.7(1.7)		McIntyre 1975
	31	1974, 1975	5.8(0.01)	14.1	0.35	Fox et al. 1980
Alberta	15	1973	1.7(0.01)	1.2(0.4)		Vermeer 1973b
	17	1969- 1973	1.51	1.09		Gilbertson and Reynolds 1974

Toone (1981) implicated it in the embryonic feminization of male birds. DDT induced abnormal development of ovarian tissue and oviducts in male gulls used in their study, and they suggested the skewed sex ratio in some western gull populations may have been caused by pollutants. The high pollutant load in California's coastal waters was thought to have been taken up by gulls breeding nearby. No one knows whether or not feminization has occurred during development of male Common Loon embryos. The gull study merely points out the potential for sexual abnormalities when chlorinated hydrocarbon uptake becomes severe, and demonstrates that even now, in the 1980s, we are still finding new side effects of environmental pollutants.

Table 11-2. A Comparison of Eggshell Thickness between Common Loon Eggs
Laid before Widespread Use of DDT and 25–30 Years Later

| Study Area | N | Date | $\bar{x} \pm$ (SE),mm | | Source |
			Recent	Pre-1947[a]	
New Hampshire	14	1975, 1976	0.59(0.05)	0.65(0.001)	Sutcliffe 1978
Ontario	14	1969	0.54(0.01)	0.63(0.01)	Frank et al.1983
Ontario	34	1970	0.58(0.01)	0.63(0.01)	
Minnesota	55	1970	0.55(0.01)	0.61(0.02)	McIntyre 1975
Saskatchewan	82	1974	0.60(0.01)	0.60(0.01)	Fox et al. 1980
Alberta	15	1973	0.57(0.01)	0.60(0.01)	Vermeer 1973b

[a]Anderson et al. 1970

Other chemicals in the environment have been released as crop sprays
or as the by-products of industry, among them dieldrin, aldrin, and PCBs.
Dieldrin delays breeding; aldrin and dieldrin both act synergistically with
DDT to compound its effects. Dieldrin increases the concentration of
DDT compounds stored in fat and blood. PCBs, too, have been implicated
as a cause of delayed breeding, enlarged kidneys, necrosis of the liver and
atrophy of the spleen, increased susceptibility to viral infection, and
decreased hatching. PCB, too, has a synergistic reaction with DDT, and
increases its retention time in the body.

No loon studies indicate changes in reproductive rate resulting from
these chemicals. Yonge (1981) monitored approximately 100 pairs of
loons for three years, and in the last year of his study, collected one egg
from each of 22 clutches. It was assumed there would not be a significant
difference in residue levels between eggs from the same clutch. These
eggs were analyzed for toxic residues; viability of the eggs remaining in
the nest followed, and it was found that there was no difference in hatching
success between eggs with high pesticide levels and those low in pesticide
residues (Fox et al. 1980). Productivity in Yonge's study area was about
0.55 young per pair, considered normal for healthy populations.

It is encouraging to note that in the past decade, levels of both DDT
and PCBs have become lower in avian tissue in general. This has been verified for songbirds, pelicans and falcons, and a recent paper confirms its
decline in loon tissue (Frank et al. 1983). The potential for trouble, however, may not be over. Stressed birds use up fat reserves, and in so doing
may inject themselves with a dose of deadly chemicals. Ten emaciated
loons were analyzed by Frank et al. They had an average of 20.5 mg/kg

DDT compounds in brain tissue; 13 healthy adults averaged only 0.83 mg/kg DDT. At times of stress, such as during winter storms, food shortages, or postmigratory fatigue, physiological response would be hindered by the inflow of toxins from fat metabolism. Fortunately, toxic materials are also eliminated through the uropygial gland, providing a way for some to be lost from the system.

Unfortunately, levels of heavy metals have not declined during the last decade. Several heavy metals are actual or potential hazards for birds. Lead poisoning was implicated as the cause of mortality for three loons that had ingested lead sinkers (Locke et al. 1982). Cadmium, lead, and mercury have all been shown to damage rods, but not cones, in the retina (Fox and Sillman 1979). This would be devastating for loons, visual predators relying primarily on their ability to see underwater.

Mercury is probably the most frightening of all the heavy-metal contaminants because it has become so widespread and its damage is irreversible. Toxic effects of mercury are familiar to us if we remember the Mad Hatter. He may have been a charming character on the pages of Alice in Wonderland, but he was not a product of an unusually vivid imagination, he was the caricature of a very real person. Hatters worked in the beaver hat industry in 19th-century England, and they frequently suffered mental abnormalities, that is, they went "mad." Mercury was used during the processing of beaver pelts, and its effects on workers were devastating to their neurological systems. Effects on loons are not very different.

Methylmercury is the toxic form, but most mercury enters the environment in another way (Fimreite 1970). Mercury cells are used during the production of chlorine and caustic soda in chlor-alkali plants, and the metal initially enters the aquatic systems as a waste product in its metallic form. Electric tension established by the difference in O^2-poor bottom layers quickly changes the mercury to an inorganic form, where microorganisms in bottom sediments of lakes and streams convert it to methylmercury.

Mercury is also used in its organic form as a fungicide for slime control in wood pulp plants. If the caustic soda used in pulp processing is also a product of a mercury cell, the plant will release a double dose of pollutant into the aquatic ecosystem. Another major pathway of entry into the environment is via agricultural seed treated with mercury. This problem has been noticed primarily through raptor mortality because raptors are the top predators of seed-eating animals in the prairie states and provinces. The problem doesn't end there, however, as everything eventually terminates in the aquatic system via runoff. Methylmercury is taken up directly by aquatic organisms. Fish may take it in through their gills, and it is easy for the mercury to get from fish to loons. Its association is with protein, rather than fat, and it concentrates in feathers, liver, and kidney tissue, with lower amounts in lung, heart, muscle, and brain, and still less in body fat (Frank et al. 1983).

In a study comparing mercury residues in loons, it was found that both total mercury and methylmercury levels were significantly higher in loons on contaminated lakes than from those living in relatively clean water (Barr 1986). Mercury was transferred from the female to the egg, and the developing embryo and chick contained very high levels. There was no indication that effective demethylation by the embryo occurred, and there was more mercury in the brains of newly hatched young than in the brains of their mothers (Barr 1986).

Birds with high mercury levels are affected by lack of motor coordination. Experimental studies with other birds showed that mercury causes difficulty in flying, walking, and eating (Fimreite and Karstad 1971). No experimental studies have been conducted on Common Loons, but lack of muscle coordination is a general effect of mercury loading, owing to its ability to break down the blood-brain barrier.

During the winter of 1983 there was a large die-off of Common Loons along the gulf coast of Florida (Alexander 1985). It was estimated that thousands died, and Alexander believes the number may be as high as 7,000 to 8,000. Extensive necropsies followed, seeking the cause of the mortality. Death resulted from hemorrhagic enteritis, or intestinal bleeding, probably caused by a high infestation of microphallid trematodes. The blue crab is the major intermediate host of this parasite, suggesting loons were feeding on crabs. This may have been the immediate cause of death, but it probably was not the real culprit. High mercury levels in many of the dead loons tested (Stroud and Lange 1983) gave a clue that parasites were there because something else may have been wrong. Loon dives were reported to be much shorter than normal, and the birds seemed incapable of staying underwater longer than 12 to 15 seconds at a time (Alexander, pers. comm.).

Nerve damage from methylmercury toxicity lowers hunting ability by reducing the fine honing that loon hunting skills must have to permit capture of swift-moving prey like fish. Lack of motor coordination combined with reduction of visual acuity may have forced them to feed on something easy to catch, such as crabs, which explains the trematode infestation. Dead and dying loons were extremely thin, some weighing less than one kilogram. Filled with parasites, weakened by starvation, and unable to feed, they could no longer hold up their heads, and they finally died by drowning.

Acid rain has been mentioned as a probable hazard to loons (LaBastille 1977). If severe acidification occurs, so that lakes are declared dead and have no living organisms left in them, loons traditionally holding territories on those lakes may go elsewhere. Eventually, if lake acidification accelerates, and living lakes are few, the impact on loons becomes obvious.

In the meantime, loons continue to return to traditional sites each summer, as their food can be secured from lakes other than the one where they nest. On acidified lakes of New York's Adirondack Park, parents feed aquatic insects and newts to their young in lieu of small fish (Parker 1985a). Young grow well for the first two to three weeks, then weaken and may die from lack of fish in their diets. Dulin (1987) also found that substitutes were being fed to Michigan chicks, but by the time young were three to four weeks old, they needed more and larger prey, principally fish. When there was plenty of food, both chicks were fed, but when there was a shortage, the dominant chick received all that was available, while the submissive sibling starved.

Alvo (1985) worked on Canadian lakes that were more highly acidified than those in the other studies. He found no productivity at all on the most severely affected lakes, and declared them truly dead. Schindler et al. (1985) reported an initial increase in total biomass in response to lake acidification. But, if acidification continues, the fish will go first, and eventually all biological organisms will succumb. Adult loons may continue to return to traditional lakes because they can forage elsewhere for themselves if they have to, but food for their young comes only from the lakes where they are raised. Parker (1985b) watched loons flying while carrying fish, but he never saw them feed them to their young. Even if they did, it is doubtful that Common Loons could, as a general practice, provide sufficient food to raise young to fledging if all food had to be secured elsewhere at high metabolic costs for the parents.

Acidification of water systems changes many chemical processes. It releases aluminum ions into the water, where they are taken up by fish through their gills. It increases the rate of release of mercury into the water column and permits faster uptake through the food chain. These kinds of chemical changes will have a longer and more lasting effect on loons than a shift in any specific food base will. It may be easy to stock lakes with low-pH-tolerant fish, but other changes may be more lasting as well as more insidious. Mercury accumulations are irreversible and eventually take their toll, and it may be that we have barely begun to witness this threat to loons.

Human impact comes in many forms. Loons can cope with some of it, because they are sufficiently flexible to alter some of their behavior in the face of moderate recreational pressures. They become accustomed to people and will continue to breed successfully even when their habitat must be shared wih humans. Simple consideration for their needs will suffice to protect them. They can adapt to artificial structures should all natural nest sites be taken by development. Environmental organochlorine levels have been lowered and may never have posed a direct threat to loons. Education can do much to prevent shooting and mortality from commercial fishing operations. Oil spills can be very severe but are localized. It is newer hazards that could spell doom for the loons. The threat of heavy metal pollution promoted by continuing lake acidification is widespread, irreversible, and deadly. We should not forget that the loons' water supply is also our water supply. Perhaps loons are to lakes and oceans what canaries once were to coal mines.

CHAPTER 12
A Caring World

At times people and wilderness seem to be at odds with each other. We are told that recreational needs can be met only at the expense of wildlife. We see conservationists pitted against economists. We hear of solutions to world problems of hunger and industrial growth on one side, while voices from the other side whisper to us, "Make a choice, a prosperous world or a natural one, you can't have both." Does this have to be? Can the magic of our northern wilderness last when we make ourselves part of it?

Loons are considered indicators of wilderness, and many authors have used poetic phrases to describe them. In 1949 Breckenridge stated that "loons put the stamp of genuineness on a North Country setting like 'Sterling' does on silver." Brewster (1924) wrote of their "plaintive, long-drawn calls and weird, quavering laughter, decidedly the most thrilling and delightful of all the voices of the northern wilderness." Others link loons and wilderness even more closely: "Of all the wild creatures that persist in New England, the loons seem best to typify the untamed savagery of the wilderness" (Forbush 1912). Norton (1915) referred to loons as the "incarnation of the spirit of the wilderness-waters." The best-known American naturalist-writer, Henry David Thoreau, spoke of loons several times, saying, for example: "The loon came, making the woods ring with his wild laughter" (1832). Another widely known author, Arthur Cleveland Bent, mentioned the "weird and mournful cry of the loon . . . what would the wilderness be without it?" (1919).

Several recent studies have assessed the present condition of wilderness by measuring the health and stability of Common Loon populations (Smith 1981, Titus and Van Druff 1981, Alvo 1985, Parker 1985). This research has been based on the assumption that loons can be equated with wilderness, and that measurements of reproductive success by loon pairs can be used to measure the quality of their habitat.

Another popular notion is that wilderness is a place without people. By definition, portions of the Adirondack Park in New York designated *wilderness* are "areas where the earth and its community of life are untrammeled by man, where man himself is a visitor who does not remain." Furthermore, wilderness lands in the park are permitted no permanent human habitation, so that from the meanest and oldest of trapper's huts to the grandest of the Great Camps, all structures on designated lands must be torn down or burned so that no human trace remains.

If wilderness is by definition a place where people don't live, and if loons epitomize that wilderness, is it possible that people and loons can live side by side? It would seem not, but a growing body of evidence says they can. With time and care, humans and loons can fish the same lakes, children and loon chicks can swim the same waters, and a loon pair can defend its territory against conspecific intruders, while nearby on the shore, landowners can erect fences to define their territorial boundaries. The key question seems to be a simple one with a complex answer: How?

There is great public interest in loons. Loons are exciting. Their calls provide the background music for the mystery and excitement of northern lake country and they are large and easy to watch, all qualities that are inducements for public enjoyment. People become possessive about loons. They go to their cottages on their lakes, and they listen to "their" loons. It is a simple progression from listening to watching, then to monitoring and recording what the loons are doing and how they are doing it, and finally to protecting the birds and introducing neighbors and friends to the wonder and excitement of loons.

Public participation in loon surveys began in 1970 in Minnesota and New Hampshire. Simultaneously, yet independently, requests for public assistance were made. I had conducted field studies for my doctoral dissertation that summer, and Jim Kimball, then a columnist with the *Minneapolis Star*, wrote about my work with loons in one of his Sunday columns. At the end of the article he suggested that readers who wanted to help ferret out information about the state bird could volunteer to monitor loons on lakes of their choosing. They were asked to write and name the lakes for which they would assume responsibility.

Hundreds of letters poured in. Some were addressed to the Loon Project, and others were sent simply to The Loon Lady, University of Minnesota. More than 400 letters arrived during the first month, and more came later, eventually to form a volunteer crew of over a thousand. This became Minnesota's Project Loon Watch, which continued its work by surveying state lakes from 1971 to 1979, and again in 1982 and 1983. Respondents answered questions about time of loon arrival in the spring, whether or not loons were in residence during the summer on a particular lake, and how many young they raised.

In 1979, Minnesota's Department of Natural Resources began its own loon survey, the Common Loon Observation Program. The program was aimed at surveying state lakes with the help of DNR personnel, as well as federal natural-resource staff, resort owners, conservation organizations, and private individuals. Support came from Nongame Wildlife Checkoff funds on tax returns. Today, results from the combined surveys indicate a stable population in Minnesota, with an estimated 10,000 adults spending the summer on Minnesota lakes and raising about 4,000 young each year.

In 1986, during the 25th anniversary of the designation of the Common Loon as Minnesota's state bird, and 15 years after the first Project Loon Watch survey, we joined forces in a combined effort to recheck all the 324 lakes that were reported during that first effort. The program, called Love a Loon Watch, permitted an assessment of population stability over a 15-year period when recreational lake use and summer home development had mushroomed (McIntyre 1988).

Minnesota's DNR designed a program to teach grade-school children about loons. Carrol Henderson is director of the Nongame Program in the state. Henderson expects that it will have traveled to every grade school in Minnesota and been incorporated into the studies of thousands of children before 1990. Another success is the loon-banding program. More than 150 loons have been banded by Minnesota DNR personnel in the last five years, nearly as many as by all other banders combined. Valuable information has already been forthcoming, and will continue to give answers to some of the many questions about loons.

Something similar was happening in the early 1970s in the eastern part of the country. At one time, loon sounds echoed across the many lakes of New Hampshire, bouncing off the surrounding mountains and hills and answering the roll call of an abundant loon population. But by the late 1960s, people noticed fewer and fewer loons. Lake Winnipesaukee formerly had dozens of loon pairs, reduced to a handful by 1970, with fewer than a dozen chicks raised there each summer. Squam Lake, familiar for its role as the setting for the movie, *On Golden Pond*, still had several loon pairs, but was becoming busy with recreational boaters. Lake residents began to voice their concerns and this turned to action as the Squam Lake Association surveyed the lake for loons each summer from 1971 to 1975.

The Audubon Society of New Hampshire picked up the momentum and carried it forward to form the New Hampshire Loon Preservation Committee in 1975. Surveys were expanded to include the entire state, wildlife students were hired as Loon Rangers to patrol the lakes during the summer, public education programs were begun, and the first loon-management program in the country was started. By 1985 the Loon Preservation Committee had helped the state loon population grow from 200 adult birds to more than 300. Residents watched as new territories were claimed on additional lakes, and they cheered as the number of fledged young doubled during the decade.

More than a thousand volunteers now help with the New Hampshire program, which employs five full-time biologists during the summer to build artificial nesting platforms, protect nesting adults and small chicks, and monitor the growing population. Each nest site is protected, with warning signs posted near each, and chicks are guarded from human disturbance. Funds have been raised to buy critical habitat, provide advice on water-level regulations, and distribute information to the public. In 1979 the Loon Preservation Committee was instrumental in securing placement of the Common Loon on the state list of threatened species.

The annual culmination is the August Loon Festival at the Bald Peak Colony Club on the shores of Lake Winnipesaukee, where enthusiasm and interest dictate that tickets must be purchased weeks in advance to assure an opportunity to attend. Recognition came in 1985 when the National Wildlife Federation presented the Loon Preservation Committee with a well-deserved honor, the President's Award for exceptional community achievement.

During the 1970s, several other groups were formed. State agencies added their personnel and assistance in some cases, and initiated efforts in others. By 1977, loon programs in Minnesota and New Hampshire had been joined by others in Maine and New York, and in the fall, Wisconsin and Vermont began their plans for loons.

Maine's Loon Protection and Research Project started in 1977 as a joint effort by the Maine Department of Inland Fisheries and Wildlife and the Maine Audubon Society. In 1983 the University of Maine at Orono became a cooperative participant in what is now a joint project combining a conservation organization, a state agency, and a university. In addition to summer-long monitoring of loon lakes by the 800–1,000 volunteers and 20 regional coordinators, Maine Audubon initiated a one-day survey including simultaneous aerial/ground coverage of randomly selected lakes. So giant and popular is this event that it made front-page news in 1983 when *USA Today* announced the upcoming survey in a story on page one.

Maine's governor proclaimed an annual Loon Day during which loon programs, loon T-shirts, loon memorabilia, and general loonmania take over. Public-education efforts include slide presentations throughout the state, 30-second public service announcements on TV, as well as distribution of written information such as newsletters, articles, and loon posters. Maine volunteers also conduct a one-day, coastal count on Lincoln's Birthday, with a March and April follow-up to assess the wintering population. The count covers virtually the entire coastline of Maine, and that's quite a feat! Much credit is owed to Jane Arbuckle from the Maine Audubon Society, who has been the guiding hand throughout the program.

And, it is exciting that Massachusetts has loons again! Loons had been extirpated for almost a century after being common residents at one time, as the writings of Thoreau testify. Then, in the early 1970s, loons were noticed again in Massachusetts. The Quabbin Reservoir, recently created, provided excellent loon habitat, and breeding was confirmed in 1975 (Clarke 1975).

Public interest was soon aroused, and the Massachusetts Audubon Society, in cooperation with the metropolitan District Water Supply Commission and the state's Division of Fisheries and Wildlife, have an active program in force. They have added a biologist to monitor the loons' progress, to build artificial platforms in some locations where there is no suitable nesting habitat, and to patrol the reservoir. At this time there is not a volunteer survey program, but Paul Lyons has been doing a wonderful job as the loon biologist. All Massachusetts loons had been nesting on the Quabbin until 1984, when a second reservoir attracted a new nesting pair. By l987 loons occupied five reservoirs or lakes (Blodget and Lyons 1988). It is hoped that this signals the addition of still more loon pairs to other lakes and reservoirs in the state, and perhaps one day a volunteer organization will be needed.

The Vermont Institute of Natural Science (VINS) took responsibility in 1977 for a program concerned with state loons. Sarah Laughlin, director of VINS, has spearheaded the program from its inception. With a network of environmentally concerned citizens, the addition of a staff member to serve as the coordinator, and assistance from the Vermont Fish and Game Department, participants are able to monitor all state lakes and provide figures about the state's population.

Over the past 10 years this population has ranged between 32 and 68 loons (Rimmer 1988). Fluctuating water levels on several Vermont lakes have caused difficulties for some nesting loons, and the Vermont Loon Project has built artificial nesting islands, focused attention on discussing problems with dam owners, and negotiated drawdown plans to include consideration for nesting loons. Slide shows and talks are given throughout the year. In 1983 an annual Vermont Loon Watch Day was begun.

After I moved to New York in 1977, I started a Project Loon Watch based on the Minnesota project. Volunteer participants began annual monitoring of lakes to check on the presence of loons, reproductive success or failure, and recreational use and shoreline development. With grants from the National Audubon Society and a contract with the New York Department of Environmental Conservation, two graduate students conducted a survey of most Adirondack lakes larger than 10 hectares in 1977 and 1978 (Trivelpiece et al. 1979). This information, added to volunteer surveys, formed a broad base for long-term studies. New York's Department of Environmental Conservation initiated a program of surveys during 1979 and 1984–1985 designed as a five-year check on the status of loon populations, work which has been funded under Gift to Wildlife, the tax check-off program. The Adirondack Council, a conservation group, added its support in 1982 and 1983, and the following year Audubon Society's New York field office coordinated a public volunteer program, summarized by Parker and Miller (1988).

Surveys were made in the Hiawatha National Forest of Michigan during the early 1970s through the efforts of biologists Charlotte and William Taylor. Concern was expressed when it was learned that only a few pairs remained where many had formerly nested. Taylor later found that many loons were being entangled in fishing nets or were caught and drowned in fish traps on waters of the Great Lakes adjacent to the Upper Peninsula. He brought it to public attention, and solutions are finally being sought to provide fish-trapping methods that do not endanger loons.

Project Loon Watch was launched by Michael Hamas at the annual meeting of the Michigan Audubon Society in 1978. Volunteers were asked to participate in a survey of state lakes. Although it was never a widely subscribed effort, it provided valuable information on locations of nesting sites in Michigan. For example, the survey found that the southernmost breeding of Common Loons anywhere in North America was in the southwestern part of Michigan. Nesting had not been confirmed there for years, but with the help of citizen surveys, a nesting pair was located.

The Endangered Species Unit of Michigan's Department of Natural Resources pulled together both governmental and individual survey efforts in 1981. Surveys have concentrated on the Upper Peninsula and were begun on lakes of the Lower Peninsula in 1985. The following year, Michigan's chapter of The Nature Conservancy sponsored a public survey program. Interest is now high, bolstered by media coverage of the Great Lakes loon mortality. It is now hoped that the loons caught by fishing nets can be identified. Are they Michigan breeders, are they migrants, moving through the Great Lakes on their way north, or are they young nonbreeding individuals?

The migration program at Whitefish Point Bird Observatory has included a loon migration segment since 1982. Under the initiative of David Ewert, careful counts showed a major loon flyway over the Great Lakes just at that location, with loons moving northward across Michigan and continuing to Canadian breeding grounds. In 1985, auxiliary surveys were made at other locations around Lakes Huron and Michigan from late April to early May to see if there was a broad and general flight moving over the Great Lakes. The findings were negative; loons funnel only past Whitefish Point, and in 1985, more than 5,000 moved along a relatively narrow pathway. During the same period, only 37 loons were counted at other monitoring sites.

Another Project Loon Watch began in Wisconsin in 1977 as a program of the Sigurd Olson Environmental Institute at Northland College in Ashland. Sigurd T. Olson authored the first monograph on Common Loons, based on his master's thesis research (Olson and Marshall 1952), and it is fitting that Wisconsin's loon program is administered by the facility named for his father, well-known author and wilderness advocate Sigurd F. Olson.

More than 700 volunteers presently assist with the survey efforts. One volunteer, Grace James, has probably done more than anyone to inject enthusiasm into Wisconsin's loon work. Paul Strong is now the full-time director of the Loon Project, which focuses primarily on public-education programs and coordination of a network of volunteers. Wisconsin's DNR staff, biologists from the U.S. Forest Service, and U.S. Fish and Wildife Service personnel cooperate with the Sigurd Olson Institute on survey work. Nearly half the state's 2,200 lakes have been surveyed, and the estimated loon population is currently between 2,000 and 3,000 adults.

Involvement of the western states is the most recent. Montana was the first, and Donald Skaar, with only one assistant and a few observers, has managed to cover nearly all sectors of the state where suitable habitat is found. At his instigation, a public support group was formed in 1985. During the spring of 1985, Rawson Wood, chairman of the North American Loon Fund, pulled together a special loon meeting in Seattle, including participants from Montana, Idaho, and Washington. The addition of enthusiastic help from the western states is an encouraging sign that soon the status of loons in that part of the breeding range will be better known.

One group deserves recognition for its determination and perseverance in spite of a depauperate loon population. In the state of Washington, two pairs of breeding loons have been confirmed. Loon Lake is not one of those places. In spite of that, a group of 130 loon lovers organized themselves as the Loon Lake Loon Association. They are determined to bring the loons back to Loon Lake and are launching an effort to lure them by artificial islands or by whatever means they can. They even have an annual Loon Festival, replete with an assortment of loon paraphernalia, and many, many enthusiastic Loon Lake looners.

Long Point Bird Observatory, located on the shores of Lake Erie in Ontario, began the first Canadian volunteer survey. In addition to enlisting public participation in surveys, Long Point has spawned research projects, and in particular, studies looking at the effects of acid rain on loons. A recently completed master's thesis that provided important data on lake acidification and loons was begun under the auspices of the loon program of Long Point Bird Observatory loon program (Alvo 1985). McNicholl (1988) summarized problems and conservation efforts across Canada at the 1987 North American Loon Conference.

Common Loons have been given special status in several states. In New York and Massachusetts they are identified as Species of Special Concern; in Vermont, New Hampshire, and Michigan they are designated as Threatened Species. Fortunately, in some states, such as Minnesota, the loon population remains healthy and there is no need for their inclusion on special lists. Recent population growth in New York and New Hampshire offers hope. The return of loons to Massachusetts after so many years is exciting indeed. Something good may be in the wind.

Techniques for saving and protecting loons have included management of both habitat and people. I had used artificial nesting islands to examine the role of islands in selection of territories and nesting success. Later I used them to position loons where they could be easily observed during behavioral studies. The Loon Preservation Committee of New Hampshire adopted artificial nesting islands to use in managing loon populations. They have built artificial islands for many years now, and they credit them with increased productivity among New Hampshire loons. With the use of islands, loon biologists were able to move the birds away from traditional nest sites located in the path of boat routes or adjacent to summer cottages. They could lure loons to places free from human disturbance, and at the same time provide them with platforms that would go up and down with fluctuating water levels and not be subjected to flooding or water drawdowns (Fair 1979).

Islands can be made in several ways. Plate 10 shows both those made from logs and those made from sections of sedge mat. In Minnesota my husband and I cut pieces of sedge mat about half a meter thick by using an old-fashioned hay saw. We pushed the one- to four-square-meter segments into the lake, where we anchored them in water about two meters deep. Small, light logs were placed on each side, corners were wired together, and small concrete blocks were dropped off diagonally opposing corners by lead lines slightly longer than the water depth. That way, as water levels rose after a rain, the island rose higher with it, and the nest was not flooded. If no sedge mat was available, we made small rafts of cedar logs and filled the center with vegetation.

In New Hampshire, artificial structures were modified and designed to be used whether or not sedge mat was available. They are made with a log frame and a wire-mesh covering for the bottom, and are then filled with large clumps of growing vegetation. These have proved successful in many places, and plans for making them are available by writing to the North American Loon Fund.

Other effective management tools include informational posters at boat landings telling about loon requirements, modification of water-level regulations on dammed lakes, and patrolling near nests and nurseries. New Hampshire has had particularly good results with its management program. Educational posters there have been highly successful, and Loon Rangers are well received when they speak individually with lake residents and campers. People often think the runs and calls that loons exhibit are exciting and they encourage them so they can watch. When they realize this is stressful to the loons and potentially hazardous to the young, they are happy to cooperate.

One of the most effective management procedures is to establish a one-on-one relationship with property owners near loon nests. They can be unbelievably cooperative when they are made aware of loon needs during the breeding cycle. I sometimes think we are too timid in making suggestions and requests to people. I have yet to encounter a fishing boat, casting in the vicinity of a loon nest, whose occupants were not willing to move when it was pointed out they were keeping the incubating birds off their nest.

The Loon Rangers of New Hampshire and forest rangers of New York have also found that people are happy to make adjustments where loons are concerned. I have spoken frequently about this with Terry Perkins, Adirondack Park ranger. He and his assistants contact every camper in person, they position campsites away from loon nest sites, and they find that people are interested in loons and happy to cooperate. Many lakes throughout loon country have lake owners associations, and they, as well as sportsmen's clubs, Audubon chapters, and conservation organizations, have formed groups whose members patrol lakes, guard loons, and speak with boaters.

Other than providing nesting islands for loons, most loon management has been people management. There are some lakes with shorelines altered by manicured lawns and rock walls, so that all natural nesting habitat is gone. But on most lakes, it is not the physical characteristics of the lake which have changed, it is the intensity of recreational use by people. Loons can tolerate some disturbance as long as consideration is given to their need for some privacy in which to nest and raise their young.

Loons swim near docks, and their curiosity causes them to circle around camps and cottages, checking, looking, observing. Some may even swim under and around anchored fishing boats. I have occasionally seen them sitting quietly on nests close to boat channels, only their heads moving from side to side as they watch the boats pass by. And very rarely, I have shared swimming space with a loon. Even with growing tolerance, there are some forms of disturbance with which they cannot cope. These include intentional chasing, continual and repeated intrusion at their nests, forcing them to display in defense of small chicks, unnaturally fluctuating water levels during nesting, and increasing water turbidity so they can no longer see their prey. If loons are given clean water, nest sites, nonfluctuating water levels, or artificial structures that rise and fall with the water, and if they are left alone while they are nesting and raising small chicks, they will be successful and continue to give wilderness quality to northern lakes.

In 1975 the Canadian Wildlife Service invited half a dozen loon biologists to Ottawa for a meeting designed to focus on common problems and to coordinate efforts to solve them. It was the beginning of communication which a decade later is more active than ever. In 1977 I coordinated a conference on Common Loon research and management in Adirondack Park, sponsored by the National Audubon Society and Syracuse University. Seven research papers were presented and reports on loon surveys were made by participants representing 10 regions. At that time the only management program was being conducted by the Loon Preservation Committee of New Hampshire, and the group shared its predator-control program and lake-restriction attempts with us. Biologists from state agencies and the U.S. Fish and Wildlife Service attended the conference and contributed to discussions aimed at expanded and coordinated efforts.

I again coordinated the North American Loon Conference at Syracuse University in January 1979. By this time, the meeting had expanded to include 44 participants, and was organized into sections devoted to research, state surveys, government agency reports, and management and public-education programs. The U.S. Fish and Wildlife Service joined the National Audubon Society in funding the meeting, and the Audubon Society published the proceedings (Sutcliffe 1979). In addition to the presented papers and reports, a five-year management plan was inaugurated. The comprehensive plan defined the primary concern as restoration of stable breeding populations in the northeastern and Great Lakes states. Goals included reducing human-caused mortality, increasing productivity, identifying critical loon habitat, and enlisting public support and cooperation (Plunkett 1979). Increasing resident loon populations in several northeastern states and good productivity in most of them attest to the success of the program. However, there is still a long way to go, and several puzzles remain unsolved, such as age at first breeding and duration of pair bonding.

Another goal of the second conference was to form some kind of visible coordinating organization, to allow for overall unification of studies, and to provide a central place to which questions could be addressed and from which information could be disseminated. At the instigation of Rawson Wood of New Hampshire, the North American Loon Fund was formed and incorporated in 1979. It serves as the umbrella organization for all other loon programs in North America and now has, in addition to individual members, organizational members from 12 states. Its Board of Trustees meets twice each year, and is responsible for the evaluation of proposals for funding research and educational projects, and for decisions on the activities of the Loon Fund. The group represents over 5,000 members of loon support groups in the United States and Canada.

Funds are raised from contributions, from the sale of a variety of loon artifacts, and from the sale of the record, "Voices of the Loon." The record was a joint effort of the North American Loon Fund and the National Audubon Society. William Barklow supplied recordings from his doctoral study and Robert J. Lurtsema lent his voice. To date the Loon Fund has awarded more than $70,000 toward research and educational programs. In addition, an endowed fund provides an annual grant of $1000 to a graduate student for a loon-related research project. Smaller research grants have been given to other researchers studying a diversity of topics on loon biology and behavior, and funds have also been made available to state survey programs. Plans are to continue funding research, management and public-education programs.

A list is available of each state and province with an active loon program and the contact person for each. If you are interested in finding out how to contact the loon program where you live or where you spend your summers, you may write to:

North American Loon Fund
Main Street, Humiston Building
Meredith, New Hampshire 03253

So, within the last 15 years, loons have captured more than public interest. They have aroused public concern, and they have spawned survey and research work, educational programs, and public support groups. Most of these efforts have focused on loons at their summer breeding grounds, and studies of their wintering and migratory biology have just begun. Die-offs continue, perhaps precipitated by a polluted and poisoned environment, and much work is yet to be accomplished.

The initial question posed at the beginning of this book asked whether or not there would be loons for our children and grandchildren to enjoy. Loons have been here for a long time. They have shared their world with us. Now it is up to us, with care and caring, to share our world with them. "Once upon a time there was a loon . . . "

APPENDIXES

APPENDIX 1
Conversion of Metric Units

Metric Unit	U.S. Equivalent
1 centimeter	.394 inches
1 meter	3.279 feet
	1.094 yards
1 kilometer	.622 miles
1 hectare	2.471 acres
1 gram	.035 ounces
	.002 pounds
1 kilogram	2.203 pounds

U.S. Unit	Metric Equivalent
1 inch	2.540 centimeters
1 foot	.305 meters
1 yard	.914 meters
1 mile	1.609 kilometers
1 acre	.4047 hectares
1 ounce	28.35 grams
1 pound	453.6 grams
1 pound	.454 kilograms

APPENDIX 2
Scientific Names of Animals Used in the Text

Common Name	Scientific Name
Crustaceans	
crayfish	*Decapoda*
blue crab	*Callinectes sapidus*
Insects	
caddis flies	*Trichoptera*
Fish	
sea lamprey	*Petromyzon marinus*
trout	*Salmonidae*
alewife	*Alosa pseudoharengus*
whitefish	*Coregonus* sp.
cisco	*Coregonus artedi*
smelt	*Osmerus esperlanus*
lake chub	*Couesius plumbeus*
emerald shiner	*Notropis atherinoides*
white sucker	*Catostomus commersoni*
bullhead	*Ictalurus nebulosus*
mudminnow	*Umbra limi*
northern pike	*Esox lucius*
muskellunge	*Esox masquinongy*
flounder	*Pleuronectoidei*

Fish (continued)

yellow perch	*Perca flavescens*
mottled sculpin	*Cottus bairdi*

Birds

Red-throated Loon	*Gavia stellata*
Arctic Loon	*Gavia arctica*
Pacific Loon	*Gavia pacifica*
Common Loon	*Gavia immer*
Yellow-billed Loon	*Gavia adamsii*
Pied-billed Grebe	*Podilymbus podiceps*
American White Pelican	*Pelecanus erythrorhynchos*
Brown Pelican	*Pelecanus occidentalis*
Canada Goose	*Branta canadensis*
Mallard	*Anas platyrhynchos*
Ring-necked Duck	*Aythya collaris*
Spectacled Eider	*Somateria fischeri*
Common Merganser	*Mergus merganser*
Osprey	*Pandion haliaetus*
Bald Eagle	*Haliaetus leucocephalus*
Peregrine Falcon	*Falco peregrinus*
Ring-billed Gull	*Larus delawarensis*
Herring Gull	*Larus argentatus*
Common Tern	*Sterna hirundo*
American Crow	*Corvus brachyrhynchos*
Common Raven	*Corvus corax*
American Robin	*Turdus migratorius*

Mammals

beaver	*Castor canadensis*
wolf	*Canis lupus*
fox	*Vulpes vulpes*
raccoon	*Procyon lotor*
mink	*Mustela vison*
otter	*Lutra canadensis*
muskrat	*Ondatra zibethicus*
skunk	*Mephitis mephitis*

APPENDIX 3

Parasites Described for Common Loons

Parasite	Source
Cestodes	
Choanotaenia ransomi	Linton 1927
Hymenolepis capillaris	Ransom 1909
H. fuhrmanni	Linton 1927
H. pseudorostellata	Joyeaux and Baer 1950
Ligula intestinalis	Beverley-Burton 1964
Neovalipora parvispine	Linton 1927, Ransom 1909
Schistocephalus solidus	Baer 1962
Tetrabothrius macrocephalus	Ransom 1909, Linton 1927
T. immerrinus	Beverley-Burton 1964
Valipora parvispine	Linton 1927
Trematodes	
Amphimerus lintoni	Linton 1928
Apophallus brevis	Miller 1942
A. itascensis	Warren 1953
Cotylurus erraticus	Dubois and Bausch 1967
Cryptocotyle lingua	Linton 1928
Dasia fodiens	Linton 1928
Diplostomum gavium	Dubois and Rausch 1967
D. immer	Dubois and Rausch 1967
Echinostoma revolutum	Beverley-Burton 1961

Trematodes (continued)

E. sphinolosum	Gilbert 1905
Erschoviaorchis lintoni	Skrjabin 1945
Haematotrephus fodienst	Linton 1928
Hemistomum gavium	Guberlet 1922
Psilostomum varium	Linton 1928
Streigea aquavis	Guberlet 1922
S. gavium	Guberlet 1922
Tocotrema lingua	Linton 1915

Acanthocephalans

Polymorphus gavii	Khokhlova 1965

Nematodes

Ascaris spp.	Fantham and Porter 1948
Splendidofilaria fallisensis	Anderson and Forrester 1974
Streptocara crassicauda	
lonspiculata	Gibson 1968

Mallophagians

Menopon tridens	Kellogg and Paine 1911
Philopterus graviceps	Peters 1936

Mastigophora

Trichomonas eberthi	Fantham and Porter 1948

Unknown Classification

Carspedoniumus immer	Emerson 1955, Brelik and Tovornik 1962
Drepanotaenia lanceolata	Fantham and Porter 1948
Mesorchis pseudoechinatus	Linton 1928
Pseudalfersia fumipennis	Johnson 1922
Hemistomum gavium	Guberlet 1922

REFERENCES

References

Abraham, K. F. 1978. Adoption of Spectacled Eider ducklings by Arctic Loons. Condor 80:339–340.

Alexander, G. R. 1977. Food of vertebrate predators on trout waters in North Central Lower Michigan. Mich. Academician 10:191–195.

Alexander, L. L. 1985. Trouble with loons. Living Bird Quart. 4:10–13.

Alvo, R. 1981. Marsh nesting of Common Loons (*Gavia immer*). Can. Field Nat. 95:357.

Alvo, R. 1985. The breeding success of Common Loons (*Gavia immer*) in relation to lake acidity. MS thesis, Trent University, Peterborough, Ontario.

American Ornithologists' Union. 1985. Thirty-fifth supplement to the *American Ornithologists' Union Check-list of North American Birds*. Auk 102:680–686.

Anderson, D. W., H. G. Lumsden, and J. J. Hickey. 1970. Geographical variation in the eggshells of Common Loons. Can. Field-Nat. 84:351–356.

Anderson, R. C. and D. J. Forster. 1974. *Splendidofilaria fallisensis* (Nematoda) in the Common Loon, *Gavia immer* (Brunnich). Can. J. Zool. 52:547–548.

Anonymous. 1985. Wisconsin Project Loon Watch 1985. Annual Report, Sigurd Olson Environmental Institute, Ashland, Wis.

Anonymous. 1986. Vermont Common Loon project. Report to the North American Loon Fund, Meredith, N.H.

Arbib, R. S. 1963. The Common Loon in New York State. Kingbird 13:132–140.

Arbuckle, J. and M. Lee. 1985. 1985 Maine loon count: aerial and ground methodology and results. Maine Audubon Society.

Armstrong, E. A. 1970a. Diver. In: Man, myth and magic. Vol. 5. M. Cavendish (ed). Marshall Cavendish Corp., New York. pp. 2836–2837.

Armstrong, E. A. 1970b. Thunderbird. In: Men, myth and magic. Vol. 21. R. Cavendish (ed). Michael Cavendish Corp., New York. pp. 2836–2837.

Armstrong, E. 1970c. The folklore of birds. Dover Publications, New York. pp. 62–70, 90.

Ashenden, J. E. The Ontario lakes loon survey . . . status report. In: P. Strong (ed.), Papers from 1987 Conf. Loon Res. Mgmt. North American Loon Fund, Meredith, N.H. pp. 185–195.

Austin, O. L. Jr. and N. Kuroda. 1953. The birds of Japan: their status and distribution. Bull Mus. Comp. Zool. Harvard University. 109: 290–294.

Baer, J. G. 1962. Cestoda. Zool. Iceland 2:1–63.

Barklow, W. E. 1979a. Graded frequency variations of the tremolo call of the Common Loon (*Gavia immer*). Condor 81:53–64.

Barklow, W. E. 1979b. Tremolo variations and their use in duetting and distraction displays of the Common Loon. In: The Common Loon, Proceed. 2nd N.A. Conf. Common Loon Res. and Manage. S. Sutcliffe (ed). National Audubon Society. Pp. 23–44.

Barr, J. F. 1973. Feeding biology of the Common Loon (*Gavia immer*) in oligotrophic lakes of the Canadian shield. Unpubl. PhD thesis, University of Guelph, Ontario.

Barr. J. F. 1979. Ecology of the Common Loon in a contaminated watershed. In: The Common Loon, Proceed. 2nd N.A. Conf. Common Loon Res. and Manage. S. Sutcliffe (ed). National Audubon Society. Pp. 65–69

Barr, J. F. 1986. Population dynamics of the Common Loon (*Gavia immer*) associated with mercury-contaminated waters in northwestern Ontario. Occas. Paper No. 56, Canadian Wildlife Service.

Bartonek, J. C. 1965. Mortality of diving ducks on Lake Winnipegosis. Can. Field-Nat. 79:15–20.

Becker, P. H. 1982. The coding of species-specific characteristics in bird sounds. In: Acoustic communication in birds. Vol. I. D. E. Kroodsma and E. H. Miller (eds). Academic Press, New York. Pp. 213–252.

Bemister, M. 1973. Thirty Indian legends of Canada. J. J. Douglas, Vancouver, Columbia. Pp. 103–107.

Bent, A. C. 1919. Life histories of North American diving birds. Smithsonian Institution United States National Museum, Bulletin 107, U. S. Government Printing Office, Washington, D.C. Pp. 47–60.

Beverly-Burton , M. 1961. Studies on the Trematoda of British freshwater birds. Proceed. Zool. Soc. London 137:13–39.

Beverly-Burton, M. 1964. Studies of the Cestoda of British freshwater birds. Proceed. Zool. Soc. London. 142:307–346.

Black, C. T. 1935. Common Loon in Illinois in July. Auk 52:74.

Black, T. L. 1976. Parent-chick behavior from hatching to 13 days old in the Common Loon (*Gavia immer*). Report, Lake Itasca Biology Session, University of Minnesota.

Blodget, B. and P. Lyons. 1988. The recolonization of Massachusetts by Common Loons. In: P. Strong (ed.), Papers from 1987 Conf. Loon Res. Mgmt. North American Loon Fund, Meredith, N.H. pp. 177–184.

Bowman, R. I. 1979. Adaptive morphology of song dialects in Darwin's Finches. J. Orn. 120:353–389.

Boyle, W. J., R. O. Paxton, and D. A. Cutler. 1979. The autumn migration: Hudson-Delaware Region. American Birds 33:159–163.

Boyle, W. J., R. O. Paxton, and D. A. Cutler. 1980. The autumn migration: Hudson-Delaware Region. American Birds 34:143–147.

Boyle, W. J., R. O. Paxton, and D. A. Cutler. 1982. The autumn migration: Hudson-Delaware Region. American Birds 36:157–161.

Brand, C. U., R. M. Duncan, S. P. Garrow, D. Olson, and L. E. Schumann. 1983. Waterbird mortality from botulism Type E in Lake Michigan: an update. Wilson Bull. 95:269–275.

Breckenridge, W. J. 1949. Birds of the Canadian border lakes. Pres. Quetico-Superior Committee, Chicago.

Brewster, W. 1924. The loon on Lake Umbagog. Bird-lore 26:309–315.

Brodkorb, P. 1953a. Subspecific status of the Common Loon in Florida. Wilson Bull. 65:41.

Brodkorb, P. 1953b. A review of the Pliocene loons. Condor 55:211–214.

Brodkorb, P. 1963. Catalogue of fossil birds. Bull. Florida State Museum 7:220–225.

Brooks, R. J. and J. B. Falls. 1975. Individual recognition by song in White-throated Sparrows. III. Song features used in individual recognition. Can. J. Zool. 53:1749–1761.

Brown, R. N. and R. E. Lemon. 1979. Structure and evolution of song form in the wrens *Thryothorus sinaloa* and *T. felix*. Behav. Ecol. Sociobiol. 5:111–131.

Burleigh, R. D. 1972. Birds of Idaho. Coxton Printeries, Caldwell, Idaho.

Bystrak, D. (ed.). 1974. Wintering areas of bird species potentially hazardous to aircraft. National Audubon Society, N.Y.

Carson, R. 1962. Silent spring. Riverside Press, Cambridge, Mass.

Christoff, M. 1979. A study of the early chick rearing period of the Common Loon (*Gavia immer*). Unpubl. report, SUNY College of Environmental Science and Forestry, Syracuse, N.Y.

Clark, R. A. 1975. Common Loons nest again in Massachusetts. Bird News of Western Mass. 15:65–67.

Cooke, W. W. 1884. Bird nomenclature of the Chippewa Indians. Auk 242–250.

Corkran, C. 1988. Status and potential for breeding of the Common Loon in the Pacific Northwest. In: P. Strong (ed.), Papers from 1987 Conf. Loon Res. Mgmt. North American Loon Fund, Meredith, N.H. pp. 107–116.

Coues, E. 1866. The osteology of the *Colymbus torquatus*; with notes on its myology. Boston Soc. Natur. Hist. Mem. 1:131–172.

Cracraft, J. 1982. Phylogenetic relationships and monophyly of loons, grebes, and hesperornithiform birds, with comments on the early history of birds. Syst. Zool. 31:35–36.

Cramp, S. (ed). 1977. Handbook of the birds of Europe, the Middle East, and North Africa. The birds of western Palearctic. Vol. 1. Oxford University Press, New York. Pp. 42–65.

Davie, O. 1898. Nests and eggs of North American birds. London Press, Columbus, Ohio.

Davis, D. M. 1949. Description of *Similium euryadminiculum*, a new species of blackfly. Canad. Ent. 81:45–49.

Davis, R. A. 1972. A comparative study of the use of habitat by Arctic and Red-throated Loons. Unpubl. PhD thesis, University of Western Ontario.

Dawson, W. L. and J.H. Bowles. 1909. The birds of Washington. Occidental Publishing Co., Seattle.

Delle Cave, L., A. Simonetta, and A. Azzaroli. 1984. A skull of a fossil loon (*Gavia*) from the Pliocene of central Italy. Palaeontographia Italica 73:86–103.

Dement'ev, G. P., R. N. Meklenburtsev, A. M. Sudilovskaya, and E. P. Spangenberg. 1968. Birds of the Soviet Union. Vol 2. Trans. from Russian Israel Program for Scientific Translation, Jerusalem. Pp. 282–304.

Desgranges, J. L. and P. Laporte. 1979. Preliminary considerations on the status of loons (*Gaviidae*) in Quebec. Report to Joint Committee of the James Bay and northern Quebec Agreement. Canadian Wildlife Service, Ottawa.

Dinsmore, J. J., T. H. Kent, D. Koenig, P. C. Petersen, and D. M. Roosa. 1984. Iowa Birds. Iowa State University Press, Ames.

Dionne, C. E. 1906. Les oiseux de la province de Quebec. Dussault & Prouex, Quebec.

Dolensek, E. P. and J. Bell. 1977. Help! A step by step manual for the care and treatment of oil-damaged birds. Suppl. Animal Kingdom, New York Zoological Society, Bronx.

Dubois, G. and R. L. Rausch. 1967. Les Strigeata (Trematoda) des Gaviides nord-americains. Rev. Suisse Zool. 74:399–407.

Dulin, G. S. 1988. Pre-fledging feeding behavior and sibling rivalry in Common Loons. MS thesis, Central Michigan University, Mt. Pleasant.

Dymond, N. 1982. Successful fostering by Red-throated Divers. Brit. Birds 75:577.

Eaton, E. H. 1910. Birds of New York. State University of New York, Albany.

Eberhardt, R. T. 1984. Recent recoveries of Common Loons banded in Minnesota. The Loon 56:202–203.

Elliott, C. H. 1978. (editorial from South Bay Daily Breeze) Redondo Beach, Calif. 12 May.

Emerson, K. C. 1955. A note on the identity of *Strigiphilis barbatus*. J. Kansas Ent. Soc. 28:144–145.

Emlen, S. T. 1972. An experimental analysis of the parameters of birds song eliciting species recognition. Behaviour 41:130–171.

Etchécopar, R. D. and F. Hüe. 1964. Les oiseaux du Nord de l'Afrique Éditions N. Boubée & Cie. Paris. pp. 19–20.

Ewert, D. N. 1982. Spring migration of Common Loons at Whitefish Point, Michigan. Jack-Pine Warbler 60:135–143.

Fair, J. S. 1979. Water level fluctuations and Common Loon nest failure. In: S. Sutcliffe (ed.), Proceed. N. Amer. Conf. Common Loon Res. Manage. 2:57–63.

Fallis, A. M. and S. M. Smith. 1964. Ether extracts from birds and CO_2 as attractants for some ornithophilic Simulids. Can. Journ. Zool. 42:723–730.

Fantham, H. B. and A. Porter. 1948. The parasitic fauna of vertebrates in certain Canadian fresh waters, with some remarks on their ecology, structure and importance. Proc. Zool. Soc. London 117:609–649.

Fay, L. D. 1966. Type E botulism in Great Lakes water birds. Trans. Thirty-first N.A. Wildl. and Nat. Res. Conf. Pp. 139–149.

Fay, L.D. 1969. Summary of the botulism surveillances. Michigan Dept. of Nat. Res. Report No. l66.

Fay, L. D. and W. G. Youatt. 1967. Residues of chlorinated hydrocarbon insecticides in loons, grebes, a gull, and a sample of alewives from Lake Michigan. Mich. Dept. Cons. R & D Report No. 109.

Feduccia, J. A. 1980. The age of birds. Harvard University Press, Cambridge, Mass.

Fimreite, N. 1970. Mercury uses in Canada and their possible hazards as sources of mercury contamination. Environ. Pollut. 1:119–131.

Fimreite, N. 1974. Mercury contamination of aquatic birds in northwestern Ontario. J. Wildl. Manage. 38:120–131.

Fimreite, N. and L. Karstad. 1971. Effects of dietary methyl mercury on Red-tailed Hawks. J. Wildl. Manage. 35:293–300.

Flick, W. A. 1983. Observations on loons as predators on Brook Trout and as possible transmitters of infectious pancreatic necrosis (IPN). N.A.J. Fish Manage. 3:95–96.

Flint, V. E., R. L. Boehme, Y. V. Kostin, and A. A.Kuznetsov. 1984. A field guide to birds of the USSR. Princeton University Press, Princeton, N.J.

Forbush, E. H. 1912. A history of the game birds, waterfowl, and shore birds of Massachusetts and adjacent states. Massachusetts State Board of Agriculture. White and Potter Printing Co., Boston. Pp. 49–58.

Forbush, E. H. 1925. Birds of Massachusetts. Part I. Commonwealth of Massachusetts, Dept. of Ag., Norwood Press, Norwood, Mass. Pp.16–30.

Fox, D. A. and A. J. Sillman. 1979. Heavy metals affect rod, but not cone, photoreceptors. Science 206:78–80.

Fox, G. A., K. S. Yonge, and S. G. Sealy. 1980. Breeding performance, pollutant burden and eggshell thinning in Common Loons *Gavia immer* nesting on a boreal forest lake. Ornis. Scand. 11:243–248.

Frank, R., H. Lumsden, J. F. Barr, and H. E. Braun. 1983. Residues of organichlorine insecticides, industrial chemicals, and mercury in eggs and in tissues taken from healthy and emaciated Common Loons, Ontario, Canada, 1968–1980. Arch. Environ. Contam. Toxicol. 12:641–654.

Fry, D. M. and C. K. Toone. 1981. DDT-induced feminization of gull embryos. Science 213:922–924.

Gabrielson, I. N. and S. G. Jewett. 1940. Birds of Oregon. Oregon State College, Corvallis.

Gabrielson, I. N. and F. C. Lincoln. 1959. The birds of Alaska. The Stackpole Co., Harrisburg, Pa.

Gauthreaux, S. S. 1978. The ecological significance of behavioral dominance. In: Perspectives in ethology. Vol. 3. P. Bateson and P. Klopfer (eds.) Plenum Press, NY. 17–54.

Gibson, G. G. 1968. Species composition of the genus *Streptocara railliet* et al. 1912 and the occurrence of these avian nematodes (*Acuariidae*) on the Canadian Pacific coast. Can. J. Zool. 46:629–645.

Gier, H. T. 1952. The air sacs of the loon. Auk 69:40–49.

Gilbert, N. C. 1905. Occurrence of *Echinostomum spinulosum* Rud. Amer. Nat. 39:925–927.

Gilbertson, M. and L. Reynolds. 1974. A summary of DDE and PCB determination in Canadian birds, 1969–1972. Canadian Wildlife Service Occas. Paper No. 19.

Godfrey, W. E. 1979. The birds of Canada. National Museum of Natural Sciences, National Museums of Canada, Ottawa.

Gray, L. H. (ed.) 1964. The mythology of all races. Vol. 1. Greek and Roman. Cooper Square Publishers, New York. P. 180.

Grinnell, J. and A. H. Miller. 1944. The distribution of the birds of California. Pacific Coast Avifauna, No. 27. Cooper Ornithological Club, Berkeley, Calif.

Guberlet, J. 1922. Three new species of *Holostomidae*. J. Parasitol. 9:6–14.

Gudmundsson, F. 1972. Grit as an indicator of the overseas origin of certain birds occurring in Iceland. Ibis 124:582.

Hadley, A. H. 1930. Oil pollution and sea-bird fatalities. Bird-lore. 32:241–243.

Hammar, B. 1970. The karotypes of thirty-one birds. Hereditas 65:29–58

Harlow, R. C. 1908. Breeding of the loon in Pennsylvania. Auk 25:471.

Harper, F. 1958. Birds of the Ungava Peninsula. University of Kansas Press, Lawrence. Pp. 31–32.

Harrison, C. J. O. 1967. Sideways- throwing and sideways-building in birds. Ibis 109:539–551.

Heilman, G. 1927. The origin of birds. Witherby and Co., London.

Heimberger, M., D. Euler and J. Barr. 1983. The impact of cottage development on Common Loon reproductive success in central Ontario. Wilson Bull. 95:431–439.

Hess, R. 1986. The Common Loon in Michigan. Report to the North American Loon Fund, Meredith, N.H.

Hickey, J. J., J. A. Keith, and F. B. Coon. 1966. An explanation of pesticides in a Lake Michigan ecosystem. J. Appl. Ecol. 3:141–154.

Hoffman, W. 1983. Florida region in the winter season. Amer. Birds 37:294.

Hunter, E. N. and R. H. Dennis. 1972. Hybrid Great Northern Diver x Black-throated Diver in Wester Ross. Scottish Birds 7:89–91.

Huxley, T. H. 1867. On the classificiation of birds and on the taxonomic value of the modifications of certain of the cranial bones observable in that class. Proc. Zool. Soc. London 1867:415–472.

Ingersoll, E. 1923. Birds in legend, fable and folklore. Longman's, Green & Co., New York.

Jamnback, H. 1969. Bloodsucking flies and other outdoor nuisance Arthropods of New York State. Memoir 19: State University of NY Press, Albany. Pp. 11–16.

Jensen, W. I. and R. B. Gritman. 1966. An adjuvant effect between *Clostridium botulinum* Types C and E toxins in the mallard duck (*Anas platyrhynchos*). In: M. Ingram and T. A. Roberts (eds.), Botulism 1966. Chapman and Hall, London. Pp. 407–413.

Jewett, S. A., W. P. Taylor, W. T. Shaw, and J. W. Aldrich. 1953. Birds of Washington State. University of Washington Press, Seattle.

Johnson, C. W. 1922. Notes on distribution and habits of some of the bird-flies *Hypoboscidae*. Psyche. 29:79–85.

Joyeaux, G. and J. G. Baer. 1950. Sur quelques especes nouvelles ou peu connues du genre *Hymenolepis* Weinland, 1858. Bull. Sec. Neuchatel. Sc. Nat. 73:51–70.

Kabem, Von U. and D. Schwarz. 1970. Der einfluss der Nasalen sekretion der vøgel auf mykosen. Der Zoolgarten 39:134–146.

Kao, I., D. B. Drachman, and D. L. Price. 1976. Botulinum toxin: mechanism of presynaptic blockade. Science 193:1256–1258.

Kaufmann, O. W. and L. D. Fay. 1964. *Clostridium botulinum* Type E toxin in tissues of dead loons and gulls. Mich. State Univ. Agri. Exp. Sta. Quart. Bull. 47:236–242.

Keith, J. A. and I. M. Gruchy. 1972. Residue levels of chemical pollutants in North American birdlife. In: Voous, K. H. (ed.) Proc. 15th Int. Orn. Congr., The Hague. Pp. 437–454.

Kellogg, V. L. and J. H. Paine. 1911. Mallophaga from Californian birds. Entom. News 22:75–789.

Kerlinger, P. 1982. The migration of Common Loons through eastern New York. Condor 84:97–100.

Khokhlova, I. G. 1965. *Polymorphus gavii* nov. sp. new species of acanthocephalan from *Gavia* spp. of Chukotka. (Russian text.) Akad. Nauk SSSR, v. 15, 196–199.

King, A.P., M.J. West, D.H. Eastzer, and J.E.R. Staddon. 1981. An experimental investigation of the bioacoustics of cowbird song. Behav. Ecol. Sociobiol. 9:211–217.

LaBastille, A. 1977. The endangered loon. Adirondack Life 8:34–38.

LaMont, T. G., G. E. Bagley, W.L. Reichel. 1970. Residues of O,P′-DDD and O,P′-DDT in Brown Pelican eggs and Mallard Ducks. Bull. Environ. Contam. Toxicol. 5:231–236.

Larrison, E. J. and K. G. Sonnenberg. 1968. Washington birds, their location and iden-
tificaion. Seattle Audubon Society.

Lee, M. 1986. Maine Audubon loon project report. Maine Audubon Society.

Lee, M. and J. Arbuckle. 1988. Maine Common Loons: a glance back and an eye toward
the future. In : P. Strong (ed.), Papers from 1987 Conf. Loon Res. and Mgmt. North
American Loon Fund, Meredith, N.H. pp. 167–176.

Leechman, D. 1968. Native tribes of Canada. W. J. Gage, Toronto.

Lehtonen, L. 1970. Zur biologie des prachttauchers, *Gavia a. arctica* (L) Ann. Zool. Fen-
nici 7:25–60.

Leland, C. G. 1884. The Algonquin legends of New England. Sampson Low, Marston,
Searle and Rivington, London.

Linton, E. 1915. *Tocotrema lingua* (Creplin). The adult stage of a skin parasite of the cun-
ner and other fishes of the Woods Hole Region. J. Parasitol. 1:128–134.

Linton, E. 1927. Notes on cestode parasites of birds. Proc. U.S. Nat. Mus. 70:1–73.

Linton, E. 1928. Notes on trematode parasites of birds. Proc. U.S. Nat. Mus. 73:1–36.

Locke, L. N., S. M. Kerr, and D. Zoromski. 1982. Lead poisoning in Common Loons
(*Gavia immer*). Avian Diseases 26:392–396.

Locke, L. M. and L. T. Young. 1967. Aspergillosis in a Common Loon. Bull. Wildl. Dis.
Assoc. 3:34–35.

Long, W. J. 1900. Wilderness days. Ginn & Co., Boston.

Loon Preservation Committee. 1979. Annual report 1979. Meredith, N.H.

Lowther, J.K. and D.M. Wood. 1964. Specificity of a black fly, *Simulium euryadminiculum* Davies, toward its host, the common loon. Can. Ent. 96:911–913.

Lysack, W. 1985. Common Loon concentrations. Blue Jay 43:56.

Manville, R. H. 1952. Loons in the Huron Mountains. Jack Pine Warbler 20:52–53.

Marten, K. and P. Marler. 1977. Sound transmission and its significance for animal
vocalization. I. Temperate habitats. Behav. Ecol. Sociobiol. 2:271–290.

Marten, K., D. Quine, and P. Marler. 1977. Sound transmission and its significance for
animal vocalization. II. Tropical forest habitats. Behav. Ecol. Sociobiol. 2:291–302.

Martin, L. D. 1980. Foot-propelled diving birds of the Mesozoic. In: Acta XVII Cong.
Inter. Orn. R. Nøhring (ed.). Verlag de Deutsches Orn., Berlin. Pp. 1237–1242.

Martin, L. D. 1983. The origin and early radiation of birds. In: Perspectives in orninthol-
ogy. A.H. Brush and G.A. Clark (eds). Cambridge University Press.

Mathisen, J.E. 1969., Use of man-made islands as nesting sites of the Common Loon.
Wilson Bull. 81:331.

McAtee, W. L. 1957. Folk-names of Canadian birds. Bull. No. 159. Biological Series No.
51, Canada National Museum, Ottawa.

McEneaney, T. 1988. Status of the Common Loon in Yellowstone National Park. In: P.
Strong (ed.), Papers from 1987 Conf. Loon Res. Mgmt. North American Loon Fund,
Meredith, N.H. p. 117.

McIntyre, A. E. and J. W. McIntyre. 1974. Spots before the eyes, an aid to identifying
wintering loons. Auk 91:413–415

McIntyre, J. W. 1974. Territorial affinity of a Common Loon. Bird-banding. 45:178.

McIntyre, J. W. 1975. Biology and behavior of the Common Loon (*Gavia immer*) with
reference to its adaptability in a man-altered environment. Unpubl. PhD thesis, University of Minnesota, Minneapolis.

McIntyre, J. W. 1977. The Common Loon. Part II. Identification of potential predators on common loon nests. The Loon 49:96–99.

McIntyre, J. W. 1978a. The Common Loon. Part III. Population in Itasca State Park, Minnesota 1957–1976. The Loon 50:38–44.

McIntyre, J. W. 1978b. Wintering behavior of Common Loons. Auk 95:396–403.

McIntyre, J. W. 1979. Status of Common Loons in New York from a historical perspective. In : S. Sutcliffe (ed.), Proc. N. Amer. Conf. Common Loon Res. Manage. 2:117–122.

McIntyre, J. W. 1983. Nurseries: a consideration of habitat requirements during the early chick-rearing period in Common Loons. J. Field Ornithol. 54:247–253.

McIntyre, J. W. 1988. The Minnesota Report: a 15-year survey comparison. In: P. Strong (ed.), Papers from 1987 Conf. Loon Res. Mgmt. North American Loon Fund, Meredith, N.H. pp. 118–130.

McIntyre, J. W. and J. F. Barr. 1983. Pre-migratory behavior of Common Loons on the autumn staging grounds. Wilson Bull. 95:121–125.

McIntyre, J. W. and J. Mathisen. 1977. Artificial islands as nest sites for Common Loons. J. Wildl. Manage. 41:317–319.

McIntyre, J. W. and G. A. Smith. 1984. Wintering loons: where and when? Winter Loon Watch Report to the North American Loon Fund, Meredith, N.H.

McKinney, F. 1965. The comfort movements of Anatidae. Behaviour 25:120–220.

McNicoll, M. K. 1988. Common Loon distribution and conservation in Canada. In: P. Strong (ed.), Papers from 1987 Conf. Loon Res. Mgmt. North American Loon Fund, Meredith, N.H. pp. 196–214.

Midtgård, U. 1981. The *Rete tibiotarsale* and arterio-venous association in the hind limb of birds: a comparative morphological study on counter-current heat exchange systems. Acta. Zool. 62:67–87.

Miller, M. J. 1941. The life history of *Apophallus brevis* Ransom, 1920. J. Parasitol. 27 Suppl. 12.

Miller, M. J. 1942. Black spot disease of speckled trout. Revue Canadienne de Biologie 1:464–471.

Milne-Edwards, A. 1868. Recherches anatomique et paleontologiques pour servir a l'histoire des oiseaux fossiles de la France. Victor Masson and Sons, Paris.

Monheimer, R. H. 1968. The relationship of Lake Michigan waterbird mortalities to naturally occurring *Clostridium botulinum* Type E toxin. Bull. Wildl. Dis. Assoc. 4:81–85.

Morton, E. S. 1975. Ecological sources of selection on avian sounds. Amer. Nat. 109:17–34.

Morton, E. S. 1977. On the occurrence and significance of motivation-structural rules in some bird and mammal sounds. Amer. Nat. 111:855–869.

Munro, J. A. 1945. Observations of the loon in the Cariboo Parklands, British Columbia. Auk: 62:38–49.

Nelson, D. H. 1983. A Common Loon nest from New Hampshire containing four eggs. Wilson Bull. 95:673–674.

Nero, R. W. 1963. Birds of the Lake Athabasca region, Saskatchewan. Spec. Publ. No. 5. Sask. Nat. Hist. Soc., Regina. Pp. 33–39.

Nero, R. W. 1972. Further records of summer flocking of Common Loon. Blue Jay 30:85–86.

Nero, R. W. 1974. Summer flocks of Common Loons in Manitoba. Blue Jay 32:113–114.

Newberry, J. S. 1857. Zoological Report No. 2. Chap. 2. In: H. L. Abbott (ed.), Report of explorations and surveys to ascertain a route for a railroad to the Columbia River. U.S. War Dept. Reports of Explorations and Surveys 1855–60. Vol. 6, Part 4. Washington, D.C.

Nilsson, S. G. 1977. Adult survival rate of the Black-throated Diver *Gavia arctica*. Orn. Scand. 8:193–195.

Norton, A. H. 1915. The Loon. Bird-Lore 17:68–71.

Ogilvie-Grant, W. R. 1898. Catalogue of the Plataloae, Herodiones, Steganopedes, Pygopodes, Alcae, and Impennes in the collection of the British Museum. In: Catalogue of the birds in the British Museum. Vol. 26. British Mus. Nat. Hist., London. Pp. 329–653.

Olson, S. 1985. The fossil record of birds. In: Avian Biology, Vol. 8. D. Farner, J. King, K. Parkes (eds.). Academic Press, Orlando, Fla. Pp. 79–238.

Olson, S. and A. Feduccia. 1980. Relationships and evolution of flamingos (Aves: Phoenicopteridae). Smithson. Contrib. Zool. 316:1–73.

Olson, S. T. and W. H. Marshall. 1952. The Common Loon in Minnesota. Minnesota Museum of Nat. Hist. Occas. Paper No. 5. University of Minnesota Press, Minneapolis.

Palmer, R. S. 1949. Maine birds. Bull. Mus. Comp. Zool. Harvard. Vol. 102. Cambridge, Mass.

Palmer, R. S. (ed.). 1962. Handbook of North American birds. Vol. 1. Yale University Press, New Haven, Conn. Pp. 21–35.

Parker, K. E. 1985a. Foraging and reproduction of the Common Loon (*Gavia immer*) on acidified lakes in the Adirondack Park, New York. MS thesis, SUNY College of Environmental Science and Forestry, Syracuse.

Parker, K. E. 1985b. Observations of a flying Common Loon carrying a fish. J. Field Orn. 56:412–413.

Parker, K. E. and R. L. Miller. 1988. Status of New York's Common Loon population — comparison of two intensive surveys. In: P. Strong (ed.), Papers from 1987 Conf. Loon Res. Mgmt. North American Loon Fund, Meredith, N.H. pp.145–156.

Perkins, J. P. 1965. Seventeen flyways over the Great Lakes. Audubon 67:42–45.

Peters, H. S. 1936. A list of external parasites from birds of the eastern part of the United States. Bird-banding 12: 9–27.

Peters, H. S. and T. D. Burleigh. 1951. The birds of Newfoundland. Department of Natural Resources, St. Johns, Nfld.

Petersen, M. R. 1976. Breeding biology of Arctic and Red-throated Loons. MS thesis, University of California, Davis.

Peterson, J. 1965. Foods eaten by aquatic fish-eating birds. Mich. Dept. of Cons. R & D Report No. 44.

Plunkett, R. 1979. Major elements of a five-year comprehensive plan of research and management for the Great Lakes and northeastern United States populations of the Common Loon, *Gavia immer*. In: S. Sutcliffe (ed.) Proc. N. Amer. Conf. Common Loon Res. Manage. 2:154–162.

Poole, E. L. 1938. Weights and wing areas in North American birds. Auk 55:511–517.

Powers, K. D. and J. Cherry. 1983. Loon migrations off the northeastern United States. Wilson Bull. 95:125–132.

Predy, R. G. 1972. Another summer concentration of Common Loons. Blue Jay 30:221.

Price, I. M. and J. A. Keith. 1975. Common Loons on Big Rideau Lake. Unpubl. report, Canadian Wildlife Service. Ottawa.

Pycraft, W. P. 1909. On the pterylosis of the Black-throated Diver. Brit. Birds 1:93–98.

Raine, W. 1892. Bird-nesting in north-west Canada. Hunter, Rose and Co., Toronto. Pp. 152–153.

Rand, A. L. 1947. Geographical variation in the loon, *Gavia immer*. Can. Field Nat. 61:193–195.

Ransom, D. H. 1909. The taenoid cestodes of North American birds. Bull. U.S. Nat. Mus. 1–141.

Ratcliffe, D. A. 1967. Decrease in eggshell weight in certain birds of prey. Nature 215:208–210.

Ream, C. H. 1976. Loon productivity, human disturbance and pesticide residues in northern Minnesota. Wilson Bull. 88:427–432.

Regalia, E. 1902. Sette uccelli pliocenici del Pisano e del Valdarno superiore. Palaeontogr. Ital. 8:219–238. (Pisa).

Richards, A. and A. Musche. 1985. Breeding status of the Common Loon in Washington, 1985. Final Report, 1985, to the North American Loon Fund, Meredith, N.H.

Ridgway, R. 1895. The ornithology of Illinois. Vol. 2. Nat. Hist. Surv. of Ill., Bloomington. Pp. 253–255.

Rimmer, C.C. 1988. The status of Common Loons in Vermont, 1978–87. In: P. Strong (ed.), Papers from 1987 Conf. Loon Res. Mgmt. North American Loon Fund, Meredith, N.H. pp. 157–159.

Roberts, T.S. 1932. The birds of Minnesota. Univ. Minn. Press, Minneapolis. Pp. 140–144.

Robertson, M. 1969. Red Earth: Tales of the Micmacs with an introduction to the customs and beliefs of the Micmac Indians. Nova Scotia Museum, Halifax.

Robertson, I. and M. Fraker. 1974. Apparent hybridization between a Common Loon and an Arctic Loon. Can. Field-Nat. 88:367.

Robinson, H. W. 1923. Dive of the Great Northern Diver. Brit. Birds 17:64.

Rummel, L. and C. Goetzinger. 1975. The communication of intraspecific aggression in the Common Loon. Auk 92:333–346.

Rummel, L. and C. Goetzinger. 1978. Aggressive display in the Common Loon. Auk 95:183–186.

Salt, W. R. and A. L. Wilk. 1958. The birds of Alberta. The Queen's Printer, Edmonton, Alta. P. 18.

Schindler, D. W., K. H. Mills, D. F. Malley, D. L. Findlay, J. A. Shearere, I. J. Davies, A. Turner, G. A. Linsey, and D. R. Cruikshank. 1985. Long-term ecosystem stress: the effects of years of experimental acidification on a small lake. Science 228:1395–1401.

Schreiber, R. W. 1977. Maintenance behavior and communication in the Brown Pelican. A.O.U. Monogr. No. 22.

Sclater, P. L. 1880. Remarks on the present state of the Systema Avium. Ibis 22:340–350.

Scott, J. D. 1973. That cry of wildness. Sports Afield (January): 77–81.

Seebohm, H. 1890. Classification of birds: an attempt to diagnose the subclasses, orders, suborders and some of the families of existing birds. R. H. Porter, London.

Seton, E. T. 1911. The Arctic prairies. Chas. Scribner's Sons, New York.

Shuffeldt, R. W. 1898. On the terrestrial attitudes of loons and grebes. Ibis 4:46–51.

Shuffeldt, R. W. 1904. An arrangement of the families and the higher groups of birds. Amer. Nat. 38:833–857.

Sibley, C. G. and J. E. Ahlquist. 1972. A comparative study of the egg-white proteins of non-passerine birds. Bull. Peabody Mus. of Nat. Hist. Yale University 32:1–131.

Sibley, C. G. and J. E. Ahlquist. 1983. Phylogeny and classification of birds based on the data of DNA-DNA hybridization. In: Current Ornithology. Vol. I. R. F. Johnston (ed.). Plenum Press, New York. Pp. 245–292.

Sim, R. J. 1923. The Common Loon. Bird-Lore 25:167–175.

Sjølander, S. and G. Ågren. 1972. Reproductive behavior of the Common Loon. Wilson Bull. 84:296–308.

Skaar, D. 1986. Montana loon study: 1986 summary. Report to the North American Loon Fund, Meredith, N.H.

Skinner, M. P. 1925. The birds of Yellowstone National Park. Roosevelt Wildl. Bull. 3:11–189.

Skrjabin, K. I. 1945. On the taxonomic position of *Haemanotrephus fodiens* Linton, 1928, within the system of trematodes. Dakl. Akad. Nauk SSSR 348:75–76.

Smith, E. L. 1981. Effects of canoeing on Common Loon production and survival on the Kenai National Wildlife Refuge, Alaska. MS thesis, Colorado State University, Fort Collins.

Smith, W. J. 1977. The behavior of communicating. Harvard University Press, Cambridge, Mass.

Snyder, L. L. 1951. Ontario birds. Clarke, Irwin, and Co., Toronto.

Stickel, L. F. and R. G. Heath. 1965. Wildlife studies, Patuxent Wildlife Research Center. In: Effects of pesticides on fish and wildlife. U.S. FWS Circ. No. 226, Washington, D.C. Pp. 3–30.

Stolpe, M. 1935. *Colymbus, Hesperornis, Podiceps:* II ein Vergleich ihrer hinteren Extremität. J. Orn. 83:115–128.

Stoner, D. 1932. Ornithology of the Oneida Lake region; with reference to the late spring and summer season. Bull. New York College of Forestry, Syracuse. Pp. 361–362.

Storer, R. W. 1956. The fossil loon, *Colymboides minutus*. Condor 58:413–426.

Storer, R. W. 1978. Systematic notes on the loons (*Gaviidae: Aves*). Breviora 448:1–8.

Storer, R. W. 1988. Variation in the Common Loon (*Gavia immer*). In: P. Strong (ed.), Papers from 1987 Conf. Loon Res. Mgmt. North American Loon Fund, Meredith, N.H. pp. 54–65.

Street, P. B. and R. E. Wiltraut. 1985. Birds of the Pocono Mountains. 1975–1985. Cassinia 6:3–19.

Strong, P. I. V. 1985. Habitat selection by Common Loons. PhD thesis, University of Maine, Orono.

Strong, P. I. V. 1987. Reuse of nesting and nursery areas by Common Loons. J. Wildl. Manage. 51:123–127.

Stroud, R. K. and R. E. Lange. 1983. Information summary: Common Loon die-off winter and spring of 1983. Report, National Wildlife Health Laboratory, U.S. FWS, Madison, Wis.

Sutcliffe, S. A. 1978. Pesticide levels and shell thickness of Common Loon eggs in New Hampshire. Wilson Bull. 90:637–640.

Sutcliffe, S. A. 1980. Aspects of the nesting ecology of Common Loons in New Hampshire. Unpubl. MS thesis, University of New Hampshire, Durham.

Sutcliffe, S. A. 1982. Prolonged incubation behavior in Common Loons. Wilson Bull. 94:361–362.

Sutton, G. M. and D. F. Parmelee. 1956. On the loons of Baffin Island. Auk 73:78–84.

Taverner, P. A. 1926. Birds of western Canada. F. A. Acland, Printer. Museum Bull. No. 41, Canada Geological Survey, Victoria Memorial Museum, Biological Series No. 10. Victoria, B.C.

Taylor, K. 1974. The loon. Adirondack Life 5:30–37.

Thoreau, H. D. 1946. Walden, or, Life in the woods. Dodd, Mead & Co., New York.

Titus, J. and L. Van Druff. 1981. Response of the Common Loon to recreational pressure in the Boundary Waters Canoe Area, northeastern Minnsesota. Wildlife Monograph No. 79., Wildlife Society.

Trivelpiece, W., S. Brown, A. Hicks, R. Fekete, and N. J. Volkman. 1979. An analysis of the distribution and reproductive success of the Common Loon in the Adirondack Park, New York. In: S. Sutcliffe (ed.). Proc. N. Amer. Conf. Common Loon Res. Manage. 2:45–55.

Tufts, R. W. 1961. The birds of Nova Scotia. Nova Scotia Museum, Halifax. Pp. 25–27.

Tyler, C. 1969. A study of the eggshells of the Gaviiformes, Procellariiformes, Podicipediformes, and Pelecaniformes. J. Zool. (London) 158:395–412.

Vermeer, K. 1973a. Some aspects of the breeding and mortality of Common Loons in east-central Alberta. Can. Field-Nat. 87:403–408.

Vermeer, K. 1973b. Some aspects of the nesting requirements of Common Loons in Alberta. Wilson Bull. 85:429–435.

Volkman, N. and W. Trivelpiece. 1980. Survival for the loon. Adirondack Life 11:26–31.

Von Braun, C., A. C. Hessle, and S. Sjølander. 1968. Smålommen (*Gavia stellata* L). beteende under ungvårnadstiden. Sårtryck ur Zoologisk Revy årg 30:94–95.

Warren, B. H. 1953. A new type of metacercarial cyst of the genus *Apophallus* from the perch, *Perca flavescens, in Minnesota. Amer. Mid. Nat. 50:*397–401.

Wetmore, A. 1940. Fossil bird remains from Tertiary deposits in the United States. J. Morph. 66:25–37.

Wetmore, A. 1941. An unknown loon from the Miocene fossil beds of Maryland. Auk 58:567.

Wetmore, A. 1943. Fossil birds from the Tertiary deposits of Florida. Proc. New Engl. Zool. Club 22:57–63.

Weydemeyer, W. 1975. Half-century record of the breeding birds of the Fortine Area, Montana: nesting data and population status. Condor 77:281–287.

Wilcox, H. H. 1952. The pelvic musculature of the loon, *Gavia immer*. Amer. Mid. Nat. 48:513–573.

Wiley, R. H. and D. G. Richards. 1978. Physical constraints on acoustic communication in the atmosphere; implications for the evolution of animal vocalizations. Behav. Ecol. Sociobiol. 3:69–94.

Williams, A. J. 1971. Ornithological observations on Bear Island, 1970. Astarte 4:31–36.

Williams, L. E. 1973. Spring migration of Common Loons from the Gulf of Mexico. Wilson Bull. 85:238.

Williamson, K. 1970. The Atlantic islands. Routledge & Kegan Paul, London.

Wilson, A. and C. L. Bonaparte. 1831. American ornithology; or the natural history of the birds of the United States. Vol. 3. Constable and Co., Edinburgh, Scot.

Winter, J. and J. Morlan. 1977. Middle Pacific coast region; The Changing Season. Amer. Birds 31:1041–1045.

Wood, R., J. Fair, C. Mauhs-Pugh and K. Neilsen. 1985. The calling continues, 1986–1985: ten-year report. Loon Preservation Committee. Audubon Society of New Hampshire. Meredith.

Woolfenden, G. E. 1972. Selection for a delayed simultaneous wing molt in loons (*Gaviidae*). Wilson Bull. 79:416–420.

Woolfenden, G. E. and J. W. Fitzpatrick. 1984. The Florida Scrub Jay: demography of a cooperative breeding bird. Princeton University Press, Princeton, N.J.

Yeates, G. K. 1950. Field notes on the nesting habits of the Great Northern Diver. Brit. Birds 43:5–8.

Yonge, K. S. 1981. The breeding cycle and annual production of the Common Loon (*Gavia immer*) in the boreal forest region. MS thesis, University of Manitoba, Winnipeg.

Young, K.E. 1983. Seasonal and temporal patterning of Common Loon (*Gavia immer*) vocalizations. MS thesis, Syracuse University, Syracuse, N.Y.

Zicus, M. C., R. H. Hier, and S. J. Maxson. 1983. A Common Loon nest from Minnesota containing four eggs. Wilson Bull. 95:672–673.

Zimmerman, D. A. 1967. The Common Loon in Sonora, Mexico. Condor 69:527.

INDEX

Index

A professor of biology at Utica College of Syracuse University, **Judith McIntyre** has been studying and writing about loon biology for more than twenty years. Her research has been conducted in Minnesota, New York, Saskatchewan, and coastal Virginia, with research-related forays to Alaska, New Brunswick, Florida, Ontario, Maine, and the coasts of Connecticut, Rhode Island, and California.

McIntyre received her Ph.D. in zoology from the University of Minnesota in 1975. Her doctoral research examined the competence of loons to modify their behavior in response to the impact of human recreational use and development on lakes used as loon territories during the breeding season. Later, her work focused on the structure and communicative role of loon calls, and is still the only experimental loon vocalization study. She has continued to monitor contaminant levels in loon eggs, initially in cooperation with the Minnesota Department of Natural Resources, and more recently with the U.S. Fish and Wildlife Service. She is currently examining the role of reservoirs as loon habitat.

McIntyre initiated the public survey programs known as Project Loon Watch in Minnesota in 1971; she soon became known as the "Loon Lady." She has been a trustee of the North American Loon Fund since 1983, currently serving as vice president, and is the founder and director of the Oikos Research Foundation. She wrote and produced an educational slide/tape program for children, *Hello, I'm a Loon!*, wrote the chapter on Common Loons for the *Audubon Wildlife Report 1986*, contributes to *Auk*, *Journal of Field Ornithology*, *Wilson Bulletin*, *The Loon*, and *Journal of Wildlife Management*, and has published in *National Wildlife* and *National Geographic*.